YOUR CAREER GAME

YOUR CAREER GAME

How Game Theory Can Help You
Achieve Your Professional Goals

NATHAN BENNETT AND

STEPHEN A. MILES

STANFORD BUSINESS BOOKS

An Imprint of Stanford University Press
Stanford, California

Stanford University Press
Stanford, California

Special discounts for bulk quantities of Stanford Business Books are available to corporations, professional associations, and other organizations. For details and discount information, contact the special sales department of Stanford University Press. Tel: (650) 736-1782, Fax: (650) 736-1784

Printed in the United States of America on acid-free, archival-quality paper

Library of Congress Cataloging-in-Publication Data

Bennett, Nathan, 1961-
   Your career game : how game theory can help you achieve your professional goals / Nathan Bennett and Stephen A. Miles.
      p. cm.
   Includes bibliographical references and index.
   ISBN 978-0-8047-5628-0 (cloth : alk. paper)
   1. Career development. 2. Game theory. 3. Executives--Interviews. I. Miles, Stephen A. II. Title.
   HF5381.B3623 2010
   658.4'09015193--dc22   2009046753

Typeset by Bruce Lundquist in 10.5/15 Minion

CONTENTS

ACKNOWLEDGMENTS

This project was only possible with the participation of a number of special people with a range of talents and experiences that are impressive for their variety, breadth, and depth. We would like to take this opportunity to thank them for their help. Of course, we maintain full responsibility for the work that follows. First of all, we want to thank the executives listed below who made time to share their career experiences with us. We are grateful for their time, their candor, and their enthusiasm for our project.

Charlene Begley, *General Electric Company*

Bryan Bell, *Bain & Company*

Ursula Burns, *Xerox Corporation*

Stephen Elop, *Microsoft Corporation*

Tamara Erickson, *Author and Consultant*

Pasha Federenko, *Bain & Company*

Ken Frazier, *Merck & Company*

Brian Heese, *Cristo Rey New York High School*

Stephen Heese, *Chris-Craft Corporation and Indian Motorcycle*

Brian Humphries, *Hewlett-Packard Company*

Muhtar Kent, *The Coca-Cola Company*

Chris Klaus, *Kaneva*

Marius Kloppers, *BHP Billiton*

Ted Mathas, *New York Life*

Liz McCartney, *The St. Bernard Project*

Dan Palumbo, *Formerly with The Coca-Cola Company*

William D. Perez, *Campbell Soup Company and Johnson & Johnson* (formerly with *William Wrigley, Jr. Company*)

Carol Tomé, *The Home Depot*

Alex Vanselow, *BHP Billiton*

Keith Wyche, *Pitney Bowes*

We would also like to thank Michael Krot and Ryan Pastrovich at Heidrick & Struggles for their research assistance. Meredith Ashby, also with Heidrick & Struggles, was instrumental in preparing the conversations reported herein, as were Emily Muhlberger, Cornelius Rouse, and Erin Russell at Georgia Tech. Additionally, we would like to thank the many Georgia Tech MBA students who shared their experiences in numerous conversations about career decision making. Finally, we want to thank Mary Wedel with Heidrick & Struggles for all she did to manage the project.

Decisions about your career are likely among the most important ones you will make in your life. Our goal with this book is to provide an accessible approach to a useful tool—game theory. With this tool, you will be able to better frame and analyze career decisions and thus improve your ability to make informed—and more strategic—decisions. By doing so, you can more productively direct your career toward the end that in your mind constitutes a "win." Thanks for your interest in our book. We would appreciate hearing your comments via e-mail to nate@careergame.org or stephen@careergame.org.

Nathan Bennett
Stephen A. Miles
Atlanta, Georgia

YOUR CAREER GAME

INTRODUCTION

For every good job opening you find, chances are there will be
hundreds—even thousands—of people competing against you for
it. There is simply no way you can kill them all.
Dave Barry, *Dave Barry's Money Secrets*

You are well aware that people compete for jobs. The more desirable the job, the tougher the competition you will face. Most people readily understand this. Fewer, we suggest, recognize how the pursuit of an open job can be framed as one "move" in a multimove game called "a career." Our contention is that individuals who quickly recognize the career game for what it is—a fascinating, complex, nuanced, real-life, multiplayer game played in real time—can develop themselves to be better players and consequently will have a better chance of successfully competing for the sorts of positions that will help them realize their goals.

Whether you recognize it as such or not, you have been making career moves for some time. Decisions about whether and where to go to college, the choice of a major, whether to join a fraternity/sorority, serving as captain of a sports team, being active in student government, internships and jobs accepted and those turned down, and even whether to read this book—each are moves that may impact your later career opportunities. Some of these moves may have been what we will call *career refining*—incremental efforts that sharpen your qualifications and focus your résumé. Other moves may have been *career defining*—these are the successful big swings that create positive disruptions and sharply accelerate your career progress. Still other moves may be blunders that produced terrible results and threaten to set back or stall your career. We call these moves *career ending* or *career limiting*—moves that could require you to leave the game or simply send you back to square one. Which one is the case will be a function of the blunder's impact on the company, your previously earned reputation, and the power and influence contained in your network of relationships. These protective factors—reputation and influential contacts—were, of course, developed through your earlier and successful career moves.

Myriad books aimed at providing career guidance already have been published. The majority of these books encourage readers to engage in a process of reflection, which in turn should lead readers to increased self-awareness and a sense of what matters to them in a job, a company, and a career. The individual, now clear as to what he or she should be looking for, is sent forward to do just that—look. This book is different. We believe that by recognizing your career as a game and by applying concepts developed by scholars working in the arena of game theory, you can develop a game strategy that will increase the likelihood of realizing your career goals. In some ways, this book is designed to begin where the work that encourages reflection stops—we presume that you have a sense of where it is you want to go. Playing off the title of the perennial best-seller, you first must determine the color of your parachute. We further presume that your desired destination is likely viewed as attractive by others. As Dave Barry's quote at this chapter's outset drolly points out, you then need to understand how you might position yourself to successfully compete for that destination. In all, we contend that understanding how to prepare to win in the competition over desirable opportunities has a dramatic impact on individual careers. Winning in competition is assisted when actions are guided by thoughtful strategy. A well-crafted strategy is an adaptable plan that takes into account your own objectives, resources, strengths, and weaknesses, as well as those of your competition. This strategy must also consider the condition of the playing field, the rules, and the time structure of the game.

In the pages that follow, we demonstrate how game theory—an economic theory in which the metaphor of a game is applied in order to model how interdependency and interconnectedness among parties should influence decision making—can help you understand how to best and proactively take charge of your career strategy. Game theory has been applied in efforts to understand a wide range of phenomena, including business strategy and decision making. For our purposes, we first show how game theory is productively applied to helping you learn how to manage the interdependencies and interconnectedness among coworkers, managers, and others in a manner that supports your personal career efforts. Second, we show how you, now understanding the "game," can become a player. The key to learning how to play the career game is a concept we have labeled *career agility*—in short, we posit that agile individuals are better game players.

Of course, achieving career success is not merely the result of planning or ability. These tools cannot substitute for demonstrations of competence over the course of a career—what it does do, instead, is help you leverage what you've got. We agree with President Eisenhower that, while plans may be useless, planning is indispensable. What we hope to offer is a new and more useful frame for that planning exercise. Of course, in order to realize the value of a career game plan—as is the case with any other plan—individuals must also faithfully execute their responsibilities and deliver results. In that regard, we favor the view of Samuel Goldwyn, who reflected on his remarkable experience as an immigrant in the United States by noting that the harder he worked, the luckier he became.

As we initially envisioned this project, the primary audience we had in mind was made up of early-career people—those in their mid-twenties to early thirties who are starting to question whether they are on the right path. This stems largely from the fact that the first author spends a great deal of his time at Georgia Tech with people in precisely this predicament. As noted above, many books are designed to help individuals test this question. We set out to offer this group a strategy for acting on its answer. Once we began, we realized that the lessons contained in a game theory approach to career management certainly apply to individuals at all career stages. For early-stage players, all that is required is a sense of the desired end state. Once a destination is in mind, the tools and concepts we present in the chapters that follow can be applied immediately to charting the best course forward. Later-stage players have, by definition, fewer moves left in their games. Consequently, making the most of each of their remaining moves is of the utmost importance. We think that the game theory approach we offer will help ensure that players do just that. Although we focus our examples on successful business people, we are confident that the lessons herein will be useful to *anyone* who is seeking an opportunity that is also desired by others and where outcomes are impacted by interdependent players. People who want to earn desirable volunteer opportunities, for example, are also engaged in a version of the career game.

The book is structured as follows. We use the first five chapters to outline and describe the game theory approach to career management. Chapter 1 begins with a presentation of our rationale for considering your career as a game. Chapter 2 provides you with descriptions of key concepts developed in game theory and explanations of how they apply to the career game. Chapter 3 is intended to help you understand the work you need to do before beginning to play the career game. In Chapter 4, we provide a number of illustrations of career moves and show how game theory can help you decide whether they are the right moves to make. As we note at the beginning of that chapter, moves quickly become very game-specific, so you will need to do some work to see how similar logic would apply to the moves in your career game. Chapter 5 focuses on one specific move that our experience shows is often poorly executed—the move out of a position. We focus on this because the way that move is made impacts the company you are leaving behind, as well as your reputation as you move ahead—both your former employer and your personal future benefit when the transition is done well. With that foundation in place, in Chapter 6 we introduce the concept of career agility and provide suggestions about how you can become a more agile player.

As a part of the research for the book, we conducted interviews with a number of people. Two were selected for their reputations as thought leaders in understanding career issues. Tammy Erickson has written extensively on the way different generations experience work. She offers fascinating insights into how Gen X, Gen Y, and the millennials each frame and then play the career game. Understanding how members of these generations are likely to approach the game can help you be ready to play with them as a manager, as a coworker, or as a competitor for an open position. Keith Wyche, president of Operations at Pitney Bowes, is widely recognized for his work as a mentor to minorities in the workplace and is the author of *Good Is Not Enough*, a book intended to help minorities understand the key to career success. In our conversation, he elaborated on the way the career game is experienced differently by minorities and how, as a result, they may need to play differently.

The majority of the conversations recorded in this book are with people who were selected because they, themselves, are in the midst of experiencing remarkable careers. We hope that these conversations will shed some light on how others have played their career games, as well as on how game theory can be used to interpret the moves of others—and that the conversations will ultimately help prepare you to make your own career moves. We tried to choose a diverse set of individuals in a range of career stages in a variety of industries. For example, Ursula Burns (Xerox) and Charlene Begley (GE) have had long and successful careers within large companies. Pasha Federenko and Bryan Bell are in the early stages of their career games, both having just accepted positions at Bain & Company at the time of our conversations. Chris Klaus, the founder of Internet Security Systems, has experienced great success as an entrepreneur. Marius Kloppers (BHP Billiton) has experienced a very fast rise to the C-suite of one of the world's biggest companies. Bill Perez (William Wrigley Jr. Company) has spent the majority of his career in leadership positions in family-held companies. Finally, Liz McCartney (CNN's 2008 Hero of the Year) is an example of a social entrepreneur—she left her career in Washington, DC, to move to the New Orleans area to assist in the post-Katrina recovery effort. After each conversation, we offer a few specific examples of how—even if the subjects did not label it explicitly as such—game theory principles were present in their career decisions. We hope you will find the conversations useful in their own right, but we also encourage you to consider how well even an implicit game theory approach served each individual—and how it might serve you as you make your own career decisions.

Together, our hope is that the material we offer in each chapter along with the lessons from the conversations we report will be useful to you as you continue to make moves in your career game.

1 YOUR CAREER AS A GAME

The indispensible first step to getting the things you want out of life is this: Decide what you want.
Ben Stein

In the film *A Beautiful Mind*, Russell Crowe plays game theory pioneer John Nash. One scene from the film succinctly captures the essence of game theory and its implications for decision making. In the scene, Nash and his classmates are together in a bar when a group of five young women walk in—one blonde and four brunettes. The group—and particularly the blonde—quickly attracts the attention of Nash and his friends. Immediately, each classmate begins to plot his next move to win over the blonde. Nash has an epiphany of sorts: If each one independently attempts to maximize his personal outcome (which, in this scenario, involves pursuing the blonde), they will undoubtedly trip over one another and, in the end, no one will "win." He predicts that, by the time their mutual failures to win over the blonde become apparent, it will be too late to turn their energy to her friends—none of the brunettes will want to be second choice. This dilemma causes Nash to comment that Oliver Williamson's classical view—that through individuals acting in their own best interests, the best interests of the group are met—does not fit the situation. If each classmate acts in his own best interest, then they will all fail.

Instead, Nash understands the situation as one in which *each individual's best move depends on the anticipated moves that other rational players can be expected to make.* Understood this way, the best course of action for each individual is to recall the dynamic—espoused in the title of the 1953 movie—that "gentlemen prefer blondes." Knowing that your classmates are likely to pursue the blonde first, a more effective strategy would be for you to attend to one of the brunette friends. That way, you maximize your chance of winning the attention of one of the women. The critical observation here is the recognition that, in many situations, *one individual's best move is often dependent on the anticipated moves of other players.* Just as an understanding of game theory might help a college student understand how to win a date, we suggest that it can help you position yourself to have a successful career.

GAME THEORY IN OUR CULTURE

Game theory continues to be a popular topic; a 2005 Nobel prize was, once again, awarded to game theory scholars.[1] It has been used to provide novel ways to look at wide-ranging phenomena including logistics,[2] investing,[3] marketing,[4] human evolution,[5] and terrorism.[6] In popular culture, strategists have used game theory to outline a winning strategy in the spate of reality television shows (*The Weakest Link*, *Survivor*, and *The Apprentice*, for example). These shows share some important characteristics. First, individuals move on to the next round—or are eliminated—based largely on the votes of other contestants. Second, early-round success depends on the contributions of all players. In such contests, the winning strategy involves finding the delicate balance between moves that cause others to conclude that you are too weak to contribute to the group tasks and those that reveal you to be so strong as to be seen by other contestants as a final-round threat. Those who fail to achieve this balance and who appear to be "free riders" in the early rounds may not survive because others conclude that they cannot help the team with early wins. Those who tip their cards and reveal their strength too early will likely be eliminated by temporary alliances of other players.

Not surprisingly, examples of game theory applications abound in competitive sports. For example, the concept of a "moral hazard" is illustrated by the greater propensity for batters in the American League to be hit by pitches than their counterparts in the National League. In the American League, the rules do not require the pitcher to take a turn at bat. As a result, pitchers may not be concerned about experiencing retribution when they throw "at" rather than "to" batters. Anyone who has spent time watching football broadcasts has heard the ubiquitous comment from "color" analysts that a team "has to be able to run to set up the pass" or "has to be able to pass to set up the run." Unknowingly, those commentators are applying the concept of "mixing motives" from game theory to the calling of plays.

Making predictable moves in a multiplayer game is rarely a winning game strategy. If your opponent knows your tendency, developing a response is quite straightforward. When a football defense unit knows a team has trouble passing, they "pack" their players toward the line to stop the run. Similarly, when either tendencies or circumstances suggest that the offense must pass, the defense knows to adjust. The best moves for an offense, then, are to first avoid getting into a situation, such as third and long yardage, in which your position telegraphs your likely play and, above all, to avoid discernable patterns of play calling.

All of us play games in our daily lives, as well. Consequently, game theory can help our understanding of a variety of routine activities familiar to everyone. For example, before leaving the office you may check online to see what the traffic report is for your trip home. Upon hearing of an accident delaying traffic on your primary route, you begin to plot a strategy using alternate roads. Other drivers who share parts of your route home are simultaneously plotting their own strategies. To the extent that you anticipate and avoid their choices, your commute home is a breeze. Should you each select the same alternative, you end up no better off than those stuck on the primary route. Here begins the game of trying to anticipate what your competitors are thinking—and their simultaneous efforts to understand what you are thinking—and each of your efforts to "outthink" the other.

These illustrations show how accessible and useful game theory can be in understanding decision making in situations with interdependent players. Our first task in this book is to provide you with a deeper understanding of the primary concepts behind game theory. Game theory provides ways for you to think about your career so that you learn to anticipate the moves others will make and to plan your own moves accordingly. The second element of this book is the focus on a key individual capability—a new concept we are calling *career agility*.

GAME THEORY IN CAREERS

Why do we think you will find game theory a useful tool when considering careers? As noted above, game theory has gained some traction as a useful tool for understanding business situations. For the most part, applications of game theory related to business strategy have focused on elements such as pricing strategy, market entry, and strategic moves. The theory has not been explicitly applied to understanding career decision making, although some figures have paved the way. Gary Kasparov, who, in 1985, became the world's youngest chess champion, has since been writing and has become active in Russian politics. He recently published a book titled *How Life Imitates Chess: Making the Right Moves from the Board to the Boardroom.* As the title implies, Kasparov feels that lessons he learned while honing his chess game are applicable to the business world. As Kasparov notes regarding chess, you can't win at your career without moral and physical courage, boldness, and daring. Kasparov also speaks to our sentiments about agility, noting that to win at chess requires intelligence and audaciousness as well as a willingness to do what it takes to unnerve the other player.

Another observation that caused us to explore this topic concerns what we view as a fairly stagnant body of literature on career management. The expression "career advice" returns nearly 14,000 recommendations on Amazon. com's website.[7] The top choice was a book called *Career Match: Connecting Who You Are with What You'll Love to Do* by Shoya Zichy and Ann Bidou. The title seems to make clear the authors' central premise. The Amazon.com search utility suggests a second title—the ubiquitous *What Color Is Your Parachute? 2009* by Richard Nelson Bolles. The admonitions proffered in these books are strikingly similar to advice that appeared fifty years ago. In 1959, an article in *Nation's Business* offered the following career advice: consider your interests, your abilities, your personality, and "everyday practicalities" and match what you are good at with what you want out of a job.[8] The state of the art in understanding career success does not appear to have changed very much. To our point of view, just as John Nash noted that Oliver Williamson's view of individual decision making required some revision, so, too, does our thinking about how to manage a career. The insights that a game theory approach offers to individuals about how to strategically manage their careers, we think, constitute a proper revision.

Once a career is understood as a game involving players who compete for opportunities, the natural next question concerns how to become a better player. We suggest that the key to developing ability as a career game player is career agility. Career-agile individuals have high emotional intelligence, are politically savvy, are comfortable with uncertainty and risk, and thus demonstrate high degrees of successful portability from position to position over time. Great players of the career game are often modest, and most minimize their own role in their success. In our experience, the most common explanation that executives will offer for their personal success is that they were lucky enough to be in the right place at the right time. Of course, as the Roman philosopher Seneca observed long ago, "luck is what happens when preparation meets opportunity." Agile executives understand how to navigate *to* the intersection of preparedness and opportunity. Whereas a concerted effort to do so would likely uncover some examples of meritless people stumbling into that intersection, it is fair to expect that most people's opportunities derive from demonstrated capability. Others describe their rises as resulting from a nearly invisible "hand up" from a mentor. Some successful individuals are more purposeful in their efforts. As one executive told us, "Some people are constantly plotting their career. I don't know where they got this gene, but it seems that they are plotting from the playpen until they become chairman and CEO."

Over the course of the rest of this book, our first goal will be to help you understand the career game; the second goal will be to help you develop your skill as a player. Game theory tools, concepts, and nomenclature will help you understand that your career is productively viewed as a game characterized by interacting, interdependent, and self-interested players. The game has rules; the players all have motives and options. Comfortable salaries, exciting work, promotional opportunities, and charismatic coworkers are among the often zero-sum prizes out there to be "won" by players. Game theory helps us frame the career game—to understand its rules, boundaries, and ways of winning. Then, understanding career agility—a characteristic that individuals can develop—is explained as the key ability to playing the game well. Each is necessary, and neither is sufficient on its own, to win at the game of your career.

In the next chapter, we will introduce you to the game theory concepts that will prove most useful in managing your career. First, however, you will find our conversations with Charlene Begley, Bryan Bell, and Ursula Burns. Charlene Begley is senior vice president with General Electric and president and CEO of GE Enterprise Solutions. She has had a long and successful career at GE and offers a number of important comments on topics, including how GE uses its size to develop careers and how you can attract mentors to your cause. At the time of our conversation, Bryan Bell was finishing his PhD in Bioengineering and had recently accepted a position as a management consultant with Bain & Company. Bell offers some great insight into early-career moves—around universities, majors, and first job decisions. Our final conversation in this chapter is with Ursula Burns, CEO of Xerox Corporation. Like Charlene Begley, she has had a long career with one employer and offers some insights into what it is about Xerox that made it possible for her to stay and grow—and what she did in order to continue to garner opportunities. These interviewees' observations provide useful clues for evaluating the likelihood of a long career with a potential employer.

NOTES

1. V. L. Smith, "A Second Nobel for Stelten?" *Wall Street Journal*, October 15, 2005, A6.
2. I. Wylie, "Mars Wins the Shipping Game," *Fast Company*, April 2003, 38–42.
3. T. Kostigen, "Where Game Theory Ends Human Nature Takes Over," October 11, 2005, www.investors.com.
4. A. Fass, "Game Theory," *Forbes*, November 14, 2005.
5. R. Wright, "Games Species Play," *Time*, January 24, 2000, 59.
6. C. Oster, "Can the Risk of Terrorism Be Calculated by Insurers? Game Theory Might Do It," *Wall Street Journal*, April 8, 2002; S. Begley, "A Beautiful Science: Getting the Math Right Can Thwart Terrorism," *Wall Street Journal*, May 16, 2003, B1.
7. Search conducted in June 2008.
8. "Guides to Career Planning," *Nation's Business* 47, no. 8 (August 1959), 72–75.

A CONVERSATION WITH CHARLENE BEGLEY

SENIOR VICE PRESIDENT, GENERAL ELECTRIC; PRESIDENT AND CEO, GE ENTERPRISE SOLUTIONS

Since stepping into her present position in August 2007, Charlene Begley has been driving growth initiatives in GE's technology, emerging markets, vertical solutions, and global infrastructure. GE Enterprise Solutions has 17,000 problem-solving employees in more than sixty countries around the world.

Begley began her career at GE in 1988. She has held a variety of leadership roles within the company, including vice president of operations at GE Capital Mortgage Services, quality leader and CFO at GE Transportation Systems, director of finance for GE Plastics-Europe, vice president of the Corporate Audit Staff, and CEO at GE FANUC Automation. In January 2003, she was appointed president and CEO of GE Transportation. And in July 2005, she was named president and CEO of GE Plastics.

Begley serves on the World Economic Forum's Young Global Leaders panel, the GE FANUC board of directors, and the board of the National Association of Manufacturers. She is a graduate of the University of Vermont. See also www.ge.com/company/leadership/bios_exec/charlene_begley.html.

AUTHORS: **You have been at GE for twenty years. How did you get started there?**

BEGLEY: Coming out of college, I knew I wanted to enter a leadership development program. It was my goal to be some type of leader—although at the time I didn't have a clear idea of exactly what I wanted to lead. As I was looking for a job, I paid attention to companies that had the best reputations for leadership development. That was my first strategy, to get into a company that had a really good reputation for developing people. I started in finance, not because I have a love for it, but because I felt understanding finance was fundamental to understanding overall business.

I went through GE's two-year financial management program, and I made a conscious decision to join the corporate audit staff because it was considered the career accelerator within the company. I wanted a chance to see other functions and to see other parts of GE, so I joined with the intent of broadening myself beyond finance. At that time, the audit staff did about 50 percent nonfinancial work, so it was actually a broadening experience. From there, the opportunities have kept on coming. Beyond the first few decisions—to join GE, to take advantage of the financial management program, and to work in corporate audit—things have happened faster than I could have ever hoped or planned.

AUTHORS: **These early steps prepared you for either a long career at GE or for a position elsewhere, since you were learning fairly portable skills.**

BEGLEY: True. I never thought about taking them out the door with me, but I certainly could have.

AUTHORS: Our observation is that many companies are quick to cut or scale back on these entry-level leadership development programs. Why has GE remained so committed to theirs?

BEGLEY: You are right about the overall trend. At GE, people and leadership development are fundamental company values. I have been on Jeff Immelt's executive council for years, and on [our previous CEO] Jack Welch's before that. We view talent development as core to our business strategy, and leadership development is a key tactic in our growth strategy. We are more committed than ever to programs that will develop our leadership. For example, we support two-year entry-level programs in finance, IT, HR, engineering, communications, design, and technology. This commitment has never wavered in my twenty years at GE. It has always been a huge priority. No matter how tough it may get from an economic and business standpoint, developing people is one priority where we never lose focus.

AUTHORS: Who has helped you shape your career?

BEGLEY: I had mentors and sponsors throughout my career. These people played a big role in why I have had such an accelerated career in GE. It was never formal or structured, and, personally, I think this is the strongest way to form mentor-mentee relationships. Early in my career, Dave Calhoun [now at The Nielson Company] was very instrumental. He was running the corporate audit staff while I was there. He noticed my work and was impressed with some of the things that I had achieved. He took interest in my career early on, and throughout my career I have called him for his opinion on particular opportunities at GE. He has pulled me out of jobs and moved me to the next level, such as the CFO job at GE Transportation. He had a lot to do with some of my career moves.

AUTHORS: Calhoun has been valuable to you because of his position and his network in the company. He is senior enough to be influential, but not so senior that he didn't notice you on the audit staff.

BEGLEY: That's right. He was an excellent mentor in this regard.

AUTHORS: As you have climbed higher on the organizational chart at GE, what has changed in terms of what you need from a mentor relationship?

BEGLEY: What I appreciate now—although it has always been useful—are peers who can give you a reality check. Having a connection to someone with enough experience and insight to understand your challenges—but who also is in a position to be objective—is very valuable. This isn't true mentoring per se, but it is an incredibly useful support system.

AUTHORS: **You mentioned that opportunities have often come to you more quickly than you might have expected at GE. Did you ever worry about moving too quickly? How long do you think someone needs to stay in a role to really have a positive impact for the business?**

BEGLEY: There have been positions that I didn't occupy for very long, and that was partly how Jack Welch wanted to run the company. Rotating people—and rotating them frequently—really has been a fundamental part of the GE culture. Under Jeff Immelt's leadership, there is an emphasis on changing this a bit so that people develop more expertise by spending more time in a job, but I have never been with one business for more four years in my entire career at GE.

There are pros and cons to this approach. Obviously, I have had the benefit of working in different functions, different businesses, and different continents. With all that comes a huge learning experience. The con is that you don't develop a deep expertise in anything.

AUTHORS: **Another result of moving around too quickly is that executives are not in place when the consequences of their bad decisions come back to roost.**

BEGLEY: Yes—that can happen. One year is way too short—to me, twelve months is a training program, not tenure in a position. As such, the business is willing to sacrifice your contributions for your learning. I think three years is about right.

AUTHORS: **What have been your toughest moves; that is, what positions had steep or difficult learning curves, and how did you successfully transition between career moves?**

BEGLEY: That's a tricky question because each new job has been so absolutely and fundamentally different from the previous role. I started with four years on the corporate audit staff. It is a perfect example of having to learn the business and the issues very quickly, no matter what the job. We would take different projects every four months, ranging from reducing the cycle times of aircraft engine designs and gas turbines, to overseas projects on compliance processes and infrastructure, to examining how we market appliances globally, to selling aerospace operations and performing the due diligence to prepare for that sale, and so on. In all of these environments, you have to learn as much as you can as fast as you can, and you need to make an impact right away. The secret to this really isn't a secret: you have to ask a lot of questions.

Next, I ran operations for our mortgage business for two years. The business was doing so well, they had really not focused on the process. As a result, it was easier to come in and make a big impact quickly. From there, I took on the Six Sigma leader for our GE Transportation business. That was a big hurdle for me because I didn't have an engineering degree; I knew nothing about the mechanics of a locomotive, and there was a perception held by some that I was favored for the position because Dave Calhoun was running that business at the time. This made it one of my toughest jobs, as I had to prove myself without having a lot of expertise in this particular technology.

As I transitioned into any new role, I treated it like cramming for a college exam. I read as much material as I could, and I set up meetings with people who knew what they were talking about and asked them a ton of questions. Eventually, you build a baseline by pulling in experts to help. However, it is very important to remember that you don't get a lot of time to study or get up to speed; you have to start contributing pretty quickly.

AUTHORS: Your next role was as director of finance for GE Plastics in Europe and India. What stands out from your overseas assignment?

BEGLEY: When I moved to Europe, I experienced an entirely different culture on top of taking on a new role in a different part of the business. This was before the euro, so there were lots of issues with understanding financial exchange, different laws, and how that all affects business. So, there were some challenges from a technical and functional standpoint, but more importantly, it was just a big eye-opener for me to see the differences in cultures between Italy and Germany and India and so forth. Plus, it was an eye-opener for me to see how different it is to be at a remote site, as opposed to corporate headquarters. When you are at HQ, you have a lot of infrastructure and support. When you work away from that base, you have to do much more on your own.

AUTHORS: **When you are away from corporate, do you need to be a bit more of an entrepreneur?**

BEGLEY: Absolutely—you have to get more done with less, which is why I think those types of assignments are some of the best professional development experiences.

AUTHORS: **What were the eye-openers when you moved from a functional (finance) role to a general management position? What helped you make this key transition?**

BEGLEY: Again, my early audit staff experience gave me some advantage because it was such a good training ground. Through those projects I learned about many different parts of the business and how each function worked and provided value to the organization. I got enough of a taste to equip myself with confidence in my ability to be effective as a general manager. Part of what I learned early on was how important it was to use process skills to break something apart—whether it's a manufacturing design process or a marketing process—fundamentally, everything is a process. Once I figured that out, it became easier to transition across, functionally. I would add, too, that working with Jack Welch from 1999 through 2001 was great, eye-opening preparation. The exposure from sitting with Jack in all those business strategy and financial meetings and traveling around the world with him gave me a huge—if not unfair—advantage of watching and learning from a master.

AUTHORS: **You are now in a position to mentor others. How do you pick the people you are going to influence and spend time with as a mentor?**

BEGLEY: I work hard to mentor individuals who strike me as having potential. The best mentoring relationships are those where the foundation began in a real business application, as opposed to assigning randomly or calling someone out of the blue and asking, "Will you be my mentor?" In some cases, mentoring means a phone call every once in a while to bounce ideas around. In other cases, it can mean being involved and consultative in career choices [mentees] are wrestling with and facing. Sometimes it means helping them by opening doors to opportunities because you know how good they are.

I have been the most senior woman at GE for a long time and I am a mother of three children, so I tend to mentor a lot of people who strive to have families and do well in their careers. It is rewarding to find people who have a lot of curiosity, who take real initiative, who don't bring problems but bring ideas about solutions and then volunteer to help solve them. You just naturally want to help people like that.

AUTHORS: **What advice do you offer to the next generation of female leaders?**
BEGLEY: First of all, it is important to realize that nothing else matters if you are not good at your job. Another thing I tell people early in their careers is to not try to plan out your whole career too soon. Early in your career, you don't have enough perspective about work—and you probably don't know enough about yourself—to understand how your career might best develop. If someone asked me early on if I thought my career would have taken all the turns it has, my answer would have been no. Also, even though I knew I wanted to be a leader, I would not have guessed that I would have served as a CEO, and certainly not as a CEO of several businesses.

When I was first starting my career, I thought being successful in business was mutually exclusive to having a full family and social life, which I wanted, too; but it is not an either-or situation. It depends on the support system you have, and on your own determination and the decisions you make along the way. I couldn't be where I am today if my husband had not made sacrifices along the way. Someone with a less supportive spouse could not have entertained the choices I have entertained. We all make priorities, we all make choices, and we have to be realistic about the fact that you can't maximize on every outcome. It is best to figure out what the priorities are for your family and stick with them.

CAREER GAME OBSERVATIONS

- Once out of school, Charlene Begley's first move was to find a position at a company with a reputation for developing people; from there, she was able to earn a spot on the company's audit staff—a position that was seen as a "career accelerator." Such opportunities no doubt change the nature of the subsequent moves open to an individual.

- During her tenure at GE, Begley has held a number of positions—she noted that, under Jack Welch, it was a deliberate strategy to move people fairly frequently. This has the predictable benefit of building breadth of experience and the predictable drawback of the individual developing a shallow depth of experience. In terms of the career game, there is an additional benefit of frequent moves in that an individual's network grows accordingly. Along with that benefit may be a drawback: since many people are moving knowledge about, awareness of your weaknesses or blunders moves, too.

- Begley offers some useful comments about how she makes decisions about whom to invest in as a mentor. Her sentiment, that she is drawn to some people who she just naturally wants to help, reinforces for early-career people the importance of finding ways to be appealing to their senior colleagues. Showing initiative, displaying curiosity, and offering solutions where others simply identify problems are all ways to get others to care about your success.

- Finally, Begley notes that it is important to not plan out your entire career too soon because you aren't the same person early on that you will be later in your career—you will likely discover that your priorities, your interests, and your abilities evolve in ways that are not entirely predictable. Just as a business strategy needs to have the ability to evolve as conditions change, so too does your career strategy.

A CONVERSATION WITH BRYAN BELL

MANAGEMENT CONSULTANT, BAIN & COMPANY

Bryan Bell earned his BS in Materials Science and Engineering from MIT in 2002. He graduated with an MS in that same field from Georgia Tech in 2004. He continued his studies at Tech, completing his MBA in 2008, and his PhD in Bioengineering in 2009.

During his undergraduate program, Bell interned with Lucent Technologies and with Ethicon, a division of Johnson & Johnson Company. He joined Bain & Company during the summer of 2009.

AUTHORS: Can you start off by just sharing the story of your decision to go to MIT and then Georgia Tech for school? What initially drew you to engineering and MIT?

BELL: I knew, coming out of high school in Gainesville, Georgia, that I was interested in science and that I was good at math. Engineering seemed like a logical major for someone with my interests. I was excited about the thought of one day working on cutting-edge technology. Out of high school, I only applied to two schools—Georgia Tech and MIT. I was accepted early to MIT, and because it is the top-ranked engineering school, that's where I went. I had grown up in Georgia, so the chance to live in another city was appealing, too.

AUTHORS: And when you went to MIT, what did you plan to do when you finished? What were your intentions?

BELL: I didn't necessarily think I wanted to be an engineer; I had always had an interest in business in the back of my mind.

AUTHORS: Where do you think this came from?

BELL: Both my parents were influential here, I think. My dad had been the president of a couple of banks here in Georgia. My mom was a role model, too. She started her own real estate appraisal business—she was an entrepreneur.

AUTHORS: After finishing MIT, you came straight to Georgia Tech and began your master's program. Is that right?

BELL: I came straight to Tech. During my undergraduate program, I held a couple of internships. I have always been interested in medical devices and was able to work one summer for Johnson & Johnson. I also worked at Lucent Technologies—that position obviously wasn't in medical devices, but it helped me explore other things. The exposure, in a way, provided a test to see if working in the medical device industry was really what I wanted to do. You know, at the time, high tech was big, so I wanted to see if that was interesting to me as well.

AUTHORS: **Did something specific happen that caused you to decide to go straight through for a master's right after your undergraduate program, rather than working as an engineer for a while?**

BELL: I knew, during my undergraduate program, that I was going to get a master's right away. I applied to several programs coming out of MIT. I applied to Georgia Tech and to three schools in California. I was looking for someplace warm.

AUTHORS: **Four winters in Cambridge was enough.**

BELL: Right—it was for me. I ended up picking Georgia Tech because of the extent of the financial support I received to attend. While I was doing my master's thesis, I was involved in engineering research. All the while, I had in the back of my mind an interest in business.

Once I was at Tech, I learned about a program that teamed engineers with business students around the development of a commercialization plan for a technology. I became interested in that program and at about the same time decided to pursue my PhD in engineering. So things changed quickly—in a fairly short time I entered that commercialization program, enrolled to simultaneously be part of the MBA program, and changed my status in the College of Engineering from the master's to the PhD program.

AUTHORS: **In the commercialization program, have you been working with a team around a technology that you identified in your PhD research?**

BELL: It was a new technology that I was working on in the lab. The program is set up to build and commercialize a plan, but honestly my research was too basic to consider commercialization opportunities. Still, the program made use of it to teach us the process.

AUTHORS: **So, as of today, you have earned your MBA and you are slated to finish your PhD in the spring, correct? You will have exhausted school options—what are you doing in terms of launching your career?**

BELL: I've accepted a consulting job with Bain.

AUTHORS: Can you talk a little bit about your decision to look for that kind of position and then, more specifically, what it was about Bain that was attractive?

BELL: Once I committed to the MBA program, I knew I wanted to work more to the business side of science and technology. I didn't know much about consulting at that point. I had spent enough time in the lab to know that research—though interesting—was not something I wanted to do for my career. I honestly wanted to interact with people a little bit more. That same desire is part of what drove me to the MBA program. There, I had the chance to work on a number of projects with outside clients. Those experiences triggered my interest in consulting. I worked on three projects in the MBA program. One was in a strategy class—it was the first group project I did with an outside company. We worked on something for Air Tran. Being forced to so quickly learn about something I hadn't known much about was a very interesting challenge. It was also great to interact with some of the top-level people at Air Tran. I did a couple of other projects in other classes. These experiences helped me realize how much I enjoy working with other people in order to deliver results that help the client. That's when I decided consulting is what I wanted to do.

AUTHORS: So, how did you land on Bain as the place to begin your career?

BELL: My job search began in the fall of 2007. At that time, I was still thinking a little bit more about how to leverage my engineering credentials. I knew that I wanted to leave academia. I wanted to work in a medical device company, but I didn't want to do research. I love science and technology, but I wanted more interaction with people and I wanted to see my work more directly have an impact on people's lives. I initially looked at traditional medical device companies, like Johnson & Johnson or Medtronic. I looked at several different types of positions, including product specialist, research scientist, and business analyst.

Product specialist positions are relatively new options for PhD students. Only a few companies have these positions for new PhD hires. Essentially, the PhD becomes the "product expert" and crosses over functions (R&D, physician interface, marketing, manufacturing, management). Traditionally, PhD students have become research scientists. These positions pay well and can provide stable careers, but it is difficult to advance from them into management positions. It is easy to get "pigeonholed" into doing the same research for an entire career. My MBA scared some companies because they want to hire research scientists who will become research experts, not someone who will use the job as a stepping-stone to something else. This question—what did I really want in my career—came up frequently during interviews. Business development positions are also nearly impossible to get directly out of school. Each company hires only a few people, and generally the positions go to new hires from the top five MBA programs or to internal hires.

So, basically, I was going to have to take a traditional research position, which I would probably have hated and would have needed to use as a stepping-stone for another job. That path probably would have required me to move to the Northeast or the Midwestern U.S.

I also spent time looking for jobs with some start-ups and VCs, but no one seemed very interested in me because I didn't really fit. I made a lot of contacts with small biotech companies in Atlanta, but it is very difficult to get a position with them as a new PhD hire. I didn't have the experience to be brought in at a high level, but at the same time, I was overqualified for the entry-level lab technician jobs that most of them are looking to fill. I also talked to a few VCs doing biotech work and got the same answers regarding my lack of experience.

During these efforts, I noticed that a lot of people in start-ups and VC firms had been consultants before becoming entrepreneurs. It seemed like the right move to make might be to reframe my search to focus on consulting companies. Of course, this became clear to me as a viable strategy in January of 2008—after the traditional recruiting cycle had just ended. This wasn't the end of the world—although I finished my MBA in May of 2008, I was still working on my dissertation.

Although I knew I wanted to get with a consulting firm, I didn't think that I would land with one of the big three. And, when I originally applied to Bain, my résumé didn't make it through their screening process. I didn't get any positive response from a number of firms—Deloitte, Kurt Salmon, and others. For a time it seemed like my lack of consulting experience might be a barrier I couldn't get over. Some were skeptical that I really understood what I was getting into in terms of consulting. Since I wasn't having much luck, I began looking for research positions. I actually received an offer from one medical research company, and I had a good interview with another. It looked like that was what I would need to do next to get some of the experience that the consulting companies were looking for. Of course, at just that time, Bain contacted me again. I ended up talking to Bain, McKinsey, Capgemini, and BCG. Bain was the first to get me through all of the rounds. I liked the people at Bain so much, I accepted that offer once I had it.

AUTHORS: **Why do you think companies are interested in you?**
BELL: I think they were interested in me because of the MBA and PhD combination. Those three companies specifically look for PhDs. They have PhD recruiting programs and PhD training programs; they are familiar with hiring PhD students. So, it's something they are comfortable with and I think some of the other companies I talked to weren't. The fact that I have a MBA and PhD combination made me stand out a lot there.

AUTHORS: **And do you think they plan on using you differently as a result?**
BELL: No, I don't—they've told me that. That's something I asked in the interview and basically their answer was no. What I am told is that they like the analytical skills that PhD students bring, and they like the credentials too.

CAREER GAME OBSERVATIONS
- Bryan Bell's early moves—to go to MIT and then Georgia Tech—were instrumental, given his interest in a career in science and technology. All the while, however, he recognized his curiosity about business. He had a general idea of what he wanted to do after school, and he was both strategic and flexible in terms of how he learned more about the available opportunities and prepared himself to pursue them.
- Once at Tech, Bell was able to leverage a program designed to provide engineers with some business acumen, and ended up earning an MBA along the path to his PhD. His move to get an MBA was interesting in terms of its impact on his job search. Generally, people would view an MBA as a career-refining move. In the science/technology arena, however, the move was career limiting: employers did not believe he would be fully committed to the positions they had available.

- Bell's PhD qualified him for research jobs at medical device companies, but by that time he had concluded that those jobs were not a fit for him. Furthermore, his MBA signaled to companies that he would likely not be happy long term in the researcher role. Medical device companies offered business-oriented positions, but his inexperience was a liability in terms of competing for them.

- Bell's next alternative was to consider positions in entrepreneurial firms or with venture capital companies. For these positions, he was overqualified on the science end and underqualified on the business end.

- Bell exhibited an example of social learning in discerning that many of the people who were in the positions he desired in the entrepreneurship space had experience as consultants. This led him to reengage with those companies. From what he has seen, this first move should prove to be instrumental and career refining.

A CONVERSATION WITH URSULA BURNS

CHIEF EXECUTIVE OFFICER, XEROX CORPORATION

In July 2009, Ursula M. Burns was named CEO of Xerox Corporation. Burns joined Xerox in 1980 as a mechanical engineering summer intern. She has since held several positions in engineering, including product development and planning. In June 1991, she became the executive assistant to Paul A. Allaire, then Xerox chairman and CEO. From 1992 through 2000, Burns led several business teams, including the office color and fax business, the office network copying business, and the departmental business unit. In May 2000, she was named senior vice president, Corporate Strategic Services, and two years later assumed the role of president, Business Group Operations. In 2007 she was named president and appointed to the company's board of directors.

Burns serves on professional and community boards, including American Express Co., Boston Scientific Corp., CASA (the national Center on Addiction and Substance Abuse at Columbia University), FIRST (For Inspiration and Recognition of Science and Technology), National Academy Foundation, MIT, the U.S. Olympic Committee, and the University of Rochester.

AUTHORS: **When you started as an intern at Xerox, did you imagine developing a long career inside the company?**

BURNS: Absolutely not. In fact, I didn't imagine a career at all. I only imagined a job, and understood that it may lead to another job at Xerox, but I thought that I would return to "the city." I considered myself a city girl—I was born and raised in New York City. I figured I would work a few years for Xerox in Rochester and, eventually, find my way back to the city. It has now been more than twenty-five years that I have spent in Rochester. That sort of longevity is certainly not the norm today.

AUTHORS: **How has Xerox been able to keep you from wondering if the grass is greener somewhere else?**

BURNS: Well, I think it's a natural curiosity to wonder about how green the grass is on the other side, but Xerox has always felt like a special place to me. I was not your typical Xerox employee in the early 1980s. I am a black, urban, female mechanical engineer—we were not a dime a dozen back then! At the time, it would have been difficult for any company to find that kind of diverse engineering talent, and perhaps it would have been difficult for me to find a place where I felt as comfortable as I did at Xerox. Fortunately, one of the most significant things Xerox did was to never expect or ask me to be anything other than who I was. Of course, they have helped me smooth out some of the edges—that is part of everyone's development. There were so many obvious differences between me and my colleagues—the way I spoke, the things I liked to do, my outlook on life. Those differences were not looked at as anything but strengths. It actually took a while for me to realize that, "Wow! They're not asking me to change to fit into this base or that base. They actually like—or at least don't dislike—the fact that I am who I am." They offered jobs to me, Ursula, and that's who they wanted in these jobs—Ursula.

AUTHORS: It is easy to understand that they made you comfortable—that would seem necessary, but not sufficient to engage someone for over twenty-five years.

BURNS: Correct. It wasn't. That was just one piece of it. What also mattered a lot was that I got real work from the day I walked in the door. In fact, it was to the point where sometimes I was absolutely shocked. They gave me a lab, a budget, a lab technician, and a problem to solve. I remember asking, "Who can help me with this?" and the reply was, "If you need specific help or specific questions answered, let us know, but you are the person who actually knows about this challenge, and you are who we want to solve it." They let me run with it. I don't think there was a grand strategy to make sure I had amazing jobs each step of the way—but that is how it turned out. I would also have to say that, 90 percent of the time, I was put in jobs that were one step beyond what I thought I could do. That is how Xerox has kept me engaged. I have been constantly tested, constantly challenged.

I remember one big job I got in business planning. Here I was, this mechanical engineer who had never done a business plan of any type before. They gave me a project to study—whether or not a certain feature on the machine was needed and, if so, how we should price it. Opportunities like that really stretched me. I was continually given jobs that were a little bigger or in an interesting part of the company.

A final piece has been that, overall, Xerox has treated me very fairly. I never felt forgotten or undervalued. I was given great work that challenged me, and I was paid reasonable money and allowed to travel all over the world to get the job done. I was treated like an adult from the day I walked in the door. I was given opportunity. True, I was given a whole lot of opportunities to fail, but there was never an expectation that I would fail. There was always an expectation that I could do it—and that I could do it while just being who I was. That support and encouragement gave me confidence, and, twenty-five years later, I still feel it.

AUTHORS: Can you talk a little bit about the role you played as the executive assistant to Paul Allaire when he was a CEO? How did that help you develop as an executive?

BURNS: It was an unbelievable role. At the time, the company was going through lots of changes, and to sit around as a "fly on the wall" during that transformative time was very exciting. Also, Paul was a wonderful match for me—especially at that time in my career. His personality is very different than mine. He is quiet and a more introverted individual—we were perhaps a bit of each other's alter ego. Obviously, he had the truly significant job, and I was just following him around learning from him, but he and I would talk about the business, and because I had a different way of thinking about things, I think I was helpful to him. We actually developed a more senior-level relationship than you would think an executive assistant and CEO would normally have. We would talk candidly about a lot of things. He was always quizzing me—asking what I thought about this individual or what I would say in that situation, and so on. It helped me formulate and understand different opinions, different views. It also showed me how tough the CEO job is. It is a demanding schedule, and the risks and pressures could be daunting. Seeing how CEOs work within that kind of a schedule and with those risks, pressures, and stresses—as well as how they jump on opportunities—was enlightening to me.

AUTHORS: **These are great experiences. How did Allaire find you for the position?**

BURNS: I had just started to work as the EA for the executive vice president in charge of all marketing and customer operations. He was a direct report to Paul, so, over time, I got to know Paul. I wasn't shy about participating in meetings or sharing my views. After six months, Paul's EA left and Paul asked me if I would do the job. I remember explaining that I thought it might not be a great idea. After all, I was just getting comfortable as EA to the EVP. I asked him why I should make the change, and he said, "Because I am the CEO and I asked." That was a pretty clear response!

Going to work for Paul was a very good decision because it showed me an entirely different side of leadership. Previously, I had not appreciated how tough the external part of the job is—the shareholder and political elements of the job, for example. I also learned how he managed and balanced his personal and professional lives.

YOUR CAREER AS A GAME

It was a great time—he and I really hit it off in an interesting way because, like I said, we had very different personalities.

At one point, we were going through a massive reorganization of the company. He appointed me to the reorganization task force as a real, participating member—not just as a fly on the wall for him. That was an interesting position because I was the only person on the task force who was not in line for any of the potential jobs—and I was fairly junior. This made it easy to participate in an objective way, as I had no personal, vested interest in the outcome. At the end of it, Paul offered me the job of running the smallest business unit that was formed. I never would have been given that opportunity without working for Paul, learning from him, and, I guess, without the opportunity of showing him my potential.

AUTHORS: One challenge in a long career in a single company is that you never really get a fresh slate. All your history—the good and bad—follows you. What are the advantages and disadvantages of that?

BURNS: You can't confuse people about who you are. Being consistent about who you are and who you are not is important. When people really know you—how you react, what you value, the expectations you have of others—it gives them a foundation.

AUTHORS: Some use the word "authentic" to describe what you are talking about.

BURNS: Authentic—yes. It isn't about being perfect—it's about authenticity and dependability, so that everyone knows that who they are dealing with Monday is the same person they will be dealing with on Thursday.

AUTHORS: What attributes in early-career employees get you excited about their potential?

BURNS: Passion about getting it better the next day, optimism about the fact that it is possible to do it better the next day, and recognition that any challenge is actually an opportunity. I would also say fearlessness. What I mean by that is not recklessness, but knowing that you can make a decision, take a course of action, and just move forward. You can always correct later, if correction is needed. Too often, I see people who sit back, studying and trying to get 99 percent of the information before making a move. Meanwhile, your options slowly run out.

The last indicator I look for to gauge potential is, frankly, being good at lots of things, or at least being outstanding at a few things. You have to be able to engage your brain without stressing to catch all the nuances. So, a part of your job needs to come easily because you are good at it, and the more of that you have, the better. As an example, I have a gentleman working for me who manages a very large piece of the company. We keep increasing his responsibilities. He succeeds, in part, because, at his core, he does a series of things extremely well. He knows how to design an organization and how to pick and nurture people. He can keep up with all we give him because these two strengths allow him to do a big part of his job without too much trouble. Having some parts of your job that you can do "at rest" is important. If you don't have a place where you are an expert, you can never relax or get comfortable with your work because nowhere is safe. Obviously, the more things you can do in this sort of automatic way, the better. Throughout your career you need to develop more and more of this ability.

AUTHORS: **As you look at talent and advise people on their career moves, what do you see as the difference between people who can recover from bad career decisions and people who can't?**

BURNS: Some of the biggest differences include patience, perspective, optimism, and not assuming that mistakes will follow you forever. This is true whether you make a mistake at work or in your personal life. People who recover from errors will often step back and be patient with the recovery. They take a longer-term perspective and they realize that they can reinvent themselves without too much damage. You don't want your mistake to define you. For example, let's say you have a car accident. You don't assume that every time you drive in the future you will have an accident. You may be a bit guarded and hesitant at first, but you learn from the accident and actually become a better driver. You fix your car, you get back on the road, and put the accident behind you. It takes time, so patience is key. We need to show this kind of patience to people who make mistakes in their jobs, and even with career mistakes.

Some mistakes are extremely hard to recover from, but most mistakes are not like that. It may be that you have to accept some lateral moves in the short term, but in my experience, well-run companies will see most mistakes as opportunities for people to learn and get better. Over time, people will gain a better perspective—that's another reason patience is important.

AUTHORS: You are active on a number of boards, of both community organizations and companies. What role have those opportunities played in your development?

BURNS: Let's talk first about the corporate boards. I serve as a board director at American Express and Boston Scientific. These experiences have been invaluable for the perspective they have provided. Since I have been with Xerox my whole working life, these positions effectively allow me to be in other businesses. I get to vicariously participate in two completely different industries. I see enough similarities to the challenges and opportunities we have at Xerox to help me validate our situation too. The nonprofit boards I am on allow for learning, but more than that, they help me stay a well-rounded person. Among all the boards, I get to observe different leadership styles and different sets of issues. My board service is rewarding in many ways.

AUTHORS: These types of opportunities are mostly open to senior-level executives. Are there ways for a more junior person to get those sorts of experiences, or would you advise emerging talent to stay focused on their jobs?

BURNS: I don't believe that junior-level people should work with their heads down and be immersed only in their organizations, but it is true that the extracurricular opportunities available to them will be different. At Xerox, we value our employees getting involved in the communities in which they live. For example, we are proud of the work we are doing to support teaching in science and technology in high schools and middle schools, and we have a great deal of employee engagement in those programs. It is a way for employees to learn and teach others through the sharing they do. Education is a passion here, and we view K–12 education as critically important to our future.

Ultimately, resourceful people can find ways to be involved in outside organizations, and they approach these opportunities as learning experiences.

CAREER GAME OBSERVATIONS

- Ursula Burns is remarkable for many reasons, one of which is her long track record of success at Xerox. Key to a long career in a single company, she says, is the ability to "smooth off some corners" while remaining "who you are." In her view, you don't have to be perfect, but you do have to be authentic.

- Her game at Xerox has been characterized by a series of jobs that always seemed to her to be one step beyond what she thought she could do. Xerox has kept her engaged, challenged, and learning as a player—all things that made her best next move always to be another position with the company.

- An important piece of wisdom is Burns' recommendation that everyone work at being very, very good at one or two elements of their jobs so that at least this part of the work can be fairly automatic in terms of execution. If every dimension of your job presents a challenge, you simply will not have enough gas to get it all done. In considering a move to a new opportunity—particularly if it is going to be a step beyond what you think you can do—make sure that at least some responsibilities will be in your sweet spot so that you can be certain you will have the energy required to succeed at the tough, new stuff.

- In regard to career agility, Burns stresses that mistakes are not destiny and they should not be managed as such.

- In regard to a network, Burns notes that it is important even for junior people to have some community involvement as a way to build their networks.

UNDERSTANDING FUNDAMENTAL GAME THEORY CONCEPTS

Begin with the end in mind.
Stephen Covey, *The 7 Habits of Highly Effective People*

Nobel prize–winner and game theory pioneer Reinhard Selten observed that people work diligently to be rational *ex post*. That is, we commonly look back at how a situation played out to try and understand how a better outcome might have been achieved. This contrasts with a game theory approach in which the goal is to develop a strategy that will lead to that better outcome *a priori*. Recognizing your interdependencies with other individuals is key in terms of developing an effective strategy. Your ability to achieve a desired outcome based on a decision is consequently dependent on your insight regarding the likely decisions and reactions of others. You can improve your ability to understand others' actions and reactions by explicitly recognizing the interdependence among parties and by making use of a host of concepts developed by game theorists. As a result, you can make better decisions.

Our purpose in this chapter is to introduce and discuss the key game theory concepts that will be useful in understanding your career as a game. We begin with an introduction to different types of games and a discussion of how the type of game that you play impacts your strategy. Next, we review the most important game theory concepts and their roles in the career game. Finally, we draw on work by John McMillan on game theory and business strategy to present and discuss the critical questions that players need to address in order to frame their career games. Answering these questions appropriately will allow you to understand the rules, players, boundaries, and time constraints of the game you are setting out to play.

UNDERSTANDING THE GAME

Game theorists have developed a nomenclature that describes central components of the theory and its application.[1] Here, we introduce and explain the terms and concepts most important for you as you develop your career game.

Rationality

Rationality on the part of players is a fundamental assumption in game theory. Rational players predictably seek to maximize their own payoffs when playing games. Choices or behaviors that do not lead to a maximum payoff are irrational. To the extent that you (a) understand the payoffs available to others and (b) can count on others to behave rationally, it becomes possible to predict people's moves and responses in a game. Without this assumption that players are rational it becomes difficult to estimate much about the likely strategies of one's opponents, peers, and assorted players. This means that a key question to ask when taking a game theory approach is "How likely is it that the other players involved in this situation are interested in maximizing their own outcomes?" Our expectation is that, when it comes to career decisions, people are generally looking to get the best return on the labor that they offer their employers.

Payoffs

Payoffs are simply the values assigned to outcomes achieved via one move or a series of moves. Since game theory recognizes that games are played by multiple players, you can think of payoffs as the results of the implementation of each player's strategies. The part that makes this tricky is that payoffs that individuals seek are not strictly monetary and are not always obvious. For example, workplace payoffs might include the chance at unique experiences to develop working relationships with key executives or exposure on a project of importance to the company. Some payoffs are awarded outside the workplace—but inside the game. An executive who turns down an international opportunity, for example, may lose financially. But, by remaining close to home, she realizes other payoffs, such as her spouse's ability to keep a great job or her child's ability to stay in school with close friends. The rationality of the decision applies to the sum total of these factors—many of which can be difficult for outsiders to even identify, let alone properly value. As difficult as it is to construct an accurate understanding, however, the payoff environment is the most important factor in making predictions about others' moves.

Sequential and Simultaneous Move Games

Games can be categorized based on rules regarding the timing of moves. *Sequential move games* are those that involve players taking turns. Chess, tic-tac-toe, checkers, and most board games are played in this way. In business, first movers, fast followers, and laggards make sequential moves as they enter markets. Winning a sequential move game relies on an individual player's ability to envision what a win "looks like" and then to reason backwards to make the current move that will push the game toward that desired end state. As chess grand master Gary Kasporov has noted, each player must calculate the opponent's moves in advance, essentially doing the thinking for two people all of the time.

In *simultaneous move games*, players make their strategic choices at the same time. This means that their choices of moves are made without firm knowledge of the choices being made by the other players. Players learn of their competitors' chosen strategies at the precise time that they reveal their own. The child's playground game Rock, Paper, Scissors is an example of such a game. Each player selects a strategy and simultaneously implements it by revealing a hand signal that represents either a rock, a sheet of paper, or a pair of scissors. The payoffs are familiar—rock smashes scissors, scissors cut paper, paper wraps rock. The key to winning a simultaneous move game involves anticipating your opponent's move, recognizing all the while that your opponent is similarly trying to ascertain your likely move. This means that each player wants to understand what the opponent views as the best choice. After all, a rational player will make the choice that provides the best payoff.

Mixed and Pure Strategies

The Rock, Paper, Scissors game is designed to have no "best move." Any of the three available strategies has an equal chance of winning. Players looking for an edge are left only with efforts to discern patterns or irrational preferences demonstrated by opponents over time. A player known to always pick "paper" will not win many games. For this reason, players are advised to adopt a *mixed strategy* (that is, randomly choosing between rock, paper, and scissors) in order to keep the other player guessing. Players who adopt a *pure strategy* (such as selecting "rock" every time or moving predictably from paper to scissors to rock) quickly become transparent, and their strategies are easily rendered ineffective. And, Kasporov notes that "when your opponent can easily anticipate every move you make, your strategy deteriorates and becomes commoditized."

Dominant and Dominated Strategies

A *dominant strategy* is one that is always best for a player to implement; a *dominated strategy* is one that can be overcome by an opponent. A strategy is considered dominant if it provides the best return to the player, regardless of the strategies employed by other players. Logically, then, a dominated strategy is one that provides a poor return to the player, regardless of the strategies employed by other players. There is no dominant strategy in the Rock, Paper, Scissors game—each strategy may produce a winner or a loser; winning is attributed to luck or perhaps the ability of one player to identify a pattern in the strategies selected by other players. Players in simultaneous move games are well advised to mix their strategies because becoming predictable (always throwing "scissors," for example) allows the opponent to consistently win.

The classic example of a simultaneous move game is represented by what is referred to as the Prisoners' Dilemma. In this case, a pair of suspected criminals—let's call them Spencer and Reid—are separated by the police and questioned. Each is individually given the opportunity to confess or to profess innocence. The payoff—the number of years' time to be served—associated with each choice is dependent on the simultaneous decision of that individual's partner in crime. Studying the payoffs presented in the payoff matrix below reveals that each player's *dominant strategy* is to confess. This is because confession yields the lowest time to serve, *regardless of the decision made by the other suspect*. Reid likely prefers serving no time in prison to serving one year in prison (the payoff if Spencer does not confess) and similarly prefers serving five years in prison to serving fifteen years (the payoff if Spencer does confess). The irony here is that by playing the dominant strategy—confessing—each player receives a worse outcome (5,5) than if both were to continue to profess their innocence (1,1). This emphasizes the importance of knowing the other players in a game and, more important, understanding payoffs, the motives of other players, and how credible they are. It also raises the importance of whether or not the players have the ability to coordinate strategies. If the police allowed Spencer and Reid time to strategize—and if the two had confidence in one another's ability to remain stoic—then they could likely receive the better outcome.

Prisoners' Dilemma Payoff Matrix

Reid	Spencer	
	Don't Confess	*Confess*
Don't Confess	1, 1	15, 0
Confess	0, 15	5, 5

In Prisoners' Dilemma, each player has a dominant strategy—to implicate the other—because no matter what the other does, the personal outcome is less severe when implicating the other. However, both would have experienced the best joint outcome if they had each refused to confess.

Information in Games

Information—and, more important, *any* information advantages or disadvantages—plays a critical role in strategy formulation. When the game history has been witnessed by players so that each knows the motives, moves, and any payoffs that occurred up until his or her move, then the game is referred to as a *perfect information* game. Chess is an example of a game that contains perfect information. The definition of winning is unequivocal, the moves available to each piece are defined, the order and history of play are clear, and so on. When this condition is not met—when, for example, some or all of the moves are hidden from some or all of the other players—the game is an *imperfect information* game. Because Spencer and Reid were separated and not allowed to communicate with each other, the police were able to create such a game. As a result, it was impossible for either Spencer or Reid to understand how to maximize his outcome. Your career game is most likely to be an imperfect information game, thus, going forward, these games will be our focus. For example, job seekers are unlikely to know all of the players or to fully understand the possible outcomes (such as salary, bonus, and relocation allowances).

Since a better understanding of the game and the steps necessary to maximize personal payoffs is possible only by having the best information possible, it behooves players to (a) work to collect as much useful information as possible and (b) work to avoid being on the wrong end of *information asymmetries*. When there is imperfect information (that is, one player knows something that other players do not), an information asymmetry results. Players in games may take advantage of asymmetries to create advantages. For example, a top public business school recently conducted a search for a new dean. A website was built as a mechanism for keeping both the university and the broader community informed about progress in relation to the search. Three finalists were identified and invited to the campus for interviews on successive weeks. The website was updated to announce each week's visitor, to provide the candidate's résumé, and so forth. What this meant is that the third candidate interviewed for the job with full information on the candidates who had come before; the second had the chance to be familiar with the first; and the first candidate interviewed with no idea as to who the other candidates were. This information asymmetry could have been exploited by the second and third candidate—they had information that could be leveraged to best distinguish their own records and capabilities from the candidates who had interviewed earlier.

Signaling

Signaling takes place in situations that contain information asymmetry—that is, games characterized by incomplete information.[2] In some situations, a player with more information will use signaling in an effort to influence another player's move. For example, years ago, before banking regulations became so well developed, it was difficult for customers to ascertain where their money would be safe. Banks signaled their legitimacy through the construction of grand places of business—an investment that a "fly by night" operation could not match. These opulent facilities were intended to influence depositors by signaling that the bank had a rock-solid foundation and a lasting commitment to the community. Similarly, automobile manufacturers offer warranties in an effort to signal something about the quality of their vehicles. In the career game, both employers and job candidates signal one another during the recruiting process. The speed at which each party moves is a signal of enthusiasm for the deal; the aggressiveness with which candidates negotiate is a harbinger of what they may be like as employees. In our conversation, Bryan Bell noted that his MBA signaled to employers seeking to fill research positions that he would likely be a short-timer and, hence, a bad fit for their openings.

Equilibrium

Equilibrium describes a situation in which no player has an incentive to make a change to his or her strategy. That is, the status quo in regard to the moves being made by the players results in the best possible payoff. Equilibrium exists when all players recognize that a change in strategy could lead to a poorer return than that earned by remaining with the current strategy. It is important to recognize that equilibrium does *not* mean that the best outcome will necessarily be earned. For example, in the Prisoners' Dilemma game, equilibrium is achieved by both players confessing—neither player has an incentive to change to the "don't confess" strategy.

Repeated Plays

The term *repeated plays* refers to instances in which a game has multiple iterations involving the same players. When repeated plays occur, two new aspects emerge in the game. First, there is an opportunity to learn about your opponent's strengths and tendencies. Second, each play becomes part of a shared history from which players can also learn to either trust and cooperate with— or to suspect and manipulate—other players. In a repeated-play game, your reputation matters and opportunities for cooperation are often present. These aspects of the game mean that players need to consider how aggressively they want to play, what sort of reputations they want to develop, and how—if at all—they want to address any opportunities for trust and cooperation that arise. In career games, repeated plays are impacted both by the bridges previously burned and, more broadly, by the reputations player have earned. Sometimes, there is no chance for a "do over," such as when you are onboarding to a company from the outside. You are the new hire only once. With no chance of a repeated play, your moves should be carefully thought out.

One commonly used training exercise illustrating these aspects of repeated plays is a version of Prisoners' Dilemma known as the Red-Blue Game. In the game, players are placed in groups and then paired with another group for play. The goal of the game is to earn points by simultaneously voting either "red" or "blue." Groups are not allowed to talk with one another and may communicate only via ballots carried by a runner to the facilitator conducting the exercise.

Once in groups, players are provided with a payoff matrix showing how points are determined not only by their group's vote, but also by the vote of the other group. When both teams vote blue, each team earns five points. When both teams vote red, each team loses five points. At this point, voting blue is clearly the dominant strategy and voting red a dominated strategy. However, if one team votes blue and the other red, the team voting blue loses ten points and the team voting red gains ten points.

Red-Blue Game Payoff Matrix

	Vernon's Team	
Janet's Team	*Votes Red*	*Votes Blue*
Votes Red	-5, -5	10, -10
Votes Blue	-10, 10	5, 5

Having run this exercise many times over the years, it has become clear that three patterns of play emerge. In one pattern, both teams begin in a trusting manner and vote blue. Having seen the other team as trustworthy (based on their voting history), they both continue to vote blue. Both teams accrue points at a modest rate. In the second pattern, both teams vote red in an effort to maximize their points at the expense of what they hope is a naïve, trusting group willing to begin by voting blue. When a red vote is met with a red vote, things tend to deteriorate—no group wants to be played as a sucker by being the first to vote blue; without communication, there is no opportunity to try to establish trust. During debriefing after the game, each team will unvaryingly recall efforts to remember who was on the other team in order to assess how aggressively these individuals might approach the game. Should the facilitator allow communication among the runners, issues always arise around convincing group members who were not party to the communication to trust their runner's judgment regarding the sincerity of the other team's runner—as well as those individuals' abilities to sway their groups.

The third pattern that emerges involves those groups that have been cooperating by voting blue. Generally, the game is introduced as having a finite number of repeated plays. Some groups do not seek to take advantage of this feature or rule of the game—they vote blue every round. However, as the final round approaches, some number of these previously trusting, cooperating groups begin to think about how to play the game to maximize their points. Clearly, by voting red in the last round, when they are certain the other team will once more vote blue, they have a chance to earn more than their customary five points and thus to take the lead. In a ten-round game, this pattern would indicate that teams so motivated will vote red in round ten. However, as is true in simultaneous move games, each team is also trying to divine what the other team is planning to do. If the other group has diagnosed the game in the same way, they will vote red in round ten. If that happens, both teams will lose five points. So, now a decision might be made by one team to beat the other to the punch, and to vote red in round nine. However, the other team is also diagnosing the situation and might come to the same conclusion, requiring the first team to vote red in round eight, and so on. Each team is trapped in the process of trying to outthink the other. This element of the game arises in cases in which the rounds of the game are *finitely repeated*. Knowing that the end of the game is near provides the impetus for this sort of strategic thinking. In a game in which rounds are *infinitely repeated*, the shared future of the players disincentivizes these sorts of moves. Players often presume that the rounds are not infinite, but at the same time they rarely know precisely when the last round has arrived. Understanding the degree to which your career game offers repeated play is important—as one executive told us, "I work in a small field and hope to have a long career." This observation implies that repeated plays will occur and that, as a result, each move you make will be remembered and could impact your game at some later point.

Credible Threats and Commitment

At times, players may use threats in an effort to influence the moves of other players. Threats are effective only when they are viewed as *credible*. A noncredible threat is one that others recognize is not in that player's best interest. For example, if one government threatens to use nuclear weapons against another to pursue its objectives, and if it is clear that the other government is prepared to respond in kind against the aggressor, then the threat of a first strike is not credible. Throughout the cold war, for example, the United States and the USSR engaged in this sort of a standoff: if either's willingness to respond to a first nuclear strike with a nuclear strike of its own had not been credible, the game may have played out differently.

Of course, in many cases the credibility of a threat is hard to discern beforehand. Recently, the ABC television program *Prime Time* featured a segment that speaks to this difficulty, filmed with game theory expert Barry Nalebuff.[3] For the segment, photographs of five overweight people wearing only very skimpy bathing suits were held in reserve. The threat was that the photographs of any individuals who did not lose at least fifteen pounds in a two-month period would be revealed on television and on the Web. Four of the five individuals successfully lost the weight to avoid the embarrassment they associated with such a public airing of the photographs—they found ABC's threat credible. However, the network chose *not* to show the photographs of the one participant who failed to lose the weight, making its threats much less credible in the future.

Research that has looked at layoff victims and their reactions to unemployment speaks to this as well. In one study, laid-off employees who felt they had received significant severance and outplacement support were less inclined to take the sorts of actions that lead to reemployment than those individuals who did not feel so well treated. The support that these individuals received reduced the threat associated with unemployment. Those who saw unemployment as a credible threat made moves that put them back at work more quickly.[4]

An additional component of evaluating credible threats concerns the player's *commitment* to them. Are the threats easily reversed? The clichéd example that appears in virtually all treatments of game theory involves Spanish explorer Hernán Cortés. One version of the story has it that, upon arrival in

Mexico, he had his ships burned so that his troops had no option but to fight to victory over the Aztecs. Once a ship is burned, it is burned—there is no reversing that move: it requires complete commitment to the strategy of fighting until victory or death. Coming at this from a different direction, Sun Tzu's *The Art of War* suggests leaving a surrounded enemy an escape route. Absent that alternative, the enemy has no choice but to remain committed to the fight. Avinash Dixit and Barry Nalebuff offer a business strategy example of a strong commitment in the actions of the Polaroid Corporation's response to Kodak's entry to the instant photography field.[5] Upon determining that Kodak was in violation of a number of Polaroid patents, Polaroid went "all out" to defend its intellectual property, investing considerable resources in its efforts to ultimately win a sizable judgment against Kodak as well as a return to a monopoly position in the industry.

FRAMING THE GAME

Now that the central terms and concepts describing game theory have been introduced, the next challenge is to understand the concept of game boundaries and how they apply in the career game. One of the challenges to applying game theory to complex settings such as individual careers arises from the potentially limitless field of play. In a board game, the field of play is quite clear—a Scrabble board has 225 squares, Monopoly has 22 buildable properties, and a chessboard has 64 individual squares. Furthermore, each player is clear on who can impact the field of play—certainly, the opponent is expected to be involved, and occasionally something unpredictable may impact play, such as the wagging tail of an exuberant dog passing by the chessboard. Players may have agreed to time limits for each move or for the entire game. In athletic competitions, the term *field of play* can be taken quite literally—in football, *in bounds* and *out of bounds* are understood, and clear time limits are in force; in baseball, each game begins with a meeting between managers and umpires to review peculiarities regarding what is in play or out of play in the venue, and each team takes a set number of turns.

In business, generally—and in careers, specifically—this field of play concept is more difficult to pinpoint. When making career decisions, there is a wide cast of possible players, the field of play may feel indeterminate, the nature and the timing of moves and the length of the game may be unclear, and so on. For this reason, the first challenge of applying game theory to career decision making is to discover a way to properly define the boundaries of the game. Once those boundaries are identified, it becomes possible to consider how to best play the game. This understanding of boundaries—though complex—is essential. Without a reasonable understanding of the boundaries of play, it would be impossible to discern what constitutes rational behavior on the part of players.

John McMillan wrote one of the more accessible books for managers on game theory for business strategy.[6] Included in the book's conclusion is a series of questions he offers managers so that they can properly frame a game theory analysis of business situations. In the next chapter, we build on McMillan's framework. But we also employ it briefly here in order to offer readers a quick tool for understanding the way a game theory analysis can be applied to career strategy. In considering each of the following questions, we offer examples of applications to the career game—along with the reminder that your particular circumstances will drive your own best answers to the questions.

Who Are the Players?

This question specifically addresses who and how many people are playing the game. All it takes to be considered a player is to be in a position in which your actions can impact the game. Beyond simply acknowledging who the players are, it is also useful to make note of their proximity to the action. Players who are closest have an easier time impacting play than players who are distant. In a job opportunity situation, the most proximate players are arguably the candidates for the position and the hiring manager. Less proximate players might include other managers at the hiring company who are involved in the interviewing process, individuals providing letters of reference for the candidates, and other employers who are also seeking to fill similar vacancies. Moving further from the action would reveal other players who should be considered, such as family members. In some circumstances, the roster of players might be properly expanded to include coworkers at each candidate's current employer, potential coworkers at the hiring company, and members of each candidate's professional network, mentors, and search firm consultants. Each member of this diverse cast of characters has the opportunity to impact the game. All of them will have their own motivations for whether, when, or how they do so. Savvy job hunters will take this into account as moves are plotted.

Which Options Are Open to Players?

Once players have been identified and sorted so that you understand how strongly each can impact your game, the second step in framing the game involves determining the different moves that are available to each player. In many board games, this is not particularly difficult to do because moves are determined by a role of dice or the draw of a card. In other games, there is much wider discretion regarding each move and, as such, a larger role for strategy. In some games, players choose not only the *direction* in which they move, but also the *force* behind the move. In chess, for example, a bishop can move diagonally one or many squares. In the career game, an available move for a player would be to recommend a candidate for a position. That move contains with it a level of enthusiasm that is also at the discretion of the player. Understanding the different moves open to the other players is a key concern because some of their options will serve your strategy better than others. Of course, understanding how to influence their moves so that your strategy is supported and not blocked is even more useful.

What Goals Are the Players Pursuing?

Each player has a goal. The goal often is simply to "win"—however the rules of the game define it. Certainly, there are game situations where winning is not the only goal a player could pursue—nor is it necessarily the case that every player has the same goal. For example, most adults locked in a game of Candyland or Mousetrap with a six-year-old child will be pursuing a different goal—to entertain, teach, or otherwise occupy that child. In all likelihood, that child has winning as paramount. The player hoping to win will likely play the game differently than the player with a goal to entertain, teach, or otherwise occupy.

To further complicate our understanding of goals, it is important to recognize that player goals may also shift over the course of a game. A couple's divorce provides a stark contrast to children's board games—but anyone who has experienced a divorce or watched as a friend's marriage unravels has likely seen how player goals can change over time—and how a change in goals makes previously irrational moves seem rational. Commonly, when parents realize their differences are irreconcilable, the language that each uses to describe their goal is to "do what is best for the children." When this is the goal, certain player moves (such as establishing a way for the children to have the healthiest relationship possible with each parent, or minimally disrupting their relationships with friends and progress at school) are expected, and they make a great deal of sense to observers. In too many cases, however, one or both parents will experience a goal change—suddenly the goal that matters is causing the most distress to his or her ex. In these situations, feuding parents turn the child from player to pawn. The shift in goals creates a new situation in which entirely different moves—even when undesirable—become "rational" (such as passive-aggressive behavior in being late for pick up/drop off, or lobbying with the child for the role of favorite). Outsiders watching the proceedings will find themselves asking "why in the world is s/he doing that?" Spouses are often similarly confused, because the ex with whom they seemed to be "on the same page" is suddenly behaving in an unexpected way. The new moves do not seem rational—until it is understood that the player has changed his or her goal and that new moves are required to support achievement of the new goal.

What Are the Benefits to Be Earned through Cooperation?

Multiplayer games are sometimes zero-sum—whatever one player wins comes at the expense of other players. In many instances, however, the outcome is not zero-sum, and by cooperating, players can actually benefit. This requires two things. First, each player has to *recognize* that there are benefits from cooperation. Second, players cooperate best when they have the *opportunity* to arrange it. Consider another version of Prisoners' Dilemma. Here, two college students, Mike and Maureen, took a weekend trip to the beach to unwind. Though they intended to be back to campus in time for a Monday morning exam, they overslept. Realizing they would not make it for the exam, Mike e-mailed the professor to explain that a flat tire had delayed their return to campus. The professor replied that they could sit for a makeup exam after they got back. Mike and Maureen were relieved and arrived later that day for the makeup. The professor sat them in separate rooms and gave them the exam. The test was going well for each until they got to the last question—worth

80 percent of the grade. The question was simply, "Which tire was flat?" The two now have only a 25 percent chance of getting the question "right." Had they anticipated the question, they could have taken the opportunity to cooperate for mutual benefit. Cooperation would have increased the likelihood of a good outcome, but the game's structure did not provide the opportunity.

The question for players of the career game is whether other players can be influenced—or whether the game can be shaped—so that other players care about your success. One way this plays out in individual careers is as follows. It is common that the early phase of the career game emphasizes how successful someone can be as an individual contributor. Strong individual contributors earn promotions for their abilities to drive results based on their personal efforts and business acumen. As the game unfolds, these strong individual contributors often face a stall in their career progression. The stall happens because these players have not developed the ability to enlist others to be willing to work with them for the good of the whole. If the executive does not recognize how the metric by which success is measured has changed, and cannot make the corresponding moves, he or she will remain stalled.

Can the Players Make and Keep Commitments?

In games that consist of more than one move, each player's reputation becomes an important part of the other's efforts to develop strategy. One element each player attempts to discern is how likely it is that they—as well as the other players—can make and keep commitments. In the Red-Blue Game described earlier in this chapter, the game facilitator may allow a representative from each team to speak to one another, in an effort to break a pattern of "red-red" voting. The representatives may commit to voting blue in the next round. However, each team will wonder—properly—whether the other representative can keep that commitment. That is, do they think the other will be able to convince his or her team members to vote blue? In the career game, the same type of questions arise—can you trust someone at their word? This really has two parts. First, when someone makes you a promise, do they intend to honor it? Second, does the person making the promise have—and will they at the necessary moment—the power to deliver? Every reader knows someone who left an employer after being passed over for promotion—in spite of promises of "next time." When players—in this case, a manager—cannot make and keep commitments, there is little reason to trust they can or will impact the game in the way that they advertise.

What Is the Time Structure of the Game?

As noted at the beginning of this chapter, time structure is an important boundary for the game. Some games are defined by a time limit (football, soccer, hockey), some by a number of turns (baseball), and others by achieving a milestone chosen to represent victory (tennis). Strategy under each time scenario is different. For example, managers and players can both budget their resources more efficiently in a time-limited game (by substituting players to conserve their energy, for example). In many companies, the game's time structure may be tied to quarterly reporting, annual budgeting, or the industry's annual trade show. In the career game, the time structure can impact play in many ways. One example regards the move to step out of a career in order to return to school for an MBA. We spoke with several executives who never "pulled the trigger" on that decision—at first because the timing never seemed right in relation to what was going on at work, and then because the window of opportunity had closed. They recognized that an investment to pursue the degree at a more advanced age would ultimately provide a respectable return. Time also matters in terms of understanding how long to stay in a position. On the one hand, some executives move very quickly, assuming the role that Michael Watkins labeled "management tourist"—someone who visits several management positions, but neither knows nor impacts any very deeply. On the other hand, some executives eschew opportunities and stay with the familiar because they feel that the time is not right to make a move. If this occurs enough times, opportunities stop presenting themselves. Finally, the time element matters in career game situations that are repeated plays—whenever individuals know that repeated plays will occur, they make a certain set of moves; when they know the endgame is near, they make different moves.

The time structure of the career game is complex because there are myriad ways to frame the game's time dimension. When individuals at or near the beginning of their careers think about time in terms of a game, they focus on the moves they want to make and how they should spend their time—the impact they want to have on the world, the things they want to experience, the importance of material possessions, the role that relationships with family, friends, and colleagues should play, and so on. Making explicit these aspects of what a "win" looks like is a key step in planning early moves. Decisions about whether or where to attend college, choices of majors, and the nature of early work experiences are all capable of influencing how these longer-term goals are met.

At the other extreme, it should be clear that comparatively discrete episodes—such as the process of applying for a job, earning an offer, and then negotiating terms of employment—can also be viewed as a game. At the risk of relying on sports metaphors too heavily, we prefer to think of the long view of the game as a season. That season is made up of a number of games. In some instances, the outcome of one game impacts the play of the next; in other instances, the games are largely independent events.

While this metaphor helps begin the process of creating a time boundary around the game, it still leaves some distance to travel. The best way to complete that journey is to recognize that the common underlying theme of the moves that players make is that together they are intended to influence a decision. The right way, then, to frame the time structure of the game is to have in mind when that decision will be made. Each particular game is over when the focal decisions—who to hire, how much to offer, how vehemently to oppose a candidate, and so on—are executed.

What Is the Information Structure of the Game?

Relevant information is vitally important in order to play a game well, and when one player has an information advantage he or she has what might be a considerable strategic advantage. Information structure refers to the degree to which players benefit from private information and also to the efforts they might employ to resolve any information disadvantage. A marked deck of cards offers poker players what most would acknowledge as an unfair information advantage; the ability to count cards at a blackjack table provides an information advantage that game hosts try to counter by using multiple decks of cards. In the career game, information asymmetries abound, and players strive to remove those that place them at a disadvantage. We consider this in greater detail later; for now, consider the following example. Hiring managers have an information advantage over job candidates because only they know how badly the company wants each particular candidate, and only they know what the top of the salary negotiation range is. Candidates have some information leverage, too, in that only they know how badly they want a position—or how many attractive options they have. Anyone who has played either of these parts has without a doubt asked clever questions that might casually reveal useful information and, thereby, reduce the asymmetry.

SUMMARY

Leaving this chapter, you should hang on to two major points that will guide you through the sections ahead. First, remember the fundamental game theory concepts that we have introduced. Knowing each and the way that they apply to the career game is essential to proactively managing your career. Understanding what rationality means to each of the players in your career game provides a context in which you can better predict moves—to support or to block you, for example. Your career strategy will be better formulated if you can recognize whether the game is characterized by sequential versus simultaneous moves: simultaneous moves require predicting what other players will do, while sequential moves require planning ahead (given each player's rational goal) and reasoning backwards to make the best next move. A proper appreciation of elements of the game, such as credible threats and commitments, signaling, and efforts to manage information asymmetries also provide players with an advantage.

Second, remember that you will need to identify boundaries and the nature of your game. Each player needs to recognize who the other players are, what their goals are, and which options they have as they pursue those goals. Players should also strive to understand how each, once the game is set in motion, can credibly make commitments to various courses of action. The interdependence of the players in the career game also means there are opportunities to cooperate for mutual benefit. These opportunities may only be recognized if players know where to look for them and how to exploit them. Finally, the time and information structure of the game set important constraints that players need to recognize in order not to find themselves out of time or out of play in their efforts to execute their career strategy.

In the next chapter, we will consider three important elements of games in greater detail: information asymmetries, player incentives, and risk. We will then focus more closely on four specific steps that help a player get ready to play. In the pages that immediately follow this chapter, we invite you to consider our conversations with Stephen Elop, president of Microsoft's Business Division; Tamara Erickson, author and consultant; and Pasha Fedorenko, a consultant with Bain & Company. Elop provides interesting examples of how disruptive moves can enhance your career game and the way that goals change over the course of an executive's career. Erickson offers great insight into the way players from different generations frame the game—particularly when it comes to the way they define winning. Obviously, different frames impact the way that different generations play the career game. Finally, Fedorenko offers a great example of doing the work necessary so that your résumé tells a great story. After he developed his résumé sufficiently, other players were drawn to him and wanted to support him.

NOTES

1. For a very useful and regularly updated and improved game theory resource, visit the webpage maintained by Mike Shor at Vanderbilt University, http://www.gametheory.net/.
2. A Nobel prize for work in game theory went to economist Michael Spencer in 2001 for his work on signaling.
3. "Testing Game Theory," *Prime Time*, aired December 20, 2006. http://abcnews.go.com/video/playerindex?id=1733511.
4. N. Bennett, C. L. Martin, R. Bies, and J. Brockner, "Coping with a Layoff: A Longitudinal Study of Victims," *Journal of Management* 21 (1995): 1025–40.
5. A. Dixit and B. Nalebuff, "The Concise Encyclopedia of Economics Game Theory," http://www.econlib.org/LIBRARY/Enc/GameTheory.html.
6. J. McMillan, *Games, Strategies, and Managers* (Oxford: Oxford University Press, 1992).

A CONVERSATION WITH STEPHEN ELOP[*]

PRESIDENT, MICROSOFT BUSINESS DIVISION

At Microsoft, Stephen Elop oversees the Information Worker, Microsoft Business Solutions, and Unified Communications Groups. His division is responsible for the Microsoft Office system of programs, servers and software-based services, Microsoft Dynamics, and business applications for small and midsize businesses, large organizations, divisions of global enterprises, and Microsoft's Unified Communications, which develops products and services that provide complete software-based communications tools to businesses.

Elop joined Microsoft in January 2008 and is a member of the company's senior leadership team that sets overall strategy and direction for Microsoft. Before joining Microsoft, he was COO for Juniper Networks, a leading provider of high-performance network infrastructure and a valued Microsoft partner. There, Elop was responsible for all of the company's product groups, corporate development, global sales and service, and marketing and manufacturing organizations.

Prior to Juniper, Elop served as president of worldwide field operations at Adobe Systems Inc., where he was responsible for Adobe's global sales organization and all customer-facing functions. Elop joined Adobe following the 2005 acquisition of Macromedia Inc., where he was president and CEO. During his seven-year tenure at Macromedia, Elop held many senior positions, including COO, executive vice president of worldwide field operations, and general manager of the company's eBusiness division. Earlier in his career, he served in a number of executive positions, including chief information officer.

Elop earned a bachelor's degree in computer engineering and management from McMaster University in Hamilton, Ontario. See also www.microsoft.com/presspass/exec/elop/.

---

* The views expressed here are those of Mr. Elop and do not represent the views of either Microsoft Corporation or any of Mr. Elop's prior employers.

AUTHORS: **What are some of your career moves that best developed you as an executive?**

ELOP: There is an expression I have used to describe what I think are key career moves: any positions for which you are "uniquely unqualified," because these are the moves that lead to the biggest career gains. A couple of examples in my career illustrate this concept. I was a consultant for many years, working in a small consulting company that got acquired by Lotus. I was doing fine there—my career was advancing incrementally in terms of greater scope and responsibility. I was given larger projects over time, and so on. This was progress, of course, but none of it was disruptive. Like a lot of people, I was doing well and earning incrementally better opportunities.

When I joined Boston Chicken, I was quickly moved into the role of chief information officer. I was uniquely unqualified for that role. It was a disruptive move—the kind that really can accelerate a career.

Similarly, at Macromedia, there were many occasions where I was put into roles for which I was uniquely unqualified. It has carried on since then in my career.

AUTHORS: **How do you earn your way into jobs where you have no qualifications?**

ELOP: In my experience, these opportunities tend to happen when you have already established some basis of credibility with key decision makers. For example, when I took on the CIO role at Boston Chicken, I had already been consulting with them. Through that exposure, they knew about my work habits. They built up some trust in me and came to respect what I could contribute, how I thought, and how I interacted with other people. From that, they were willing to grant me the right to do something, even though I really didn't have the résumé to stake a claim to the position.

When I went to Macromedia from Boston Chicken, the initial position I had was not a disruptive one. I moved into a role at Macromedia that had an unusual title—"SVP of the Web." But it was effectively an amplified CIO role, a bigger role than I had at Boston Chicken, but not really a disruptive move. Once within Macromedia, I did make some disruptive moves. For example, when I became the leader of the field organization, there was nothing on my résumé that would have said I should do that. But, because I had shown some abilities and potential of what I could do, the company was comfortable putting me in the role. When I succeeded in that role, my career took off, and I got more of those disruptive opportunities.

Quite often I see people looking to make a move to another company into a role for which they are not qualified, but also without any prior relationships or history with that company or team. They want to change companies to work their way up the promotion ladder more quickly, but this tactic isn't always as successful as it could or should be, because the expectation when you enter a new company in a new role is that you actually are qualified for the role. Your new colleagues are not willing to give you extra latitude because you haven't earned their respect yet. But once they understand what your strengths and weaknesses are, there is more of a willingness to grant you something that allows you to successfully move through a disruptive step in your career. So, my advice is that people should look for those potentially disruptive moves within a context where they have already earned the trust that will help them stretch.

AUTHORS: **What if you find yourself "over your head" in one of these stretch roles?**

ELOP: To recover from being uniquely unqualified, it helps to think about the fundamental principles of what makes good leaders. My friends at Juniper have developed a set of leadership principles that I admire. They believe that one of the most important attributes of a good leader is self-awareness. If you can look in the mirror and admit to yourself first—and then to others—that you are in over your head, then the problem is more than halfway solved. You have to say out loud that you need help. Then you get help by building the team around you, by reaching out to other teams, your boss, your board, whatever is available to you, and saying, "I have a problem here, and I need help with this issue. This is what we need to do." It begins with self-awareness, and then transparency follows—that is, not trying to hide a weakness. How can others help you if you aren't honest about where your gaps are? In the end, you will earn respect and trust—others will realize you are insightful enough to know what you don't know—and that you are not afraid to ask for help.

Both of those are tremendously important if you want to survive in a position where you are uniquely unqualified.

AUTHORS: **How do you choose the people you will mentor?**

ELOP: In any role, you only have so much time in the day, so of course you want it to be well spent. You should focus your mentoring on people who you think will really appreciate and learn from it—and who will perhaps use it to help the company overall. I think about the people that I naturally want to mentor. It's not necessarily the person who just sends me an e-mail asking me to be their mentor. I am always willing to chat with people, but in terms of really engaging in the process, it tends to be with those people who I realize are smarter than I am or that have some assets that I don't have and from whom I can, therefore, learn. If I invest in them, it will help me and the organization. It is certainly easier to invest in people who are going to help the organization advance. There are certain individuals at Microsoft I am mentoring now whom I believe could be our future leaders. They are helping me deal with the really hard problems and will succeed me at some point. So, these mentoring relationships help them, me, and the organization.

AUTHORS: **What causes mentoring relationships to end?**

ELOP: In some cases, your protégé may become your peer—or even your boss. As the official reporting relationship between the two of you changes, chances are the mentoring relationship will need to evolve.

The key to making mentoring relationships work is a sense of humility on each party's part. If each can demonstrate humility, then it is always possible to learn—even if there are status changes between the two of you.

Humility was a big part of the culture at Juniper. I haven't seen too many other company cultures that feature humility front and center. Humility is important because of the sort of behavior it drives in companies. It positions people to be always learning, to be more open to accepting criticism or suggestions about how to improve, and more importantly, it keeps people grounded.

As far as outgrowing someone's ability to mentor you—I am less certain about that. I mean, if you maintain humility, should you or will you ever outgrow a mentor? What does outgrowing a mentor mean from a humility perspective? It means, "I guess I am now better than them. I have learned every-thing they know and I am moving beyond them." That's not right somehow. I have someone in mind who was one of my professors many years ago. He really has little direct knowledge of what it is that I do now—he has no foundation on which to advise me specifically, but I so deeply respect his intellect and his thoughtfulness that I still learn from him. He can bring me back to earth somewhat. He isn't necessarily familiar with what it is like to manage a $20 billion enterprise, but he can remind me of things he taught me that I may be overlooking.

The truth is that, as your career evolves, different things become important and you need to look for mentors who can help you through them.

AUTHORS: **How has the career game changed in recent years?**

ELOP: It has evolved for me due to professional and personal maturity. What seems so important early in your career tends to moderate over time, or perhaps you just get a more mature perspective on it. Early in my career I was concerned—like many of my colleagues—with climbing up the corporate ladder. The game was a quest to get a position of increased responsibility, a more impressive title or level. At some point, though, most people figure out that it is more important to be challenged, it is more important to have an impact, it is more important to enjoy what you are doing, and it is more important to enjoy the people around you. Titles, perks, all that really becomes less important. The way you play the game clearly changes as you grow through your career. Exactly why that happens I couldn't speculate, but I know I definitely have a more sanguine view on my life, and it changes what I am looking for in the game.

That said, there are some elements of the game that I would bet don't change. What I mean here are the characteristics of an individual that tend to stay constant; work ethic, for example. I work at a certain degree of energy, and I can't imagine ever doing anything differently. My work ethic has contributed to the success of my career; it contributes to my belief that I have had a good day and that I got a lot done, that I accomplished something and helped others and delivered results, etc. There are certain aspects of the game that are relatively constant. These may be more the parameters of who you are and how you function, and perhaps as a result, they are very hard to change despite others' best efforts—for example, when your spouse has to plead you to stop working for the day.

AUTHORS: **How do different generations play the career game?**

ELOP: I can compare my father's generation to my son's generation. It is safe to say that the expectations keep shifting toward earlier results or rewards in response to the efforts you put into your career. My father worked in essentially the same company in the same role for his entire career, and my son's generation is looking for results, looking for action, looking for a payoff much earlier. I see a greater degree of impatience from people in their twenties, and there are higher expectations in terms of money and personal recognition. This attitude may not be well aligned with the realities of today's business environment, which implies that there will be greater dissatisfaction, a higher propensity for people to change jobs more often to look for that holy grail, and so forth. I find myself about midway on that trend.

AUTHORS: **What distinguishes people who make bad career moves and recover, from those who never recover?**

ELOP: It relates back to being in over your head. When you are in a situation and you are unsuccessful, recovery from that starts with being honest with yourself about what went right, what went wrong, and what you could have done differently. The people who recover are those who can get past it by looking in the mirror and understanding what just happened and how they contributed to the problem. The person has to accept their share of responsibility, and that can be a very unpleasant and even an embarrassing situation. We all make bad decisions—but the career-threatening decisions tend to be remarkable. Putting everything on the table that was associated with that sort of failure is a very, very difficult process. Talk about requiring humility! These are public failures, where everyone has opinions, where often the rumor mill is running rampant.

If you want to survive, you have to be self-aware, to be willing to learn and take ownership of your role in the problem's creation or mismanagement.

Lastly, a key to recovery is adaptability. You got in trouble for a reason—something was off with the way you were doing things. To avoid history repeating itself, you have to adapt who you are. It's not only adapting to a circumstance that didn't work out, but also, in general, learning to adapt to your environment.

CAREER GAME OBSERVATIONS

- The concept of finding positions for which you are uniquely unqualified is an interesting one to consider. As Stephen Elop notes, these opportunities can be thought of as "disruptive" career moves—the sort that can really accelerate your progress in the game. "Uniquely unqualified" means that, although you have the sense of getting in over your head, others believe that all the ingredients for your success are present—and they trust you to deliver because of your track record.

- Elop mentions several attributes of good game players—self-awareness, adaptability, and humility are all characteristics that will contribute to your career agility.

- His comments on mentoring provide an example of the game theory concept gains from trade. For example, he is most interested in mentoring people from whom he can learn. Effectively, Elop is reminding you that mentoring relationships are not one-way—each partner needs to bring something to the relationship for it to work well. As you think about mentors, one of your evaluation criteria should be whether or not you think the executives you plan to approach will benefit from a relationship with *you*—particularly as compared to others they could choose to mentor.

- As his career has played out, Elop has reconsidered what he perceives as winning. He is looking for different things now, such as the chance to work with interesting people, and would be expected to make moves supporting that new strategy. This way of winning usually can be more broadly met than the goals of promotional opportunity and the accumulation of assets and, as a result, creates greater mobility.

- Elop's comments about the generational differences in the career game, comparing his father and his son, are an interesting addition to those expressed later in our conversation with Tammy Erickson.

A CONVERSATION WITH TAMARA J. ERICKSON

AUTHOR AND CONSULTANT

Tammy Erickson is a McKinsey Award–winning author and widely respected expert on organizations and innovation, on building talent and enhancing productivity, and on the nature of work in the intelligence economy. Her work is based on extensive research on the changing workforce and employee values and, most recently, on how successful organizations innovate through collaboration.

Erickson has coauthored four *Harvard Business Review* articles, including "It's Time to Retire Retirement," winner of the McKinsey Award, an MIT *Sloan Management Review* article, and the book *Workforce Crisis: How to Beat the Coming Shortage of Skills and Talent*. She also authored one of *Harvard Business Review*'s Breakthrough Ideas for 2008, "Task, Not Time." She is currently writing a trilogy of books on how individuals in specific generations can excel in today's workplace. *Retire Retirement: Career Strategies for the Boomer Generation* and *Plugged In: The Generation Y Guide to Thriving at Work* were published in 2008, and *What's Next, Gen-X? Keeping Up, Moving Ahead, and Getting the Career You Want* in 2009. Her blog "Across the Ages" is featured weekly on HBSP Online (http://discussionleader.hbsp.com/erickson/).

AUTHORS: **What are some of the career "games" of baby boomers compared to Gen-X (thirty-something) and Gen-Y (twenty-something) employees?**

ERICKSON: Let's start with some context. The underpinning of my research and my perspective is developmental psychology. We know that many of the conceptual models people have were formed when they were 11–13 years old. That is when we start to try to understand how we want to live our lives and the role that work and a career will play. As a result, looking at what was happening to someone during those ages provides some interesting clues as to the way they are going to frame the situations they confront later in life as adults.

In terms of how they play the career game, baby boomers have jumped right in and played by the rules established by previous generations—and with very few questions around "do these rules make sense and do we want to change them?" It is a bit ironic because, typically, baby boomers are known for being antiauthoritarian, but when it comes to work, their competitive instincts override any tendency to question the rules—they become more inclined to follow the rules as written.

AUTHORS: Why?

ERICKSON: The explanation begins with remembering what these kids' lives were like when they were 11–13 years old. Many grew up in a world where they had to attend high school classes in temporary structures behind the main building because there weren't enough classrooms. Metaphorically, boomers have long faced the fact that there just weren't going to be enough seats for all of them. I think that reality overrode many antiauthoritarian ideals and instead created a group that basically said, "Boy, I'd better run around as fast as I can and make sure that I get a seat."

AUTHORS: **True, the boomers have heard about the sheer size of their generation their whole life. How does this impact the way a baby boomer would play the career game?**

ERICKSON: A lot of boomer career moves have been focused on self-advancement and emphasizing ways to secure their own seats, as well as the next seat up the organizational chart. Baby boomers—much more than any other generation—have a single destination in mind for their next stop.

AUTHORS: **How does this compare to the Gen-X workforce?**

ERICKSON: Gen-X employees plan their careers much differently. There was a lot of social change happening when Gen-Xers were young teenagers. Michael Hammer's *Reengineering the Corporation* symbolized that period well. There were massive layoffs, rising divorce rates, women entering the workforce, and the emergence of latchkey kids. When I interview people in their thirties and forties, it is common to hear at some point during the conversation, "*If something bad were to happen . . .* " In other words, Gen-Xers have lived surrounded by what-ifs. They are focused on making contingency plans because, even if things are good today, they may be quite different tomorrow. Whereas boomers play the game with the view of "How do I drive for the goal?" the Gen-Xer thinks more "How do I plot my moves so that if I get blocked somewhere I can still move forward in another direction?" When Gen-X employees describe their career paths to me, they invariably say something like, "I am doing *this* right now, but I've thought of *that* and I've started on *something else* and I've got contacts out for *this other thing*." They have multiple options, directions, and contacts in mind.

I also find that many Gen-X employees are frustrated with their careers. They feel they entered the workforce at a time when jobs were tight, the economy was bad, or they took a first job that was beneath their level of educational credentials. From the start, they feel that they have been forced to play the game in a marketplace that doesn't give them much room for negotiation. They feel that they've marked their time, waited their turn, paid their dues, and done the dirty work. In fact, that is how many Gen-Xers describe their careers thus far. They are waiting for that glorious moment when the boomers finally clear out.

AUTHORS: **But boomers aren't leaving as fast as we thought. Given the slowing economy and also how boomers are defining "retirement" these days, they either can't afford to clear out or they don't want to. How does that affect Gen X?**

ERICKSON: It adds more frustration, and to make things worse, there are optimistic Gen-Yers bouncing around on their heels. As a result, Gen-Xers tend to feel sandwiched between two big generations—one isn't leaving and the other wants to take over.

When you hear about Gen-Yers, most of the focus is on the way they interact with technology, but I don't think that's the most interesting element of the generation. What fascinates me is that they grew up in a world that was obsessed with talking about terrorism—terrorism around the world, school shootings in the U.S., and so on. True, baby boomers grew up during the Vietnam War, but if you go to war, there is a reasonable expectation that something bad could happen. That isn't supposed to be the case if you go to school or to work in the city, where you have essentially no expectation that something terrible is going to happen. Gen Y grew up with a concept of "bad things could happen at any point to anyone"—a randomness that other generations didn't experience as teens.

AUTHORS: So, how does that sense of randomness impact the way Gen-Yers play the career game?

ERICKSON: This translates to the workplace in that the single biggest complaint I get from employers about Gen-Y employees is their sense of impatience. I would argue that impatience is a normal reaction on the part of the Gen-Yers, given their upbringing. If your view of the world is that something bad could happen tomorrow for no reason, then living life to the fullest today would be the logical reaction. Gen-Yers want to enjoy the moment versus "putting in time," like Gen-Xers, and they plan mostly around "Is what I am doing today enjoyable, meaningful, challenging?"

So, boomers are focused on reaching goals, winning against many others, and having lots of metrics to keep score; Gen-Xers are focused on being self-reliant, and they will maintain many options so that they always have something that could work under different scenarios. Gen-Yers are focused on living life fully today.

AUTHORS: What generation is being formed now?

ERICKSON: Today's 11–13 year olds are exposed to financial, resource, and environmental issues that will shape how they view the world. Kids today are enormously aware of penguins, polar bears, melting ice caps, and all that kind of stuff—and many also know that they took a vacation in the backyard because of high energy prices. They are getting doused with a bucket of cold water that the somewhat more happy-go-lucky Gen-Yers ahead of them didn't experience. Gen-Yers grew up in a pretty rosy economic climate and, as a result, have a natural optimism. The generation forming now will have much more of a sense of realism. If the economic crisis continues to deteriorate, the realism could turn into pessimism. I suggest that we call this new wave the "ReGeneration"—playing off the realities they will face and also the kind of renewal that they are going to need to focus on.

AUTHORS: Have these generations been able to effectively change the career game, or do they just apply different tactics?

ERICKSON: The career game itself hasn't changed a lot so far, but that may change with the Ys. The boomers did not try to change it—they took the rules as a given and played as hard as they could to win. Gen-X employees have not felt that they could change it—they don't think they have much leverage as long as the boomers are still in place. In fact, many Gen-Xers feel that the only option they have—for example, to substantially increase salary—is to move to another company. Gen-Yers have both the attitude and the leverage to push back and change the game. They are motivated by what works for them here and now, and they will try to change the game to fit their ideal.

AUTHORS: **How will companies have to adapt to a workforce that is calling the shots?**

ERICKSON: It will behoove companies to figure out that they have to effectively rerecruit their Gen-Y employees every day. Gen-Y employees have to wake up every morning and still feel your company is the best place for them to work.

AUTHORS: **So, how does an employer do that?**

ERICKSON: By offering continuous learning opportunities and looking for ways to reduce the monotonous elements of any work stream. Gen-Yers want flexibility—not just in coming in at nine o'clock instead of eight o'clock in the morning—they want true flexibility that gives them the opportunity to go away for a couple of weeks if they want. If companies want to attract and keep the best of the Gen-Y generation, they will need to begin moving much more firmly in the direction of professional development and progressive talent management.

AUTHORS: **So, companies will need to have different incentives, policies, and systems in place for boomers, Gen-Xers, and Gen-Yers? This can be complicated for employers.**

ERICKSON: That's right. The most important thing from a Gen-X point of view is to create an environment in which people feel that they have more options by staying with you than by leaving. It has to feel like there are six other things in the company that they could do after their current assignment—that there is a portfolio of options available for them in the organization. Gen-Xers need to see that there are a variety of paths within one firm in order for them to stay and shape a career.

With the Gen-Yers, companies need to create jobs with enough excitement and challenge to keep them engaged. I also suggest to companies not to over-train Gen-Yers. They don't want a 52-step checklist of how to do this job exactly the way you did it. They'd much rather have the task and maybe the names of half a dozen people who've done it in the past or have something to contribute to how it can be done in the future. They tend to prefer to learn by conversation, as opposed to training. They want to figure things out on their own, so let them go forth and sort it out themselves.

AUTHORS: **How does each generation define "winning" the career game?**

ERICKSON: Boomers would have the traditional view of winning—being on top, being the victor, getting the prize, having the most prestigious outcome. One experience I had recently with a company illustrates this. I recommended that the company create opportunities for boomers to decelerate a little bit over time, since many boomers would like a little more time off in some way or another as they get into their sixties and seventies. The company couldn't get anyone to take advantage of the program until they made it a competitive process. Employees weren't interested until they had to "win" in order to slow down! That turned the tables. All of a sudden, taking time off was prestigious because you had to win in order to be allowed to do it.

For Gen-Xers, winning is more an internal measure around confidence in their ability to survive multiple permutations in the world around them and envisioning how they could survive multiple scenarios. Because it is an internal measure, it is much more difficult for a company to know when a Gen-X employee has achieved that. So, it may be more difficult for companies to know how to keep these employees satisfied and productive beyond offering broad training, lateral career paths, and multiple career options.

With Gen-Yers, the feeling of winning is going to be something very personal, because it is based on how much they enjoy what they are doing at the moment. Challenges, learning, and winning can only be defined by the individual. I have a story that captures the essence of how Gen Y views winning. I had a knock on the door of my house this past summer. I opened the door, and there was a very nice, clean-cut man, and he said to me, "I'd like to work here." I said, "This is a home," and he said, "I know—I've driven by many times and it looks very nice, and I'd like to work here." I said, "I wasn't really thinking of hiring anybody, but tell me something about yourself," because by now I'm curious.

He told me that he had gone to college with all of his friends, but that he hadn't found it particularly stimulating or relevant, so he got a job, but he didn't find that particularly challenging or meaningful either. He had been driving by, and saw our place, and thought it looked like a really nice place to work. I asked, "What are you thinking about money," and he said, "Oh that doesn't really matter since I've moved back in with my parents." That night, when I told my husband about the young man, he said it sounded ridiculous, and added, "Of course, you said no, right?" I said it didn't seem that ridiculous to me. He sounded like a Gen-Yer. He wanted something that was meaningful and challenging and relevant, and this looked like a fun place to spend the summer. We live on a little farm, and we have horses and other animals. So I hired him, and he spent the summer doing manual labor around the farm and enjoying the sunshine and the animals, and when fall came he moved on to something else. He was winning just by living in the moment.

CAREER GAME OBSERVATIONS

- The key takeaway from our conversation with Tammy Erickson concerns the way the different generations playing today frame the career game.
- From her extensive research, she suggests that boomers view winning as getting to the top of the game (as they each define it); Gen-X players view winning as having options and the self-confidence that, if something were to block their aspirations, they could find a way around it; Gen-Y players take a more personal approach to winning, and their game is structured with a very short time horizon.
- Because each generation views the game and winning differently, it should not be surprising that they play it differently. Erickson observed that boomers are engaged in efforts to charge up the hierarchy, Gen-X players work on developing viable contingency plans, and Gen-Y players make moves that help them to fully live in the present.
- These differences in the way generations frame and play the game may impact the sorts of employers that each prefers. Boomers may be more

comfortable in large companies that offer security and a tall pyramid of an organizational chart to climb; Gen-X and Gen-Y employees may prefer smaller companies where they think their future is less at the whim of an anonymous decision maker far removed from their performance. Gen-X employees are going to be very reluctant to make any move that could be viewed as career limiting, and Gen-Y employees prefer the fact that, with a smaller employer, it is easier to see how they are making a difference.

- The implications of these differences are obvious for companies as players. And evidence is emerging that companies are adapting to the game as played by their workforces—as seen in the adoption of tools like Twitter for organizational communication and Rypple for the instantaneous feedback that Gen Y craves, and in the appearance of advice such as that contained in a 2008 *Economist* article titled "Managing the Facebookers."

- You should use Erickson's insights in two ways: first, to understand the way you might best play the game, based on your generational affiliation; and second, to understand your competition, their motives, their likely moves, and their likely responses to your moves. Erickson's comments essentially provide one take on those elements of other players in your game. By understanding them, you will be in a position to better anticipate and account for their game strategies.

A CONVERSATION WITH PASHA FEDORENKO

MANAGEMENT CONSULTANT, BAIN & COMPANY

At the time of our conversation, Pasha Fedorenko was completing his PhD. in Electrical and Computer Engineering at Georgia Tech. While working toward his PhD, he also earned his MBA from Tech in 2008. Fedorenko grew up in the Ukraine and earned a BS in Electrical Engineering from Worcester Polytechnic Institute in 2004. He has recently started his career as a consultant with Bain & Company.

AUTHORS: When did you first come to the U.S.?

FEDORENKO: I first came for an exchange program for a year as a high school senior. I lived with a family in Harwich on Cape Cod, Massachusetts. I wanted to see something different, and it was a wonderful opportunity to learn American culture from the inside. It was a great experience, and the family was fantastic. The tough part was fitting in to a new high school as a senior. But after that, transition to college and making friends there was a breeze. I stayed for the school year, and then I went back to the Ukraine for my final exams and to graduate.

AUTHORS: Had you intended to stay in the U.S. for college when you first arrived?

FEDORENKO: Possibly. But the way things have worked out for my studies is that it hasn't really been about what I want to do—it has been about what I have been able find a way to do. What I mean by that is there was no way my parents would have been able to spend the money necessary for me to just say, "I want to go to school in the U.S." I only got to do it because I could find support to do it. The way it worked is that college applications in the Ukraine are done in early summer. While I was here for the exchange program, I applied to several schools in the U.S., knowing that I would hear from them before I had to make any decisions about applying to universities back at home. If I got in and was able to get financial support, then continuing in the U.S. would be an option. I was accepted to Worcester Polytechnic Institute, and after visiting the campus I decided I really liked it. I did receive some scholarship money from WPI, but my host family on Cape Cod offered to pay the difference between my scholarship and the true cost of attending. I am very thankful to them for giving me that opportunity. I am not sure how many people in the world would have the heart to spend that kind of money from their savings on the education of a 16-year-old kid from a foreign country who had basically been randomly assigned to live in their home.

AUTHORS: You are at an interesting point in your career. What are your plans after you complete your PhD?

FEDORENKO: I am in the middle of making that decision now. I have an offer with Bain here in Atlanta, and after the Thanksgiving holiday, I have an interview with McKinsey in Belgium. Both are great opportunities—those are my target employers. Once I got the Bain offer, I was able to decline some other opportunities because I knew I would be very happy at Bain. But I also want to see how things turn out with McKinsey. I would like to learn as much as I can about both firms so that I won't second-guess myself after making the decision about which to join.

AUTHORS: **When you came to Tech, was it your goal to end up at work with a consulting company?**

FEDORENKO: It really wasn't. I came as an engineer and decided to apply to the MBA program after completing the first two years of my PhD program. I thought that after graduation I would end up working for a large engineering company. I did hope to end up in a managerial role at some point and, ultimately, I wanted to start my own business. I can say that a reason Georgia Tech was attractive to me was that I might have the opportunity to work on the MBA while working on my PhD.

My interest in consulting began after I enrolled in the MBA program. Previously, I really did not understand what "consulting" really meant. I was curious about it, though, and went to some information sessions that consulting companies had on campus. As a result of those sessions, I did apply for a summer internship at McKinsey. I made it to the final round, but was rejected. The great thing about that experience is that they provided feedback about why I was rejected—they didn't just call you and say, "thank you for your time"— they told me why they made the decision to take a pass on my résumé. They told me that I had done a great job on the cases during the interview process but that I lacked business leadership experience. I couldn't disagree with them, so I took the feedback to heart. I knew there wasn't a lot I could do to remedy this because I was still very busy with the PhD program. I did try to find ways to take on some leadership positions within the school.

AUTHORS: **Can you tell us a little about those efforts?**

FEDORENKO: I knew that I wanted to look more attractive to consulting firms, so I took every opportunity for a leadership role on something of strategic importance. I started evaluating every big initiative I undertook based on whether it would (a) get me out of school quicker or (b) get me the job I wanted when I graduated. Last year, I participated in the Board Fellows program. It is a program where MBA students have the chance to sit on the board of a nonprofit in the Atlanta area. I picked a nonprofit that was smaller and certainly not well known, but that had a great working board—the Sullivan Center. The Sullivan Center works on the prevention of homelessness. That is, they don't work with the currently homeless—but they intervene when a family's financial situation changes so that they are at risk of losing their home. Up to date, it has been the best experience I have had in my time at Tech.

AUTHORS: **What did you do there?**

FEDORENKO: I recruited and led a team of very motivated MBA and PhD students that performed internal and external assessments of the organization to help the board with its strategic planning process that had been initiated earlier that year. The project lasted five months, and when we were done, we presented our final results to the board. Working on that project was a great experience, and certainly a very interesting one—the board was made up mostly of business people, and the center is run by a Catholic nun who has been doing social work for fifty years. The center was started twenty-five years ago, and like most other nonprofits, their metrics have been primarily focused on "feel good" numbers, but the expectation these days from the companies and individuals who give money is that they want clear outcome-based results and accountability.

During the project, among other things, we found convincing evidence of that trend and presented it to the center's leadership. In the end, the board used our analysis and recommendations to better identify the mission of the center and the key strategic areas on which to focus. As a result of our work, the board requested that a deputy director be hired to manage the day-to-day operations and to institute systems for reporting results. It turns out the impact of our work has been pretty large. One of the board members decided to take the full-time deputy director position. Since the summer, he has been restructuring programs and implementing profound changes at the center, and already brought revenues up by 15 percent in the middle of the financial crisis.

AUTHORS: **This experience certainly gave you some interesting stories to tell the next time you interviewed.**

FEDORENKO: Exactly. This is something that I think really set me apart from everyone else. As you know, when firms like Bain and McKinsey come to campus to interview, everyone they talk to has or is working on an MBA. My PhD work differentiates me, but is pretty esoteric to those running the interviews—I am not sure they always know what to make of it. But this experience was a great opportunity for me to stand out. I feel so strongly about its value that I am working to start a pro bono consulting operation for the MBA program at Georgia Tech.

AUTHORS: You began your studies as an engineer—how did you end up in the MBA program?

FEDORENKO: I always wanted to do business and management, but I didn't view an undergraduate business degree as that valuable. Both of my parents are engineers, so I grew up with that influence. Growing up in my house, the choice of a career was not so much "Do you want to do arts or sciences?" It was "Do you want to do electrical or mechanical engineering?" So I knew where I would start—and I had the MBA as a goal one day. My original plan was to work in a company for a couple of years and then go back and get my MBA. What ended up happening is that when I earned my undergraduate degree in 2004, the economy was not great. I did get some offers, but they were basically offers to do things I already knew how to do. Going straight to graduate school was a much better option.

AUTHORS: As you look at the Bain and McKinsey opportunities, what attracts you to them?

FEDORENKO: In both places, I will have opportunities to do international work. At Bain, I would likely start with more time spent in the U.S., but eventually it would involve international work, if I choose to do that. If I end up at McKinsey in Brussels, about 40 percent of their work is in Belgium, but the rest of the work is all over Europe, Africa, and Brazil—odds are I would have international experiences more quickly working with McKinsey out of that office.

AUTHORS: How important is that to you?

FEDORENKO: A little. There will be a lot to learn for me wherever I start. I do think experience in different cultures is important, and I want to get experience in both developed and developing economies. They face very different problems, and the way you have to solve them is very different. At the same time, I think the U.S. is a pioneer in business. And work experience acquired in the U.S. is viewed as very valuable around the world. It is a great place for a start of an international career.

CAREER GAME OBSERVATIONS

- The advice to build on your strengths is common and intuitive. One reason this is so is that building on strengths is simply easier than the hard work of remediating weaknesses and overcoming bad habits. Pasha Fedorenko provides a great example of receiving constructive feedback in his McKinsey interview about one of his weaknesses, and then taking a series of strategic steps to turn it into a strength.

- In the end, his efforts to find real leadership experiences that he could include on his résumé provided an important differentiator in the job market. Everyone he competed with had an MBA, but few of his interviewers could readily understand how his PhD research might be leveraged. The story of his work with a nonprofit, however, was something that everyone could grasp—and which few of his competitors could match. This ability to offer more than just a résumé was echoed in a number of our conversations and also has been the focus of career research (see, for example, "What's Your Story?" in the January 2005 issue of *Harvard Business Review*).

- Fedorenko made a move to ride out a bad job market in school—and he was very resourceful throughout his schooling to leverage modest resources to move his game along. A number of critical players also made moves that supported him—primarily his host family in Massachusetts and his family in the Ukraine who supported his desire to come to the United States.

- In all, Fedorenko has been very strategic about his career game. He took advantage of the time elements of the game in terms of applying to U.S. schools for his undergraduate degree, knowing that he would still have the opportunity to return to his home country if necessary. He has created a situation in which other players are very committed to his career success. He made moves during his graduate program that helped his résumé tell a more compelling story and, in doing so, negated specific criticisms that he had received about his experience. In deciding between Bain & Company and McKinsey, he carefully weighed what each would signal about him—particularly in terms of his experience—in competition for future opportunities.

WHAT YOU NEED TO KNOW TO PLAY

If you must play, decide on three things at the start: the rules of the game, the stakes, and the quitting time.
Chinese proverb

As the proverb above admonishes, you are wise to make an investment in understanding any game you are getting ready to play. Knowing the rules, the stakes, and the quitting time is useful because it helps prepare you to play, to form your strategy for the first few moves, and to evaluate your strategy's effectiveness as the game evolves. This is true for the career game, as well, although we offer a slightly revised proverb. Certainly rules, stakes, and quitting time are relevant in the career game. When it comes to getting yourself ready to play, however, the most important features of the game to study are *information asymmetries*, *player incentives*, and *risk*. These three factors together underpin the career game. Our first goal in this chapter is to outline a schema to help you build just such an understanding. Then our second goal is to describe how that effort can lead to the specific considerations players must entertain before making any moves: *the conditions of the playing field, the actions a player needs to undertake to be ready to play, an assessment of the other players, and the time structure of the game.*

INFORMATION ASYMMETRIES, PLAYER INCENTIVES, AND RISK

As we noted, an *information asymmetry* exists when one player knows something another doesn't. Asymmetries are a result of the *information structure* of a game and often can be leveraged to the knowledgeable player's advantage. Consequently, players who feel at a disadvantage are encouraged to take steps to learn what they must to level the playing field in terms of information. Take as an example a classic job search situation involving three players: an employer, a candidate, and a retained search firm. Each has information that might inform their moves and, as a result, their position in regard to other players. Employers know, better than the other players, the true content of a job, the potential for growth in the position, the quality of the team, the actual level of resources available to support the new hire, how strong the other candidates are, and how badly they want this particular candidate. Candidates know how badly they want the position, how many attractive alternatives they have in play, and how little they would accept in salary to obtain the position. Search firms know what the company has told them about the position, what the hiring firm thinks about the candidate, and who the competitors for the position are. Each player clearly knows things that—if other players could discern them—would shape their strategy and consequently their moves. And each clearly has moves they can undertake in an effort to reduce the asymmetry.

Understanding *player incentives* is a second element in building a foundation for the game. Where incentives are or can become aligned, then gains from trade arise; when incentives are in conflict, then strategy becomes paramount. Employer incentives for which the career game has impact might include being concerned with organizational performance, enhancing workforce diversity, leadership development, building bench strength, or facilitating culture change. Candidate incentives might include obtaining interesting work, promotional opportunities, challenge, a comfortable work/life balance, building wealth, and so on. Search firm incentives might include their search efficiency (since contracts are typically based on a fixed rate), earning future business from the employer, building a relationship with a candidate, and enhancing firm reputation.

The third foundational element involves understanding the *risks* each player faces. Employers face the risk of making a bad hire. They also face the risk of wasting time attempting to land a desirable candidate who may ultimately jilt the company, thus jeopardizing the hiring of a second choice. Candidates risk family conflict, the loss of relationships with current coworkers, and the security of their current positions. Search firms risk failing to bring a search to a successful close, as well as the loss of future business and reputations.

The specifics describing information asymmetries, player incentives, and the risks you face will be unique to your career game. Being truly ready to play requires that you become a savvy diagnostician of these game elements. Once you develop a clear understanding as to where you face information disadvantages—by recognizing the motivations of the many players and by identifying where risks lie for each—you can then position yourself to take actions that improve your game.

THE CONDITIONS OF THE PLAYING FIELD

Broadly speaking, the playing field for the career game is represented by the labor market. *Labor market* is a term that describes a "place" where individuals with particular skills and employers with open positions exchange labor for compensation. It is likely you have in mind as a measure of your career success your ability to reach a particular "spot" on the playing field: first violinist with your city's orchestra, a respected pediatrician, third baseman for the Boston Red Sox, the world's most recognized investment banker, a successful entrepreneur. As you prepare to play your career game, a key undertaking is that you invest to understand how the labor market is best defined. Players competing for jobs that have a global labor market are playing on a different field from players competing for jobs that have a national, regional, or local labor market. Whereas the shape and size of the playing field varies, the features that describe its condition are largely the same. Basic economic conditions impact the field of play and consequently the behavior of players. For example, most MBA program admission officers will quickly agree that economic slowdowns are great for their business. During such times, prospective students recognize that the opportunity costs for interrupting their careers are low. The playing field is such that it is a good time to return to school. The result is predictable: twenty-one months later, a large crop of newly minted MBAs are competing for jobs that may or may not have emerged since the downturn that drove them all back to school. Conversely, when the economy is growing rapidly upward, pressure is exerted on salaries. As a result, the decision to step away from a job to attend graduate school becomes an expensive one. Similarly, trends such as the offshoring of work can influence the conditions of the playing field. Student interest in certain majors declines when they are perceived as leading to "offshore-ready" jobs, such as we have recently seen in information technology, engineering, and computer science. As Thomas Friedman notes in *The World Is Flat*, an entire new set of players is now competing for jobs on what has recently become a much larger and more easily traversed playing field. This offshoring trend is driven by employer desires to reduce costs, but is only possible due to the rise of quality educational programs for these disciplines in India, China, and elsewhere. Finally, the playing field is shaped by government policies regarding immigration and the issuance of work visas. These political decisions impact where you can chose to play—and they influence who can chose to compete in play with you.

Internal and External Labor Markets

It is useful to make a further distinction between internal and external labor markets. The *internal labor market* is defined by the organizational chart—it consists of the positions and players currently in a company. The internal labor market is also shaped by both supply and demand characteristics for skill sets. Company culture, politics, and norms around career succession are all factors that influence the internal labor market. Individual player reputation, as well as acts of sponsors or mentors inside the organization, can also impact the game. Naturally, outsiders face considerable information asymmetry as compared to insiders when trying to understand the internal labor market. Players can learn more about the internal labor market in a variety of ways. One source is publications such as *BusinessWeek*'s "Best Places to Launch a Career" or the *Wall Street Journal*'s "Top Small Workplaces" or *Fortune*'s "100 Best Companies to Work For." Company websites, annual reports, and the like are additional sources of information. In our conversation with Keith Wyche (see Chapter 6), he reinforces the importance for women and minorities of leveraging these and other resources before signing on with a new firm, in order to reduce information asymmetry with regard to the company's culture.

From a game theory perspective, it is interesting to consider how a company's appearance on one of these lists might impact the game. A designation as a "best place to work" undoubtedly increases interest in a company. That interest would arguably drive up demand for positions at the company, and with it the quality of the competition for those positions. Players need to consider whether the wiser move is to join the fray or to find uncontested space—what might be called a career "blue ocean" (to borrow the phrase from W. Chan Kim and Renee Mauborgne's work on business strategy).[1] Such was the career strategy reported in our conversation with Stephen Heese (this chapter). As you will read, Heese realized during his MBA studies at the Harvard Business School that it would be difficult to get ahead of the crowd after graduation if his strategy was to follow the crowd to Wall Street.

The *external labor market* contains all of the relevant pieces of the playing field that are outside the confines of a company. How far flung the external labor market is will vary based on a job's educational requirements, licensing requirements, or the industry involved. For some jobs, the external labor market represents a small geographic area, while for other positions it may be global in scope. The Web is emerging as an easy resource for learning; websites such as www.careeronestop.org provide tools that can help players assess the condition of the external labor market.

To play the career game well, it is important to understand the opportunities and constraints that the conditions of the external labor market impose on play. Speaking broadly, labor markets can be described in regard to their *permeability*. Permeability describes the number of alternative jobs, organizations, and occupations open to players.[2] By definition, entry into more permeable labor markets is much more straightforward than entry into markets that would be labeled impermeable. Factors such as immigration policy and the supply of work visas are political features that impact the external labor market through the mobility barriers that may be created. The supply and demand for skill sets, as well as language and cultural barriers, also are important elements of the external labor market. Employment law in different parts of the world—or different parts of the country—impacts the condition of the external labor market.

The Interconnectedness of the Labor Market

A final important characteristic of the labor market is the degree of *interconnectedness* among the players. In a tightly interconnected labor market, everyone knows everyone—and it may at least seem that everyone knows everything. This means that the career game may be close to a perfect information game. As a result, play may become very political. Although small labor markets are not, by definition, tight labor markets, the two characteristics do often go together. This has led some to use the cautionary expression "small field, long career" to describe such markets. This expression reinforces the way that politics and reputation can have long-lasting and strong effects on the way the game is played. Mistakes can stay with you. In contrast, a loosely interconnected labor market is more likely to be forgiving of mistakes because information is not perfect—not every player has the same access to information. The degree of interconnectedness of the labor market has several implications for the way the career game is played. For example, in a loosely connected labor market, information asymmetries can work either for or against players. As a result, players should work to remove the asymmetries that disadvantage them and to leverage the ones that provide advantage. When the labor market is tightly connected and players are engaged in a full information game, each needs to recognize how important it is to develop and protect his or her reputation.

GETTING READY TO PLAY

As in any other competition, deliberate preparation is a hallmark of successful players. Players can prepare themselves for the career game in three ways. First, they need to understand and then build strategies to leverage their skills. Second, they must develop their personal networks so that these become value-added resources during play. A critical element of this process constitutes the third step in getting ready to play: the identification, recruitment, and retention of mentors and sponsors.

Understanding and Leveraging Personal Competitive Advantage

Analyzing what you haven't got as well as what you have is a necessary ingredient of a career.
    Orison Swett Marden (1850–1924)

Developing an effective career strategy requires players to understand and then leverage personal *competitive advantage*. The process involved in developing a personal career strategy can parallel the process used in formulating a business strategy. In that process, managers draw on a variety of tools in order to identify and then leverage a company's competitive advantage. Competitive advantage comes from a company's ability to deliver benefits to customers at either a lower cost (cost advantage) or in a better manner (differentiation advantage) than competitors. Companies that are able to create a sustainable competitive advantage outperform the competition. Analogously, the challenge for career game players is to identify and then develop what could be considered their competitive advantage. This requires players to conduct an honest inventory of personal strengths and weaknesses. Just as a company's top management team might conduct a *Strengths-Weaknesses-Opportunities-Threats* (SWOT) analysis as part of an effort to formulate business strategy, so could career game players. In considering the results of the SWOT analysis, special attention should be paid to areas where the player has or could reasonably be expected to develop competitive advantage. In this evaluation process, some key elements of competitive advantage should be considered. Specifically, preference should be given to those attributes that are *unique*, *durable*, and *inimitable* because these are more likely to provide a player with a sustained edge. Players also need to keep in mind the relevant labor market when identifying places to invest. As we have witnessed with the "flat world" phenomenon, the introduction of large numbers of skilled players in China and India has eroded the competitive advantage of players elsewhere in the world. Take as an example the many U.S.-based software engineers who, over the past several years, have discovered that their competitive advantage was imitable and thus neither unique nor durable. Add to that the availability of players willing to provide that expertise at a very low cost, and it quickly becomes apparent that an effort to compete on either cost or differentiation was unsustainable.

Developing Your Network

Career books are rife with advice on the importance of developing a network. University-based career services professionals are fond of the expression "network or not work" in communicating to students the importance of this process. The Internet has created opportunities for easily building networks—Wikipedia lists over one hundred active social networking sites. These sites range from business-oriented services (such as those provided by Linked-In .com) to social-networking sites (such as facebook.com, reunion.com, and myspace.com) to sites that connect individuals with more specific interests (such as travelbuddy.com and vampirefreaks.com). It may be that the challenge now is not about convincing people of the importance of social networks. Rather, the challenge may be to understand how to effectively build and then leverage their networks.

A *Harvard Business Review* article by Herminia Ibarra and Mark Hunter summarizes their research on the way successful executives do just this.[3] They distinguish three types of networks, based on the executive's objective for each: operational, personal, and strategic. Operational networks are designed to help get work done and are made up largely of contacts inside the organization. Often, membership in operational networks is determined by the task and company structure, rather than being left to the discretion of the executive. Personal networks are created to help executives develop personally and professionally. These networks are typically made up of external contacts, particularly of those who are in a position to help an individual recognize her or his specific interests. As a result, membership is determined by the efforts of the executive. Finally, strategic networks exist to help executives understand future priorities and build stakeholder support for their pursuits. Membership is based on the way in which each contact can support the strategic goal for the network. In all, operational networks are evaluated by the depth of the relationships developed; personal networks, by their breadth; and strategic networks, by the ability to leverage member capabilities. All three types of networks have implications for the career game. Certainly, the operational network is critical to ensure today's success—that is, the foundation upon which next moves will be based. Personal networks most closely resemble what many hold as the default definition of a career network: the greater the breadth of the network, the greater the odds that a player can find a connection between a network member and an opportunity that he or she would like to pursue. Strategic networks may be the most useful tool for the career game because they connect and leverage key relationships inside and outside the company in a context that has potential career-enhancing characteristics.

Regardless of the type of network under consideration, there are commonalities to all *social networks* that are important to understand. The term itself refers to the pattern of ties or connections that one individual has with others. These ties can be described as either strong or weak. *Strong ties* are defined as emotionally intense and involving frequent contact between individuals. They are likely the ties that individuals have with others who relate to them in multiple roles—for example, you are likely to have a strong tie to the friend who is also your advisor and coworker. *Weak ties* are those that reach outside an individual's "normal" set of contacts and are more likely to be one dimensional—that is, someone you know only as a coworker or a neighbor. Sociologists have long been interested in how social networks develop and how individuals make use of them. Much of the foundational work in the area was done by Mark Granovetter, a sociologist now at Stanford University. His research determined that weak ties are more useful than strong ties in terms of job search behavior. He explained his finding by observing that weak ties provide a bridge—from what could be a fairly insular group connected to one another by strong ties, into another group that may possess novel information and other nonstandard resources. Individuals who share strong ties share largely redundant information and have access to essentially the same resources—due to their familiarity, proximity, and history. The career advice emerging from Granovetter's work is that individuals should work on finding opportunities to establish weak ties to new groups. Linked-in.com tries explicitly to leverage this in its marketing materials. The company's marketing messages contain repeated reminders that, by participating in Linked-in.com, you stay connected not only with your contacts, but also with your contacts' contacts.

In other research on making the most of networks, it has been found that weak ties impact career success.[4] Weak ties led to more contacts, although these contacts were negatively related to the ability to access information and to career sponsorship. Considering our game theory framework, this finding makes sense. Individuals with whom you share weak ties are not likely to be very invested in your success, which suggests that you should take action to compel them to want to invest in your success. It also serves as a reminder that perhaps strong ties can supply support and sponsorship, but not necessarily the door to the next great opportunity.

Although it may be self-evident, it is important to mention the importance that your manager plays in your network, even if he or she does not function as your sponsor or mentor. Managers have access to important resources such as information, rewards, opportunities, and higher-ups in the organization. When they care about your career success, managers are more likely to make these resources available as a show of support. The game theory approach reinforces the importance of compelling your manager to see your success as important. The best way to do this is by recognizing what is important to your manager and then delivering on it. Essentially, managers and subordinates are engaged in a series of exchanges. Productive relationships exist when both parties are happy with what each has to offer the other. Your manager has the resources noted above; you have your effort, skills, abilities, and attitude to offer in return. When you present these qualities to your manager in terms of accomplishing his or her goals, your manager will be inclined to provide you access to the resources in his or her control. What is required of you, then, is to make sure you are not merely a "mug-lugger"—the friendly but unproductive individual who lugs a coffee mug from office to office each day—but, rather, someone who the manager can count on.

An interesting final point concerning relationships with managers concerns the degree to which players should be open about their aspirations. After all, it may be that the next desired position is the one the manager holds. Depending on the size of the company and the rate at which promotional opportunities arise, an ambitious subordinate can be seen as a threat. If a manager reaches this conclusion, it is rational for him or her to do what is necessary to block the subordinate's efforts. Players need to keep this in mind as a factor in their decisions about how open to be about their aspirations. Company culture, the nature of their relationship with their manager, and their manager's standing in the company are all factors that might influence moves in this part of the game.

Mentors and Sponsors

Mentors provide coaching and support to their protégés, and they help their charges understand company culture and the political landscape. In specific situations, mentors can coach through interpersonal conflicts or job-related challenges. In addition to the direct help that mentors offer, some indirect benefits can accrue, such as access to their networks of contacts. In some instances, mentors are formally assigned by a company; in other instances, mentoring relationships emerge more naturally. The primary benefit to formal company programs is that junior employees cannot wiggle out of being assigned to a mentor. These programs also serve a function from the perspective of the employer as a player in the career game by *signaling* to candidates that the company has an interest in their career acceleration. As a result, companies' recruiting and retention efforts may benefit. There is, however, a potential downside to these formal programs: not all mentors are created equal, yet company programs often are designed as if they are. And, because so much of effective mentoring relies on deep trust between partners, chemistry between the two is critically important. Arranged relationships often do not result in an ideal match.

A sponsor's role differs from a mentor's in that its primary function is to make certain that a protégé stays visible with upper-level management. The goal here is to ensure that the protégé receives consideration when opportunities become available or as career planning takes place. Sponsors are primarily counted on to keep their protégés visible; that does not require a relationship with the same level of interpersonal intensity that underlies a meaningful mentoring relationship. The importance of chemistry between parties is less critical, thus the matching is not as complicated as it is with mentors.

Mentors and sponsors can be among the most impactful players in your career game. The ability to draw on their insight and experience can be an incredible resource for players. In fact, this is precisely how good game players should view these allies in the career game—*as a resource that should be proactively and strategically managed.* Many of the executives we interviewed offer insight into just how they have done this over the course of their careers.

There are three elements to mentoring and sponsoring relationships that are often neglected and can be brought into clearer focus by adopting a game theory approach to career management. First, the "right" mentors and sponsors need to be identified. Second, you, as the protégé, need to build a case for these important players so that they want to see you win at your career game. Mentors and, to a lesser extent, sponsors are expected to make investments in the careers of their protégés. And, as is the case with any other rare skill— something we think that effective mentoring represents—it will be in high demand. You should not take recruitment of mentors and sponsors for granted. You need to be deliberate about how you make the case that time invested in you will provide a better return than time invested elsewhere. Third, what you need from mentors and sponsors will change over the course of your career. Mentors who are effective early on may not be as effective later on—and likewise for sponsors. Part of your success, we argue, will be dependent on your ability to manage transitions from mentor to mentor, sponsor to sponsor, in a strategic manner as your career needs change.

Finding the Right Mentor or Sponsor

The first step here is to recognize just what your requirements are from a mentor or sponsor. Your relationship with a sponsor is less dependent on your career stage and is thus easier to address. The key elements to look for in sponsors are twofold: first, how well networked they are inside their companies, within the industry, and elsewhere; second, how likely they are to actively and articulately advocate for you when opportunities arise that make sense for your career. The "right" mentor is quite likely going to change over the course of a career. Holding that constant for the time being, the key elements to look for in mentors are threefold: First, are they individuals with whom you can quickly become comfortable? Second, are you confident you can trust them in your most insecure moments? Third, can you count on them to not hold back in the way they provide feedback to you? If you cannot answer these three questions in the affirmative, then you have not found your mentor.

Building a Case to Earn Others' Investment

When it comes to decisions about how to invest their time, mentors and sponsors have many choices. It behooves you to take some time to build the case that you provide the best return on that investment. Showing initiative and energy are important—as is a positive attitude—because, unless the relationship is organizationally mandated, mentors and sponsors *elect* to spend time with a protégés. Even in cases in which the relationship is formally announced, mentors and sponsors still control how hard they work at providing help. If, for example, the protégé is miserable company, not too many will make the effort to help.

Mentors and Sponsors Over the Course of Your Career

Since the purpose of a mentor is to provide guidance, understanding the right sort of mentor for each career stage simply involves identifying the key challenges someone is likely to face. Early in your career with a company, the key goal is for a mentor to help you "learn the company." This involves coming to understand and appreciate the company culture. In the middle career stage, the key is to find someone higher up on the organizational chart to pull you along—similarly to the way bikers in the Tour de France allow team members to draft off one another. Crucial here is to find mentors high enough above you so that you pose no threat to them as they play their own career games. Also, the closer they are to you organizationally, the less they add in terms of access beyond what you could develop on your own. In our earlier reported conversation with Charlene Begley, she provides an example of finding such a person in Dave Calhoun when the two of them were at GE. Finally, later in your career, the ideal mentor is someone at a very high level who will be brutally honest with you about your strengths and weaknesses, who will not be timid about confronting you with your failures, and who will vigorously challenge your thinking. In our conversation, Brian Humphries describes how the mentoring he received evolved along these lines over the course of his career. He had an early mentor who eased his entry into the company by providing coaching and support. He then found a mentor who was instrumental in creating some stretch opportunities. Currently, he has the benefit of close relationships with other executives, including Mark Hurd, his CEO at HP.

Research supports our recommendation that mentoring needs to take on different forms over a career. Monica Higgins at Harvard University has done considerable work in this area. In one study, she and her colleague, David Thomas, found that the quality of the relationship with the early-career mentor affects short-term career outcomes such as satisfaction and intent to stay with the employer. However, over the long run, what they labeled the "constellation" of development relationships was found to be more important. What happens in the first few years is an investment for the rest of the career, but the constellation of mentors ultimately plays a critical role—that is, no single mentor matters more than the others. This observation is consistent with how Keith Wyche, in our conversation, described his "Board of Directors" methodology for mentors and sponsors. As you think about how you might assemble the board of directors of your career, we encourage you to keep in mind lessons from Granovetter's work on weak ties; a board composed of members with overlapping strong ties will likely not be as valuable to you as one whose members have many distinct and unmatched connections to you, otherwise referred to as weak ties.

ASSESSING THE OTHER PLAYERS

As noted earlier, players are those who can impact the game. Making a definitive list of those players can be a daunting task, as we will explore below. Part of playing the game well entails developing an understanding of the players and of how they might impact play. Understanding how you might be able to influence them to impact game play in a manner that favors you is critically important. For now, hold in mind the idea that it may become important to understand what these other players have done to prepare to play, their motives as they pertain to the play of the game, and the options they have available to them. While each situation has its unique characteristics, generally, fellow players are likely to be:

- Competitors for positions that interest you
- Your current boss
- Your current colleagues
- Other representatives from your current employer
- Your mentors
- Companies that offer jobs that interest you
- Hiring managers at companies with interesting positions
- Human resources managers at your current job and those of potential employers
- Your family
- Members of your personal network
- Search firms
- Government agencies

Recall that what makes a player a player is simply his or her ability to impact the play of the game. It is not necessarily the case that all players see themselves as such. Nor is it necessarily the case that every player will take the opportunity to influence every game in which they are involved. Not knowing whether a particular player will decide to actively participate simply means that candidates may find it foolish to ignore the potential impact of any of them—the game plan should allow for the eventuality of their participation.

And, as mentioned above, savvy players will also develop plans that attempt to influence players to participate in ways that create advantage for them.

What Can Players Do to Tilt the Field to Their Advantage?

When players are cognizant of their status and have clear interests in how the game plays out, the most clever among them will seek ways to tilt the field to their advantage before the game even begins. From the preceding list, employers best suit the purpose of illustration because it is easy to imagine that (1) they see themselves as players and (2) they want to seek and leverage all possible advantages. What sorts of things might employers do to tilt the field? Employment policies are a good place to begin because they create mobility barriers that result in disadvantages for employees in game play. Reward systems can be used in a number of ways for this purpose. Vesting and seniority systems are two examples that are designed to make it costly for employees to leave. Similarly, employers may have in place options or bonus plans that work to create "golden handcuffs" for employees, making it difficult for them to rationalize moves to other employers. Noncompete and nondisclosure agreements have the same effect. Less obvious, but often similarly effective strategies would involve employer investment in employee development of firm-specific skills, rather than skills that might easily transfer to benefit another employer. Many executives have decried the demise of management development programs in companies that determined they could not risk developing what would become the competition's talent. Finally, efforts that employers undertake to build their brands as "employers of choice" can also create advantages. Companies such as Google, Ideo, SAS, and Southwest Airlines are just a few of the many that have created and now continually leverage positive employment brands as a strategy to gain advantage in the labor market.

What Options for Play Are Open to Players?

Players have a number of options about the moves they might make. Some of these moves will have the effect of supporting the candidate's efforts; others will be hurdles the candidate has to overcome. Some of these moves will have been intentionally made with a clear understanding of the impact they have on the candidate, others less so. Naturally, candidates have an interest in encouraging moves that support their career strategies and in suppressing moves that do not. The ability to accomplish this goal begins with understanding these options and then in understanding each player's goals.

A useful example here is the candidate's current manager. Managers have an option about the way they express support for a candidate's interest in promotional opportunities with the company. How enthusiastic, genuine, and public are their statements of support? Managers also have an option about how much to invest in preparing the candidate to compete for the promotion. Some may invest heavily in job-enrichment strategies that help build a foundation that readies the candidate for the next step on the corporate ladder; others may chose not to make such an investment. Some may look for opportunities to feature the candidate—to share the spotlight. Others may choose not to. Some more "toxic" managers might actively try to dissuade the candidate from pursuing opportunities; some may actively try to sabotage the candidate by sharing or creating damaging information about him or her. The manager has options about how much to share with the candidate about the next position, the competition for the job, and the factors considered desirable by the company as an indication of a candidate's readiness. Clearly, some of the options available to managers are supportive, while others would serve to erode the candidate's efforts to earn promotions.

Competitors for positions also have interesting options. Take, for example, the job-search process familiar to anyone who has attended business school. At some point during the program, students will begin the process of looking for their postgraduation jobs. Many companies work with college career services staffs to arrange information sessions, during which representatives make short presentations and then take questions from potentially interested students. Companies then follow up with on-campus interviews in order to develop a short list of candidates, who are usually then brought out to the company for further consideration.

On the one hand, the students who are part of this process are competing with classmates—first for a finite number of interview slots and, ultimately, for a finite number of positions. On the other hand, a larger—though clearly less influential—goal is at work concerning the greater good: students want companies to think well of their schools. After all, each student and alum benefits from the school's reputational halo. With this in mind, students have options about how much information they disclose. They can choose to horde information in an effort to create an information asymmetry advantage, or they can choose to share information with an expectation that others will share with them. The information might revolve around company research done prior to the recruiter's arrival on campus; it might involve early interviewees sharing the questions asked and impressions gleaned from those to be interviewed later in the day. One consequence of sharing information may well be to create stronger competition. Another consequence is to create a position from which to demand reciprocity from classmates when the next company makes a campus visit. Of course, the stronger the set of students that recruiters see, the better the school's reputation—something that benefits all players.

Family members are another set of players with interesting options. They can choose how supportive they want to be when a candidate expresses interest in a new career opportunity. In offering or withholding support, family members arguably are using their positions to influence candidates. Family members will have opinions on relocation, the proper work/life balance, salary and lifestyle issues, and perhaps also concerns about dual-career issues and educational opportunities for children. As family members assess the new opportunity a candidate is considering, conclusions about how it affects their positions will translate into their demonstrations of support or nonsupport.

Candidates themselves make choices as to the aggressiveness of their candidacies, how overtly or covertly they show interest, their efforts to build or remove information asymmetries, and to what extent they aim to differentiate themselves from others.

What Goals Are Players Pursuing?

Given that a variety of options are open to players, the logical next question is how candidates can best predict—and ideally influence—how those options are exercised. Key in this effort is an appreciation of the goals that these other players are pursuing. Just as candidates want to make moves that are instrumental in winning their career games, the other players should also be expected to behave in a manner consistent with the achievement of their goals. To illustrate this we can revisit the examples above involving the current manager, competitors, family members, and the candidates themselves.

The current manager may have any one or a number of goals. Framed positively, the manager—or anyone in a mentoring role in relationship to the candidate—may be interested in developing a reputation for effectively developing people. This goal would motivate managers to make investments in subordinates and to be alert for opportunities to "place" their people in contests where they can win new opportunities. In contrast, some managers may not be eager to give up a productive employee to an opportunity elsewhere in the company. Managers with this goal would thus be expected to "hide" their talented employees—or to hide opportunities from them. Acting in equal self-interest, some managers may welcome the opportunity to off-load what they perceive to be a problem employee. Such managers would be expected to be very strategic with regard to information disclosed and withheld about the employee and, as in the first case, to be constantly on the watch for opportunities that might attract their problem employee.

In the example of the on-campus recruiting, all students benefit directly when their institution's reputation is elevated. This goal might motivate students to share information with classmates so that, collectively, they look impressive in the eyes of the recruiters. Such behavior is a demonstration of what game theory calls a *gain from trade*. Students do not view every opportunity as equally attractive—sharing behavior should be expected to differ based on how desirable each opportunity is to each student. Students who are confident in their own capabilities should feel less threatened by the idea of sharing information, while those who are relatively less confident would feel more so. Further, students may have a selfish interest in that their relative positioning among the remaining job seekers improves as stronger classmates accept job offers. Sharing to help strong classmates make a decision that takes them out of consideration for future competition may serve their own interests.

In the case of family members, a very wide range of goals exists. With new-career players, parents will likely express goals regarding job security. After all, one of their goals might be to avoid a child having no option but to move back home. As candidates make what sociologist Howard Becker labeled "side bets" (getting married, having children), they add players to the game. Spouses may have goals regarding upward mobility, lifestyle security, dual-career issues, and the like. Children may have goals or needs regarding schools, friends, and extracurricular activities. Both spouses and children may have goals about the candidate's work/life balance.

The wide cast of characters we have positioned as players with interests in the candidate's job search also include the hiring manager. The ultimate goal of this player should be to hire the person who is the best fit for the position. Candidates with relevant experience, who have a great track record, and who can quickly climb the learning curve should be advantaged over those with less promise. However, best fit may also be a subjective notion that is driven by self-interest. And, it may simply be difficult to objectively assess. In the former case, political considerations may make a less qualified individual a better fit. In the latter case, the hiring manager may be left to play a hunch in an effort to divine the best-fitting candidate. An even more discouraging occurrence results from managers who publicly exhort that a goal in hiring should be to "hire better than we are" in order to improve the company's capabilities over time, while privately working to be sure that no one is hired who might rise to be a threat to their own success. Human resources managers have goals for hires that involve EEOC compliance, affordability with regard to salaries and additional support, and wage compression and inversion challenges with the overall workforce. Coworkers may see a benefit in an employee's departure because of the opportunities it creates inside the work group. As well, a colleague placed in a more important position within the organization increases the value of his or her professional network.

What Are the Possibilities for Cooperation Among Players?

As the game unfolds, players may become interested in understanding where opportunities for cooperation come into play. Cooperation is nothing unusual in business; after all, organizations are, by definition, driven by cooperation which is aimed at creating something that individuals cannot create on their own. Where cooperation becomes interesting from a game theory perspective is when either the game is zero-sum or, more generally, when player self-interests are not aligned. In some instances, cooperation in the game may be fleeting—interests among players may be in alignment for only a portion of the game. Take, for example, the board game Risk. In that game, players move their armies around the board in an effort to first deplete and eventually destroy other player armies in order to take over the world. During play, two players may find it useful to cooperate in a momentary alliance to eliminate a third, recognizing all the while that, ultimately, they will turn on each other. The short-term alignment of interests supports cooperation; however, the long-term, zero-sum nature of the game guarantees that cooperation is only short lived. Players in this uneasy alliance are motivated to sacrifice as little as possible of their own army to defeat the third party, hoping that their "ally for now" may overextend and ultimately weaken its own position.

In other circumstances, the gains from trade may suggest that a more enduring form of cooperation makes sense. Let us return to the example of student placement out of a university. Campus career development staff members are evaluated, at least in part, based on placement results—particularly the percentage of students with jobs and the salaries commanded by those students. Company recruiting efforts are evaluated based on the quality of the candidates they bring on board and their efficiency in doing so. Career development people need recruiters to return to campus year after year—and to ensure that they do so, they help companies efficiently find good people. Company recruiters want access to the students who provide best fits for their companies. They expend fewer resources if the career development staff can make their search efficient; similarly, career development staff personnel can reallocate resources to the not yet employed as students accept jobs and remove themselves from further competition. Here, the two players' interests are aligned in terms of achieving quick matches, and cooperation would be expected.

But, at this point, their interests diverge. Companies want the best match with a few students, whereas the career development office wants to find appropriate matches for all students. Career development staff members benefit when employers offer high starting salaries and signing bonuses; employers prefer to pay only what is necessary to acquire qualified candidates. Player motives are no longer in alignment, and consequently there is little interest in cooperation over these issues.

Gains from trade exist when companies collude—tacitly or otherwise—not to pursue the same candidates. Resources that might have been wasted on courtships that lead nowhere can be reallocated to potentially more fruitful efforts. Numerous examples of how the Internet impacts the play of the career game are now visible on blogs and websites, such as www.irrblogmill.com, that help track who is hot and who is not. The greater the perceived accuracy of the blog, the more useful it may be in shaping the game. Internally, companies manage this process as well, cooperatively moving individuals through assignments to increase their future value to the company.

What Commitments Can Players Make and Keep?

Cooperation requires an understanding that those involved can keep the commitments they make. Player commitments are credible only to the extent that others believe in them. In terms of shaping the play of the game, the most impactful players are those with established reputations that define them as capable of delivering on commitments. Paradoxically, the stronger your reputation for delivering on promises, the more transparent your motives and the more predictable your play will be to others. This means that, although the moves of credible players are impactful (they can be counted on to occur), they may not always be effective. Just as the occasional bluff makes a poker player more effective, it may also make for a more effective career game player. Of course, bluffing is acceptable in poker, while its acceptability in the career context is more complicated. Both candidates and employers may bluff during negotiations over such issues as salary, bonus packages, and moving allowances. In some cases, writers of recommendation letters are effectively bluffing when they describe candidate merits. Many would likely agree that, in these instances, some amount of game playing is to be expected. That said, when managers fail to deliver on promised opportunities, when contacts do not provide the promised introductions, or when a family member decides late in the game not to support a geographic location, their credibility for future play is eroded.

TIME STRUCTURE OF THE GAME

The time structure of the career game impacts moves in a number of ways. In the case of filling a position, for example, most experts will agree that, when a company is interviewing a number of candidates for a job, it is better to be among the last than it is to be among the first. The recency of the impression you make on interviewers—assuming you make a good one—can influence their ultimate judgments about your suitability for the position. MBA students are often quick to point out that when a company does campus recruiting over multiple days, the best interview slot is the morning (when the recruiter is fresh) of the last day (when the benefit of recency effects is most likely to impact postvisit reporting). Early in the day, recruiters are still attentive; it is only natural that later in the day they have often begun contemplating their trips to the airport and the flights home. When a company is on campus for only one day, the later you are in the schedule—as the lore goes—the better.

Another example of the way in which time structure impacts the game occurs during the negotiation phase. When candidates are quickly contacted about their interest in a position, it signals that they are at or near the top of the company's list. This knowledge should be used to shape their stance during negotiations. Similarly, candidates who are left waiting for a call for some time would likely be correct to presume that they are not a first choice. The passage of time in this context might impact a candidate's view of the job. Once back on the hiring company's radar, he or she may now want to explore why it is that the preferred candidates—those who had the company's attention for the previous weeks—chose *not* to take the job. The company for, that matter, may have been softened up a bit by the disappointment in not landing its top choices. This, too, should influence the way the current candidate approaches negotiations. Alternatively, early movers in a job market may benefit by the ability to land qualified but risk-averse employees at salaries that are perhaps a bit discounted. More generally, as it gets late in the game, some players likely become more desperate. The desperation might be based on the condition of the playing field—specifically, the external labor market. In a buyer's market, candidates become desperate; in a seller's market employers become desperate. Understanding one player's growing anxiety creates strategic leverage for the other. In all, understanding how it is an advantage to be an early or late mover in this game is a function of understanding other players' motives, risk tolerances, and the condition of the playing field.

Finally, understanding the time structure of the game provides insight to the succession planning process. Many individuals take a position with an understanding—accurate or otherwise—that it is intended to turn from the current opportunity into an even more desirable one by a given date. These expectations represent what the individual sees as a credible commitment. When things do not happen as planned or scheduled, that commitment is broken, the employer's credibility is eroded, and consequently the employer's ability to use commitments as future moves is diminished.

SUMMARY

The purpose of this chapter is to show you the work that you must undertake to get yourself ready to make moves in the career game. First and most important, you should devise a method for uncovering and then removing information asymmetries that, left unaddressed, will disadvantage you. Next, you should identify the incentives and risks faced by all of the game's players. Together, this understanding of what players know about the game—what each could "win" and what each is willing to risk—will be very useful to you in predicting their moves, as well as their reactions to your moves.

With those factors accounted for, you should next study the internal and external labor markets that frame the field of play. For you to be an effective career game player, you must continually reassess the conditions of the track. Just as jockeys have to reconsider strategies when a horse race is run on an ungroomed track, labor market conditions should impact your strategy. Supply and demand for different skill sets and the interconnectedness of the labor market are just two elements that can impact the moves you select as your game unfolds.

After developing an appreciation for the playing field, your next step in getting ready is to conduct an honest inventory of your strengths and weaknesses. The more objectively you understand these, the better positioned you will be to leverage your personal competitive advantage on the market. This advantage is based on those things you can do better than competing players. Your competitive advantage in relation to the other players in the career game may serve as the source for cooperation with other players, which will benefit you from gains through trade. Your strengths, when combined with those of another player, may create a non–zero-sum situation that allows both players to win a bit. Of course, recognizing potential gains from trade requires that you understand the commitments other players can keep. If you partner with players who cannot deliver their ends of the deal, you will end up having been played as a sucker.

In the next chapter, we talk about a number of career game moves. As we have observed elsewhere, most moves are idiosyncratic to your game. We think of some moves, however, as having broad relevance; we will focus on those in order to help you develop an appreciation for the way moves impact career progress. But, first, we report our conversations with Ken Frazier, Brian Heese, and Stephen Heese. All three made interesting—and what you might consider discontinuous—career moves. Frazier is EVP and president, Global Human Health, at Merck & Company, Inc. His major moves involved his career shift from being a partner with a major Philadelphia law firm to his current role in which he is responsible for marketing and sales worldwide for a major pharmaceutical company. Brian Heese left his position on Wall Street with Merrill Lynch and is now the director of Corporate Work Study at Cristo Rey New York High School, which serves disadvantaged children in Harlem. Finally, Brian's brother, Stephen Heese, is both the president and CEO of Chris-Craft Corporation and president of Indian Motorcycle. His career moves since earning his MBA at Harvard have involved deliberately going where others are not. From these three interviews, you should begin to develop a sense of how players create and utilize strategies and how, in doing so, they prepare for career moves.

NOTES

1. Chan Kim and Renee Mauborgne, *Blue Ocean Strategy: How to Create Uncontested Market Space and Make Competition Irrelevant* (Harvard Business Press, 2005).

2. R. S. Belous, "Flexible Employment: The Employer's Point of View," in *Bridges to Retirement,* ed. P. B. Doeringer (Ithaca, NY: ILR Press, 1990), 111–29.

3. H. Ibarra and M. Hunter, "How Leaders Create and Use Networks," *Harvard Business Review* (January 2007).

4. S. E. Seibert, M. L. Kraimer, and R. C. Liden, "A Social Capital Theory of Career Success," *Academy of Management Journal* 44, no. 2 (2001): 219–37.

A CONVERSATION WITH KEN FRAZIER

EXECUTIVE VICE PRESIDENT AND PRESIDENT, GLOBAL HUMAN HEALTH, MERCK & COMPANY, INC.

Ken Frazier leads all of Merck's marketing and sales organizations worldwide for the pharmaceutical and vaccine businesses. He is also a member of Merck's Executive Committee, the senior management group that evaluates and makes strategic decisions for the company.

Frazier joined Merck in 1992 as vice president, general counsel, and secretary of the Astra Merck Group. Prior to that, he was a partner with the Philadelphia law firm of Drinker Biddle & Reath. He was elected vice president of public affairs in 1994 and, in 1997, assumed the additional responsibilities of assistant general counsel, Corporate Staff. Frazier was promoted to vice president and deputy general counsel in January 1999. Later that year, he assumed the position of senior vice president and general counsel, overseeing Merck's legal and public affairs functions and The Merck Company Foundation. In November 2006, he was promoted to executive vice president and general counsel. He was appointed to his current position in August 2007.

Frazier is a member of the Council of the American Law Institute, the American Bar Association, and the Council on Foreign Relations. He sits on the boards of Cornerstone Christian Academy and Ithaka Harbors, Inc. (a nonprofit information technology organization). He earned a BA in Political Science from Pennsylvania State University in 1975 and a JD from Harvard Law School in 1978.

AUTHORS: **Can you begin by sharing a little bit about how your upbringing has shaped the way you have approached your career?**

FRAZIER: The way I was raised has had an enormous influence on my approach to work. I was born and raised in the inner city of Philadelphia. My mother died when I was very young, and I was raised by my father. That is a bit different than what most would picture as a single-parent family. More than anything else, it was my father's approach to life that shaped me. His approach was simple—make no excuses for anything. My father was one of the most resilient people I ever knew, and one of the most resourceful, too. He was born in 1900 in South Carolina. As an African American child at that time and in that area, he only had the opportunity for the equivalent of a third-grade education. In spite of that, he taught himself basic literacy skills and became self-educated to a significant degree. He believed that if people worked hard and had the right instincts for how to treat other people, they would be successful. I have tried to approach my career that way.

AUTHORS: You attended Penn State and majored in political science. What drew you to that major?

FRAZIER: When I started at Penn State, I intended to study chemistry but ended up in political science because, during my freshman year, I found that I was more inclined to those topics. My interest in chemistry was not really hardwired—it was just that, an interest. I had always found law fascinating, so it wasn't a difficult life decision to change majors.

AUTHORS: That's part of the undergraduate experience—the chance to explore a bit.

FRAZIER: It is, but at the same time, some people quickly seize on their major without second-guessing their decision. For example, my daughter is a sophomore at the University of Pennsylvania now. When she left for college, she knew immediately and with all certainty that she wanted to major in biomedical engineering. It strikes me as somewhat narrow, but she is enjoying it.

AUTHORS: What would you say activated your interest in the law?

FRAZIER: My interest in the law was primarily because I grew up in a period when there was great social change going on inside the U.S.—the civil rights movement being the most significant example. Many of my heroes—the Thurgood Marshalls of the world—were lawyers. There was a lawyer in Philadelphia at the time, Cecil B. Moore, who was a very strong civil rights advocate and leader. I found those people to be very compelling. I saw lawyers as heroes and as people who could actually change the world in positive ways.

AUTHORS: When you started law school, what did you think you would do when you got out?

FRAZIER: I thought I would probably be a criminal defense lawyer. That was my intention.

AUTHORS: But that isn't how it played out. What happened during law school to change your focus?

FRAZIER: When I got to Harvard Law School, I was exposed to a type of law practice and a type of legal career that I wasn't aware existed—corporate law. Harvard is oriented toward business and corporate law. I learned that major law firms represented businesses, and the expectation was that Harvard law students would join a large, prestigious law firm and eventually become a partner. I accepted that as a good way of beginning one's career, and that is what I ended up doing. I joined a large law firm in Philadelphia.

AUTHORS: What drove your decision to leave the law firm to join Merck?

FRAZIER: Merck was my client at the firm, and I did a lot of trial work for them over the years. I enjoyed having Merck as a client—it appealed to the same part of me that had thought about majoring in chemistry. The application of science to health problems is something important—and obviously interests me greatly. When I represented Merck, I was always drawn to the scientists at the company and what they were trying to do for humanity. I admired the company, as I think many people did at the time, and when they offered me a position, I was inclined to accept it. I enjoyed being a partner at the law firm, and frankly, I never had a perspective that I wanted to do anything other than be a partner in the law firm until the Merck opportunity presented itself.

So I decided to experiment and try the opportunity. There was also a personal issue that happened at that time. When my daughter was born, my wife suffered some health complications. That caused me to be a more involved parent and it also helped me see how much time was being spent in the billable rat race for the law firm. Of course, as it turns out, I haven't worked any less [at Merck] than I would have for the firm—but I had hoped, I guess, that the corporate job would allow me more time for my family.

AUTHORS: **What were some surprises when you began working inside Merck?**

FRAZIER: One difference should have been obvious—perhaps it was so obvious that it was easy to underestimate. The business of a law firm is law, and the business of Merck is the discovery and development of life-changing, pathbreaking drugs. So I found myself in a milieu where being a lawyer was an enabler of a broader strategy, as opposed to the strategy. That was a big change for me. Being in a situation where the hardest problems to be solved were multidisciplinary in nature required me to learn other people's skill sets. Knowing the law was not enough. Being around finance people, researchers, manufacturing people, human resources people, and the like caused me to be aware of—and more interested in—disciplines other than mine.

AUTHORS: **How did you make the transition to a discipline outside of legal?**

FRAZIER: Originally, I was hired as the general counsel for a joint venture between Merck and another company called Astra-Merck. After only a year in that position, the then-CEO Dr. Roy Vagelos hired me as vice president for public affairs. So, after just a year into my Merck career, I was taken out of the legal department and I spent about five and a half years on the business side of the company. That really forced me to be much more open to understanding how the business ran. Dr. Vagelos felt it was a useful move for Merck to develop me into a more well-rounded person, and it was fortunate for me to have the opportunity. That said, it was one of the hardest career decisions I ever made.

AUTHORS: **Why was that?**

FRAZIER: Law was my chosen discipline, and I wanted to believe that I could contribute to Merck in my chosen discipline. When I was asked to take on a new discipline—one that I had no experience or affinity toward—it was a very difficult choice. I felt like I was leaving the law behind. It turned out to be the best choice I could ever make in my career because I was exposed to a different level of the business than otherwise would have been possible.

AUTHORS: **What do you think they saw in you that made them confident it was a good strategic move to develop you?**

FRAZIER: I can only guess. At that time, my primary experience was as a trial lawyer and my skill set was heavily based on being able to deal effectively with people, influencing others, and being an effective public speaker. I probably demonstrated in my early time in the company that I had the ability to think more broadly about business issues.

AUTHORS: **A remarkable series of events around the Vioxx drug has been at the center of your work at Merck. Can you reflect on how that experience helped you develop as an executive?**

FRAZIER: To some degree, I am still thinking through the Vioxx issue. The experience was all-consuming. It was a circumstance that threatened the very viability of this company. The Vioxx issue required us to conceptualize a different approach for how we develop and market drugs and, frankly, to have the guts to confront it and deal with it.

AUTHORS: **Perhaps some of your dad's emphasis on resilience helped you.**

FRAZIER: Perhaps so, but I can tell you I wouldn't want to repeat the experience. It was definitely an overrated development opportunity! One positive element was that I was lucky enough to enjoy the full force and confidence of my CEO and my board, and that is fortunate because things didn't start off well for us at all.

AUTHORS: **How did you earn that level of confidence?**

FRAZIER: The key was that they believed I had the right strategy. They were fully supportive of it at the most challenging time, and as such, we were able to pull through in a way that exceeded everybody's expectations in terms of the size and finality of the settlement. The outcome is that Merck is well positioned to make important discoveries for many years to come.

AUTHORS: **You were recognized by the National Legal Aid Defender Association as the 2008 recipient of their Exemplar Award for your pro bono work. Do you see that work as instrumental to what you do at Merck, or is it a separate part of your life?**

FRAZIER: I don't see it as a separate part of my life. I like to think of people as an integrated whole—everything you do can potentially help you be better at other things. I have done a lot of pro bono work. I taught in South Africa during apartheid and have done other things that were interesting to me. I believe that varieties of experiences like these can shape one's ability to go into different environments and have confidence to make things happen. My recent pro bono work was a death penalty case. We had a client with an execution date. When I took over that case, there wasn't much hope that he would avoid the death penalty, but we went to work, and we won. Not only did the court reverse the death sentence, but ultimately they reversed the conviction and freed our client. An experience like that—overcoming long odds—gives you tremendous confidence that even when things seem hopeless they are not hopeless. I learned this lesson during the Vioxx work, too. Instead of being paralyzed by worrying about the overall outcome, the best approach is to hold yourself accountable for the outcome, put your best effort into it, and make progress day by day. If you can do that, you can eventually get to a place that, maybe at the beginning, seemed unreachable. I'll say it another way—what I really learned from my father is that the future isn't something that just happens to you. You can, in many ways, "speak it into being" by committing to making something happen. It won't always work—but it certainly won't happen if you don't try.

AUTHORS: **It's an attitude more than anything else.**

FRAZIER: That's right. I always make this point when I do public speaking. My younger sister is a concert pianist. She is in Europe now, traveling around and making her living playing the piano. I ask people to imagine how hard it is to do that. By comparison, becoming an attorney or an executive is not that tough! My sister was raised, as I was, in the inner city in humble circumstances. My father raised a concert pianist in a Philadelphia ghetto—that just doesn't happen by chance. It happened because he believed in her talent, insisted that she live up to her talent, and worked tirelessly one day at a time to remove the barriers in her way. In 1963, the thought of her living this life existed only in my father's head; it existed nowhere else in the universe but in his head. If it had not existed in 1963 in his head, it could not be true now forty-five years later. One last thing I hope to convey is that a lot of people are afraid to fail.

Not having that fear of failure, actually, is a tremendous advantage in one's career because everyone has to be willing to go into situations for which they aren't really prepared. One has to have the willingness to fail at something in order to achieve success at it. If you aren't willing to fail at some things, you won't succeed at much.

CAREER GAME OBSERVATIONS

- Ken Frazier's approach to his career was strongly shaped by influences in his childhood. His father was a tremendously influential player in the career games of both of his children. Frazier's description of his father's dedication to the tasks involved in supporting his kids—removing obstacles, cheering, motivating—is heartening.

- His comments demonstrate how important role models can be in helping people shape the outcome they are looking for in their career game. Effectively, people such as Thurgood Marshall and Cecil B. Moore were historical figures with roles as players in Frazier's career game.

- Frazier's path has taken some unanticipated turns, but the net effect of the moves has been to bring him closer to his career goals. He thought he would practice criminal law out of law school but ended up in corporate law. He did not imagine working at a company like Merck in a position outside of law, as he now does. However, Frazier is clearly working on something that matters to society—a trait that he admired in the individuals who were his role models early on.

- In making these moves, Frazier had to demonstrate a great deal of career agility. The shift from the law firm, where the business was law, to Merck, where the business was drug discovery, was a significant one.

- Frazier also had to demonstrate agility in moving out of the legal position at Merck. To do so, he leveraged the skills that Merck management saw in him—such as communication skills and the ability to be effective in influencing others.

A CONVERSATION WITH BRIAN HEESE

DIRECTOR OF CORPORATE WORK STUDY, CRISTO REY NEW YORK HIGH SCHOOL

Brian Heese received his BBA from Loyola University in New Orleans and began his career working for Price Waterhouse as an audit manager. He entered the MBA program at Wharton in 1994, and upon graduating went to work for Merrill Lynch as an investment banker with a focus on debt-financing products. Most recently, he was the manager of the structured note origination desk. He left Merrill Lynch in the spring of 2008. At the time of our conversation, he had just accepted the position he now holds at Cristo Rey High School in Harlem (www.cristoreyny.org).

AUTHORS: You recently lost your position at Merrill Lynch due to cutbacks. What are you—now in your mid-forties—planning to do next?

HEESE: I have always toyed with the idea of finding some sort of an opportunity that would help me give something back. During the past several years, I have been doing a variety of volunteer activities with area kids—mostly around coaching soccer. It has been rewarding, but I really have wanted to find a way to leverage my business experience in a way that would benefit kids.

There is a high school up on 106th in Harlem here that I've done a lot work with and got to know pretty well. Three or four years ago, the priest who married my wife and me introduced me to the guy who started the school. The school operates on a great model. The kids come from low-income families. They are placed in jobs one day a week and attend class the rest of the week. The money they earn, along with a small contribution from the family, is used to pay their tuition at Cristo Rey. When I was at Merrill, I helped set Cristo Rey up there. The kids worked in the mail room and in IT support. In IT support, for example, some would run around changing out toner cartridges throughout the facility, others would do triage—as calls for help came in, they would log the request and assign it to the right IT resource for service, and so on. The kids learned about the responsibility associated with working in a corporate setting and could be proud of the fact they were earning their chance at a great education.

The kids get a reasonable job where they learn the tools they need to succeed. The whole idea is to give them positive role models and get them beyond working just in fast food or something like that.

I have just accepted the position there as the director of Corporate Work Study. I'll be the one to make the relationships at the various companies. I will be responsible for finding placements for the kids and then also for helping prepare the kids to go to work.

AUTHORS: **How are the kids picked for the school?**

HEESE: They have to meet two requirements: they have to pass what is called an independence school examination—the exam kids take to go to private school—and they have to demonstrate enough maturity and poise so that we know they will be acceptable to the employers we have partnered with.

AUTHORS: **How big is the school now?**

HEESE: It has almost 360 kids in grades 9–12—the school is still relatively new. Plans are to have about 100 a class. Each student works in a four-person team, so that means we need to have about ninety jobs to make the whole thing work.

AUTHORS: **This is quite a big career change from Wall Street. How long do you envision being here?**

HEESE: You know, there are a lot of reasons why I took this job, and I am really excited about it. I am excited about the chance to give something back because I see I've been really lucky and I see a lot of people who didn't have the same role models that I had. I want to see if I can share some of the business knowledge I have with other people. So that is my goal right now.

At the same time, I think this job will be helpful in that it will keep me in touch with the major employers here in New York City. This is a "give back" job that doesn't really take me out of a business network if I decide I want to go back to the industry.

AUTHORS: **How have you prepared financially to make this move?**

HEESE: Amy (my wife) and I sat down and studied this very closely. When we looked at it, we figured that, based on my severance and our savings, we could afford to stay in New York City for about nine years—that's key because that is when our youngest son will finish high school. That plan means not living extravagantly while we are here—but it does mean we can still travel some and make sure the kids are in good schools and all that. Obviously, the longer I stay in the position the more we will spend the capital I accumulated while at Merrill. How long I do it will more be a function of how much I am enjoying it—and whether or not the school and I think I am being effective.

AUTHORS: **If Merrill hadn't cut you loose, do you think you ever would have pursued something like this?**

HEESE: Even though the writing was on the wall at Merrill for some time—given everything that was going on there—I never found the guts to pull the trigger myself. In hindsight, I think that was the smart move—I don't think you should pull the trigger on yourself. You always let them pull it for you because you tend to get paid better on the way out.

AUTHORS: **So, tell me what a day is going to look like for you.**

HEESE: The kids check in at the school in the morning. Each day of the week, a different class goes out—so, one day the freshmen are working and the other three grades are in class. The next day, the sophomores go out, and so on. We take the kids by subway to three or four drop-off points in Manhattan—they find their way to work from those points by nine in the morning. The kids bring work slips to show they attended work back to that same point, where we pick them up at five thirty. While the kids are at work, I will be splitting time between activities on campus to help continually develop the work readiness of the students, and working out in the business community to identify more job opportunities.

AUTHORS: **What do you see as your first big challenge in the job?**

HEESE: One of the strategic challenges I'm going to face is that the entry-level job in Manhattan is continually requiring a higher-level education. We are going to have to work hard to make sure our kids are prepared to be successful out there.

AUTHORS: **Has the school been around long enough to get a sense of how successful the program has been with the students?**

HEESE: The school opened in 2004, and it recently graduated its first class. All forty out of the forty kids are going on to college—they are not all going to four-year schools, but these kids are going and they'll get a good education and much better opportunities as a result.

AUTHORS: So is this a job for you or a new career?

HEESE: At a minimum, it's another cool adventure. Long term, it might be a career, but who knows?

AUTHORS: What would your next move be, if you loved this job? A larger school? An administrative position? Or are you going to use this as a break, and then head back to Wall Street?

HEESE: That's a very interesting question. I guess, right now, I have two concerns about a return to investment banking—one more macro and one more micro related. The macro-related issue is I think the financial services sector is going to be doing a massive contraction over the next ten years. In the 1990s and the first half of this decade, banks lent money to their clients to enable them to have enough money to buy the products that the banks created. Now, that lending spigot has dried up. If clients have less money to buy the products, then they won't buy and banks will need fewer people to create those products. So, the financial services business needs either a massive new innovation or it needs to contract.

Another thing is that the investment banking world at a large firm is really a young person's game. I was an anomaly—you find very few people who are 45 years old in that business. And, the only people who are 45 are people running businesses. At Merrill Lynch, there's a huge bubble from the age of 25 to 38, but very few people older. While I always got along great with my clients, I didn't really have much in common with my coworkers. Our kids are older, and so on. So, in a few years the people there will all still be 25 to 38, and I will be pushing fifty.

AUTHORS: So, what is this job preparing you to do next?

HEESE: I would say the thing I thought of is it prepares you better for an administrative role in not-for-profits, as it gets you networks in that community as well. So, that might be something interesting to do. I want to see if I actually do want to teach. You know, part of what I will be teaching is a business prep course to these kids, and I'll see how I like that. I am experimenting—I don't have a grand master plan—I never have.

AUTHORS: Let us challenge you on that. You went to Loyola University [in New Orleans] and studied accounting. Then you went to work for a prestigious accounting firm. After that, you were persistent about getting your MBA—not just any MBA, but an MBA from Wharton. And then you went to Wall Street. That wasn't a grand master plan?

HEESE: Looking backwards, that's fair. The job that I had at Merrill Lynch was the job I went to Wharton to get. So now, I've done that. Looking forward, I think I have a different philosophy. I have learned from a very stressful job that the best way for me to cope is to focus very much on one day at a time. So, in that way, I don't have a grand master plan now. I have an opportunity that excites me—I can afford to pursue it for a while—and I am not too terribly concerned now about what comes after that.

I am very curious to see how this goes. As my wife pointed out to me, my job is basically going to be to run an employment agency for 360 high school kids. This is a complete departure from anything I have done in the past, but it feels right to me nonetheless.

I know this is what I want because, as I get older, I see the next phase of my life focused on this process of transferring skills.

The business of Wall Street was so damned complex that in order to stay far ahead of the guys I was competing against I had to be ridiculously driven: smarter, faster, up earlier, and all that. As I go to the next phase in my life, one of the things I want to do—I want to dial it down a little. I don't know if this job will allow me to dial it down a little, but it's probably a step in the right direction.

AUTHORS: It will probably involve a lot less pressure from the corporate powers. The pressure is going to come from different places. You are going to find out that you really like these kids and you don't want to let them down. Or a kid that you've really invested a lot in will make a bad decision and let you down. That's going to be really frustrating. It will come at you differently.

HEESE: That's right.

CAREER GAME OBSERVATIONS

- Brian Heese provides an example of someone who has made a career move that represents a significant departure from a fairly established career trajectory with a well-understood sequence of moves—accounting major to an accounting firm, to Wharton for an MBA, and then to Wall Street. However, like other sound career moves, he is leveraging his capabilities and experiences to accomplish a new career goal.

- The decision to start a new career trajectory was clearly influenced by other players—Merrill Lynch (the former employer) and his family both impacted his play, the former by providing him with the opportunity to save money that might be necessary to subsidize the move, and the latter by committing to the lifestyle changes that could result.

- Heese's analysis of what the future at Merrill would hold is interesting. He looked ahead and saw that a variety of circumstances could make his work less interesting if he were to stay with the company or in the industry.

- As to his leaving Merrill Lynch, the observation that it is better to let the company "pull the trigger on you" rather than to "pull the trigger on yourself" is instructive. At least in his experience, the former strategy resulted in a more attractive severance package and, as a result, a better position from which to plan his next moves.

- It is clear that, though Heese is committed to this new position, he recognizes that it might not be where he ends his career. As a result, he is working to add to and maintain his network—something that will happen naturally in his new position—and also, he is looking for ways to learn more about opportunities that are related to his current job. The fact that his new position is different from his former one on so many dimensions means that he will be adding many nonredundant players to his network.

A CONVERSATION WITH STEPHEN HEESE

PRESIDENT & CEO, CHRIS-CRAFT CORPORATION; PRESIDENT, INDIAN MOTORCYCLE

In addition to his roles at Chris-Craft Corporation and Indian Motorcycle, Steve Heese is also a partner of Stellican Limited, the British Investment firm. Prior to Chris-Craft, he spent twelve years at Erico International Corporation in a variety of roles, including managing director of the Europe, Asia, and Australia regions, president of Erico Products Australia Ltd., and vice president of Sales & Marketing for Erico Fastening Systems. Steve also spent three years at Price Waterhouse in Tampa, Florida, as a member of the management consulting group. Heese has a bachelor's degree in accounting from Tulane University and a master's degree in business administration from Harvard University's Graduate School of Business.

AUTHORS: **You have made a number of moves during your career—some that might have been perceived as at least atypical and perhaps as risky. Can you tell us a bit about how you have approached and evaluated these opportunities?**

HEESE: One thing I have learned from my experience and from watching those around me is that people often misunderstand risk. I guess a better way to say it is that they don't take enough time to really understand the actual level of risk. So, in my career, things that might have looked like risky moves to an outsider really were, from my perspective, great opportunities. It may sound trite, but often the fact is that there is often great opportunity for those who are willing to go where others fear to go. Going "where the crowd isn't" can be a good move.

AUTHORS: **So, one atypical move was your decision after finishing your MBA at Harvard to join Erico, a company in the Midwest that makes supplies for construction—metal fasteners and the like. Not the stereotypical "off to Wall Street" move that most would predict was your path.**

HEESE: Out of HBS, there was certainly a well-beaten path to investment banking and to strategic consulting. Before coming to HBS, I worked for Price

Waterhouse. In school, I carefully listened to my classmates who had come out of those industries—those people were tortured about going back there, even though the compensation was compelling. None of them was happy with their work experience. These people never talked about being happy with what they were doing—their job was something to endure so on the back end they would have money to do what they really wanted to do. These people resented everyone where they worked.

I'm sure I could have gone into investment banking or consulting out of HBS. And I probably could have made a lot of money at it. But my thinking is, if you follow the crowd, you are going to have a hard time going further than the crowd. I figured there was more fun and excitement going in another direction.

AUTHORS: So, that explains why do didn't make those choices. Why did you pick what you did?

HEESE: I reflected back on my experience at Price Waterhouse. While I worked there, I spent a lot of time at NationsBank. At the time [mid-1980s], RBC, NationsBank, and Bank of America were buying numerous banks in Florida. There was a lot of work to do to integrate the systems. It wasn't very intellectually stimulating work, but it was something I needed to explore.

I also had some manufacturing clients, and I realized that I loved working with them. I loved the realness of watching things get designed and built, watching things get shipped, watching everything that went into creating something tangible. And my main manufacturing client was the Jim Walter Corporation. It was the largest company in Florida—a Fortune 150 building-products company at the time. And, after reflecting on it during my MBA program, I decided manufacturing was something I wanted to do. I'm sure my classmates who are still at Goldman Sachs are worth a lot more than what I'm worth and make a lot more than I make, and I'm okay with that because I have had an incredible journey of my own.

AUTHORS: Tell us a little about your decision to go to HBS.

HEESE: A lot of people view the Harvard MBA as the place to go because it provided the ticket to so many opportunities. That was the surest bet to get to their destination. I wanted to go back to school because I saw a big gap between what I was doing at Price Waterhouse and what I wanted to do. And, more importantly, I realized I was sitting on one side of the divide with no rope, no bridge, nothing to get me across. The MBA program was the way to get across.

I needed to leave my job because I really just didn't like what I saw as my future there. I worried that so many great coworkers were leaving. The company had no trouble reloading each year, but I feared that over time those finally making partner and leading the firm were "who was left" not "who was best." The job was going to change, too. I was moving from doing the work to being responsible for selling the work. That just wasn't something I relished.

So, the question is what do I do? The doors I wanted open were not open. There were things I knew I did not want to do. For example, at the time, lots of people in Florida [Heese was in Tampa] were getting into real estate. I really didn't want to go into real estate—it didn't seem exciting to me—perhaps because I didn't fully understand it. I understood better what I did *not* want to do than what I did.

So, out of restlessness, I decided to go to business school. And I figured, if you are going to go to business school you should try to get into the best one you can. I was very fortunate to get in to HBS. I didn't think I had enough of the right experience. I didn't like my essays. But something worked, I suppose.

AUTHORS: **After a time at Erico, you made another major move in taking on an international assignment. Can you tell us a bit about that decision? Was there strategy at work here?**

HEESE: On one level, it was about fun—at the age of twenty-nine, I was looking for adventure. Again, I didn't really see it as risky because it was early in my career and there wasn't a lot at stake. I did have a ton of debt—HBS was kind enough to lend me the money to attend—but I was confident I could make something work. On another level, it was strategic in that it was another example of going where the crowd wasn't.

When I joined Erico, my first assignment was a turnaround attempt of a struggling division. It ended up only 50 percent successful, and we wound up selling half of the company and shutting the other half down. The parent company was giving me projects to do while they figured out what to do with me. They wanted to keep me, but they weren't sure what they should have me do. Being back on project work was too much like being at Price Waterhouse. My plan at that point was to quit. I finished a project and, before they could start me on another, I was going to quit and go to Colorado and ski. I was twenty-nine at the time; I had no wife, no kids. I was going to go and ski for the winter and figure out what my next step was. In the meeting where I was going to quit they offered me the job of general manager of their company in Australia—another turnaround. A pattern was evolving in my résumé— turnaround, turnaround, turnaround, turnaround.

AUTHORS: So, to your earlier point—there is opportunity in turnaround because many people will see it as too risky to undertake.

HEESE: Yes—people think turnarounds equal risk, just like they think bank-ruptcy auctions equal risk. But in reality, turnarounds are huge opportunities; bankruptcy auctions are huge opportunities because everyone else runs for the exit. There are, very often, very few people standing at a bankruptcy auction, which means that what sells at the auction goes for maybe 20–25 cents on the tangible book value dollar. And I think turnarounds are tremendous because people don't expect a lot out of you.

AUTHORS: So, that's what took you to Australia.

HEESE: Yes. The job they couldn't find anyone else to do. I worked with the company there, expanded it to nine countries in Asia, and then ran the whole company from England over the next twelve years.

AUTHORS: Tell us about how that ended with your decision to move back to the States and your decision to buy Chris-Craft.

HEESE: I was married and had children by that time—this was late 1999. Our daughter was four and the twins would have been two. I was gone all the time— I was totally absorbed in the company, probably overly absorbed, in hindsight. My wife kept harassing me about missing our kids' growing up, quite correctly, pointing out to me that I was gone thirty-four weekends in 1999. I was gone for two weeks at a time, living in England, but working in Korea, in South

Africa, in New Zealand, in India . . . places where I couldn't fly home for a weekend. She eventually helped me see the light, like she's done before.

So, I agonized over leaving, over what to do. I figured out that I couldn't really look for a new adventure while I was doing my job, and there were things happening within the company that helped me see it was time to leave. That said, I owned a chunk of the company, so I couldn't just quit and walk away. That wouldn't have been my style anyway after working so hard to build the thing. So I gave the company six months' notice. We didn't announce it to anybody at the company until three weeks before my last day, but it gave the board six months to figure out what they wanted to do and recruit my replacement.

I moved back to Tampa without a new job, knowing that I could support myself for a couple of years while I found a new challenge to sink my teeth into. Not in high style, but certainly I could pay bills. I knew that I was going to find a company to buy. I gravitated toward the loan workout departments at the local banks, which, in my Price Waterhouse days, were the people that I loved talking to the best. The trust officers at the banks who knew all the rich old guys who might want to sell their businesses and the loan workout guys— that's who I called on. With that latter group, I knew there was opportunity. I figured that you could buy a dollar for 50 cents or less and you wouldn't have a lot of pressure. There's no market for businesses that are broken. Private equity firms won't touch them because they want to sit on the boards without actually doing the messy work. Every bank has a few opportunities like this on their books, and they don't know what to do with them. Even the larger private equity firms will have a few of them, and they hope and pray that some option will materialize. That's the opportunity—going where the crowd isn't.

With Chris-Craft, the deposit to enter the auction room was $2.5 million. We were the only people there, and we walked out with everything for $5 million. We then wrote the business plan for the company's turnaround, and got a $10 million bank loan. After selling the inventory, we paid ourselves a $4 million dividend. One way to look at it is we bought the company for $1 million. It is funny—people line up to buy businesses with little upside; we were the only ones who were willing to pay $1 million for Chris-Craft—a company with physical assets worth far more, plus it is an incredible American brand.

WHAT YOU NEED TO KNOW TO PLAY   115

AUTHORS: Why have so few people figured this out? Or, at least why are so few willing to take a closer look?

HEESE: It's interesting what it is that's driving the decision making. Some of it is the lemmings' march into and then out of B-school. My classmates and I worked in accounting or in consulting, then we got our MBAs, and then we returned to these jobs or similar jobs without a whole lot of thought really given to "What new tools have I really learned and where are the other places that I could use them?" It just doesn't occur to people, I guess.

I also think lots of people operate within a very narrow band where true success and failure are not—at least how I define them—on the range of possible outcomes. They make conservative choices about their careers. In some ways, there is no more conservative choice than going to HBS.

I stay in touch with lots of my HBS classmates. Some of them have ten, fifteen, twenty years in at an investment bank. Something happens, and they get laid off. There's an oversupply of these people, and their skills are not transferrable. In some ways, the decision to go to Wall Street is higher risk—and it is risk about a market you can't control.

This wasn't what I set out to do out of HBS—I learned this. It really just sort of dawned on me. If you do your homework before a bankruptcy auction, you can figure out the inventory in the backyard is worth $5 million. If you can move it, the worst thing that will happen is you will get buildings and land for free.

AUTHORS: Why do people view that as risky?

HEESE: In fairness, not just anyone can do this—you must have the money to write a check at the end of the auction. You can't go to the bank and say, "Hey give me a bank loan because I'm going to a bankruptcy auction." That's never going to work. And, you need to be able to move quickly. You might have six weeks or you might have a month to get the deal done—so you have to be liquid, be able to work very hard for a four- to eight-week period to analyze the deal. Oftentimes, the work comes to nothing, when you learn something that kills the deal. If you have a full-time job somewhere else, you can't dedicate yourself. I was fortunate coming out of Erico that I had the time and money available.

AUTHORS: So, you have completed the deal to acquire Indian Motorcycles, another iconic American brand. What is next?

HEESE: We had thought about raising a fund and using that fund to go out and buy distressed assets. One of my heroes is Leon Black, the guy that owns Apollo. They buy good businesses with bad balance sheets. What I've done is buy good businesses with no balance sheets! On the other hand, we have taken very, very hands-on approaches to our business—first with Chris-Craft and now with Indian. That makes our model pretty limiting. You either have to have your own time or the time of someone you trust very deeply in order to get it done.

CAREER GAME OBSERVATIONS

- Steve Heese focuses on understanding the real risk associated with different career moves. Specifically, he raises the question of whether the greater risk is following a crowd or looking for what we call a career "blue ocean." To use his wording, it is difficult to go further than the crowd if your strategy is to follow the crowd. His early career moves (accounting major to an accounting firm to a top MBA program) did not represent deviations from the crowd, but they did provide the foundation from which to make later moves that were true departures. Virtually every career move since leaving Harvard has been to go where others are not.

- Heese makes a number of useful observations about his decision to leave Price Waterhouse. His thinking provides a good example of a "thinking ahead and reasoning back" career strategy. He also effectively imagined how the game might play out if he stayed—that is, if he made no move.

- Over the course of his career, there are several illustrations of how family players in the game—or the lack thereof—influenced moves. Early in his career, Heese was in a position to take some big swings because only his future was at risk; later in his career, he has made moves that work for his family.

- Heese has also demonstrated the ability to conduct an honest inventory of his career competitive advantage, and he has leveraged it in each of his moves.

- Like Alex Vanselow at BHP Billiton (our conversation with Vanselow appears later in the book), Heese found that situations offering the chance to fix something are career enhancing and actually contain less downside risk than many people expect.

MOVES IN THE CAREER GAME

> The biggest break in my career was getting into the Beatles in 1962.
> The second biggest break since then is getting out of them.
> George Harrison

Because games are characterized by a series of moves, there is no more central concept to understanding your career game. In this chapter, we offer a typology to distinguish different kinds of moves. Some moves that you make will be *instrumental* because they help you move closer toward your goal. Unfortunately, some of your moves may turn out to be *blunders* that you will then struggle to overcome. Other moves will be *incidental* in that they have little impact on your game other than to have allowed you to fulfill an obligation to take a turn. After that, we discuss some of the most common examples of these types of moves.

When considering each move, the central objective is to understand the most probable impact that it has on the play of the larger game. For example, what does the move reveal about your strategy? How might you expect other players to interpret and then react to your move? In our discussions below, we will make an effort to explore how a player's goals—the way he or she defines winning the game—as well as other situational factors, impact the quality of various moves. A challenge here is that, while, with hindsight, it is relatively easy to label a move a success or a misstep, our approach advocates giving priority to developing an appreciation for the utility of a move *before* it is made. Further, because the career game can be very nuanced and personal, it becomes your challenge to understand the way in which the prototypical moves that we illustrate would impact your game.

A TYPOLOGY OF MOVES

As mentioned above, we suggest that moves belong to one of three categories: *instrumental moves*, *blunders*, or *incidental moves*. Because this last type of move has, by definition, little or no bearing on the career game, we will focus greater attention here on instrumental moves and blunders. Of course, one caveat is that post hoc labeling of a move as incidental is important if the player's intent was to accomplish something with it. If the player had intended for a move to be instrumental, and it failed, it might look, in hindsight, like an incidental move. A better accounting for such an outcome is to recognize the opportunity cost that resulted from "wasting" a move's instrumental potential.

There are two consequential types of instrumental career moves: *career defining* and *career refining*. Career defining moves involve what some would label "big swings." These are moves that represent greater risk but offer the potential of a greater reward. Individuals might have opportunities to experience some number of these over the course of a career, but they are likely to take a relatively small number of such swings. Career-defining swings often have their biggest impacts early in a career because they can influence the career game over a longer period of time—changing a career trajectory by a few degrees early on can have a big impact over the entire flight. Making moves that are big swings early in one's career is also a good strategy because, as former GE CEO Jack Welch explained recently to an audience of eager MBA students at Georgia Tech, there is little to lose and plenty of time to recover. Welch stated that, over the course of their careers, most executives become more cautious, and for understandable reasons. As their careers unfolded, as they started and expanded their families, and as they became accustomed to particular lifestyles, they decided that there was too much equity in the status quo to risk taking big swings. Big swings become possible again if personal wealth is not a central concern when building a career. This freedom—whether due to having amassed great wealth or simply having redefined priorities—reduces the risk associated with a move that could be a blunder.

Whereas career-defining moves are often discontinuous and game changing, *career-refining* moves are smaller swings that are incremental in nature and, over time, position the player for greater opportunities. In large conglomerate companies such as GE, the potential to make career-refining moves may appear to be practically infinite—chances exist to gain international experience in virtually all corners of the globe and to work in industries from consumer appliances to power generation to financial services. Obviously, most people do not work at places that afford that level of opportunity; as a result, they have to search more broadly for opportunities that allow career-refining moves in order to enhance their career preparation. When these opportunities require a change in employment, they are associated with a greater degree of risk, thus conservative players may feel more comfortable at conglomerates such as GE. Players who need to employer-hop in order to refine their careers should look for greater returns on their career refinement efforts to balance the greater risk. For the most part, the research shows that changing employers usually does lead to greater total compensation—companies understand that they need to pay a premium to dislodge someone, whereas internal candidates often can be attracted less expensively precisely because they are taking less risk.

Blunders also occur in degrees. Minor blunders can be thought of as *career distracting*; major blunders may be *career limiting* or *career ending*. Career-distracting blunders for an executive with a long track record of success could be career ending for someone lacking similar credentials. More typically, *career-ending* moves are sometimes demonstrations of unethical business judgment, such as those famously displayed by Jeffrey Skilling at Enron, Gary Winnick at Global Crossing, or Dennis Kozlowski at Tyco. They may also be demonstrations of bad behavior at work, as was speculated when Starwood announced that Steve Heyer was abruptly leaving after just two and a half years at the company's helm. In other instances, they involve poor judgment about life outside of work, actions that serve as career-ending moves, such as when HBO CEO Chris Albrecht was forced out by Time Warner after his arrest for allegedly assaulting his girlfriend in a casino parking lot or when Elliott Spitzer stepped down as governor of New York for allegedly using the services of an escort.

It is important to recognize that there are instances in which it is precisely the use of good judgment—not a blunder at all—that carries with it the consequence of ending a career. Here, we are referring to blowing the whistle on improprieties at work. Making the move to go public with concerns about your employer's unscrupulous activities appears to be akin to making the move to become an author and speaker. Based on the experience of some recent notable whistleblowers, it is clear that those moves have ended not just relationships with employers, but also careers. In addition, it appears that there are effectively very few next moves open to those individuals: chief among them is starting or joining a nonprofit dedicated to the cause of whistleblowers or becoming a speaker/writer on the ills of company culture. Take, for example, Joanna Gualtieri, once an employee of the Canadian government. She exposed improper and extravagant spending practices in the Office of Foreign Affairs. After reporting her concerns—which the inspector general and auditor general of Canada found legitimate—she faced retribution at work in the form of harassment and reductions in authority. Effectively, her job was made meaningless. Since then, she has been engaged in a long, drawn-out legal battle with her former employer. She left to form FAIR, an organization that supports Canadian whistleblowers.[1]

Another career-ending whistle blow was sounded by Jeffrey Wigand, a former executive of Brown & Williamson. He appeared on the CBS program *60 Minutes* to expose B&W's practice of manipulating the effect of nicotine in cigarettes. After his termination, he taught chemistry and Japanese at DuPont Manual Magnet High School in Louisville, Kentucky, and was eventually named Teacher of the Year in the state of Kentucky.

Peter Rost, a former Pfizer VP, blew the whistle on accounting irregularities at the company. For a time, he was effectively quarantined inside Pfizer—removed from participation in any meaningful work—and then he left the company. In September 2006, he published his experiences in the book *The Whistleblower: Confessions of a Healthcare Hitman*. He presently works as an expert witness, speaker, writer, and blogger (see http://peterrost.blogspot.com/).

Cynthia Cooper, the VP of Internal Audit at WorldCom, chose to report to the board's audit committee that the company had covered up $3.8 billion in losses through phony bookkeeping. Cooper was named one of the "People of the Year" by *Time* magazine in 2002. She now works as a public speaker and author. Cooper's book, *Extraordinary Circumstances: The Journey of a Corporate Whistleblower*, about her experience with the WorldCom fraud was published in 2008.

Finally, Sherron Watkins is considered by many to have been the key to uncovering the wrongdoing at Enron. Like other whistleblowers, since leaving Enron, she has been active on the speaking circuit and coauthored a book about her experience titled *Power Failure: The Inside Story of the Collapse of Enron*.

As experienced by these whistleblowers, career-ending moves create situations in which players need to exit one game and search for another. Even if such dramatic moves are not required, the likelihood is that plans will have to be heavily revised. Some very interesting work on the moves that are necessary to execute comebacks has been conducted by Jeffrey Sonnenfeld and Andrew Ward.[2] In their book, they provide sage counsel to victims of what might be seen as career-ending moves. Their research indicates that only 35 percent of ousted CEOs return to active roles with public companies within two years of their exits. For all practical purposes, nearly half of those (43 percent) ended their careers and went into retirement. Certainly, some individuals who face the consequences of bad moves late in their careers are well positioned to retire. Some, in fact, receive very large sums of money to do just that. However, many more do not have that luxury and thus need to focus on how to orchestrate comebacks. Sonnenfeld and Ward offer several pieces of advice gleaned from their work with defeated executives, starting with moves that are complementary to our admonitions. First, executives must make decisions about how they plan to fight back (that is, about the playing field and the rules of the game). The plan of how best to fight needs to be informed by an honest accounting for what went wrong and why; however, overemphasizing the failure may merely open up additional opportunities for others to attack. Once a plan is formed, the next step is to recruit others to join the battle. Effectively, this involves determining who the other players are and how they can be motivated to make supporting moves. Finally, the plan must be executed in a manner that helps regain what Sonnenfeld and Ward label "heroic status."

As the authors point out, their advice is based on observations of many successful individuals "firing back" after career disasters—Martha Stewart, Jamie Dimon, and Mickey Drexler, for example. Martha Stewart built a wide-ranging enterprise in Martha Stewart Omnimedia and was considered one of the most powerful women in business. In 2004, she was found guilty of conspiracy, obstruction, and making false statements in regard to her sale of ImClone stock after receiving inside information about the company. She served a five-month sentence and has since rocketed back with her business enterprise. Jamie Dimon rose to prominence working alongside his long-time mentor, Sandy Weill, only to ultimately be fired by him. Since that setback, Dimon has worked his way back to the top as the CEO of JP Morgan Chase. Mickey

Drexler was the widely admired CEO of The Gap. When the company fell on hard times in 2002, he was unceremoniously dumped by the board—led by Gap founder Donald Fisher. He has reappeared to lead J.Crew in what pundits have labeled a redemption effort.

SOME COMMON MOVES

Under close analysis of any individual's career, it quickly becomes evident that everyone's career game is idiosyncratic. Sometimes players make similar moves but do so to satisfy different motivations; in other cases players take very different paths to ultimately get to similar destinations. This means that it is difficult to discuss unequivocally the merits of any particular move. In short, moves must be evaluated in context. We discuss some common moves below in order to provide examples of how career game players can begin to consider the utility of each of these moves in their particular circumstance. The reputation of the person who precedes you when you take a new position; whether, where, and when to return to school; the relative merits of being a big fish in a small pond; and the decision to opt out are a few of the moves we discuss broadly.

Following a Sinner; Following a Saint

Once you accept a position, developing a deep appreciation for the person you succeed can be an enlightening experience. Specifically, we refer to the aura that surrounds the previous occupant of your position. Perhaps you face the challenge of following a "saint"—someone whose performance was remarkable and whose reputation is larger than life. Such was the challenge that confronted Craig Barrett when he succeeded Andrew Grove as CEO of Intel. Grove had been with Intel since 1968. During his tenure as CEO (1987–1998) the company's market capitalization grew on average more than 40 percent a year—from $4.3 billion to $197.6 billion. In fact, Grove was *Time* magazine's 1997 man of the year.

Or, perhaps you face the challenge of following a "sinner"—someone whose actions brought a sense of shame to a company. This was the situation Jay Grinney had to overcome when he followed Richard M. Scrushy, the CEO of HealthSouth Corporation. Scrushy had been convicted of a variety of offenses and sent to prison, a bondholder threatened to push the company into bankruptcy, the company was being investigated by the Securities and Exchange

Commission and by Medicare, and investors were suing.[3] Both scenarios can provide opportunities for the successor if he or she takes good measure of the challenges that each poses.

Following a Saint   Jack Welch is, by many accounts, one of the most admired executives of our time. During his tenure, GE had a tremendous run. Further, several of his practices have become management lore—the A-B-C–tiered ranking system for employees, the admonition either to be number one or two or to exit a business, and so on. What a challenge this presented to Jeff Immelt when he took over as Welch's handpicked successor. As GE shares tumbled, pundits were quick to point out Immelt's failures. Articles with titles such as "How Jeff Immelt Is Tarnishing Jack Welch's Self-Image" and "Most Foolish CEO: Jeffrey Immelt" began to spring up—some pundits no doubt emboldened by Welch's own public (and later recanted) expressions of dissatisfaction with Immelt's performance. Although Welch apologized for his comments and tried to temper them by recontextualizing them—the point is hard to deny: he was not pleased with his successor's work.

Immelt's experience at GE has been similar to those of each new GE CEO since the company's founding. Writing for *Fortune*, Jerry Useem pointed out that the pattern is quite predictable—whether it has involved Owen Young, Reginald Jones, or Jack Welch, when the outgoing executive is hailed as a genius, the public comparisons put the newcomer at a strong disadvantage.

Following a Sinner   In 2002, Tyco International grabbed headline after headline with stories about the excesses of CEO Dennis Kozlowski. A long-time Tyco employee, Kozlowski served as CEO during the 1990s—a time when the company was aggressively acquiring businesses and enjoying very good financial performance. Kozlowski was known for his free-spending ways, based on events such as a birthday party for his wife that was disguised as a corporate event, and purchases such as the now infamous $6,000 shower curtain. Ultimately, Kozlowski was convicted and sent to prison for his part in a financial scandal that was said to have involved misappropriation of over $400 million of company assets. His successor, Ed Breen, faced a very different leadership challenge than did Immelt at GE. Breen had to restore the public's faith in the company and prevent the events surrounding Kozlowksi's departure from corroding employee attitudes and performance.

How to Win When Succeeding Saints and Sinners   Opportunities exist when making the move to follow former leaders of either extreme. Seizing those opportunities requires understanding the challenges that are unique to each situation. When following a sinner, the keys to success begin with developing and maintaining an appreciation for the nature and depth of damage that has been done to the company, its culture, its people, and its customers. Early moves in the successor's tenure need to be about repairing broken elements. For example, employees are often exasperated—either because of frustrations they experienced while toiling under the command of the sinner or because of embarrassment over the way the sinner has tarnished the company. In many cases, sinners have led by sheer force of personality; the corporate culture has been designed to revolve around them, and in their absence there may be a sense of the company going adrift. Sinners usually do not leave their positions in an orchestrated manner. Indeed, some triggering, "last straw" event often precipitates their departure, and it is thus not uncommon for the successor to have been inadequately prepared. In some instances, a sense of urgency around getting the company back on track might lead to an insufficient onboarding process. In our experience, even the best potential successors often opt out of offers by companies previously led by this sort of personality in favor of opportunities at less chaotic companies.

Following a saint entails its own challenges. Most obviously, people tend to be tremendously loyal to that leader—perhaps even more so than they are to the company. For much of their tenures, saints are generally seen as people who can do no wrong—and, when they do misstep, they enjoy the benefit of the doubt from others who are appreciative of their track records of success. Successors don't have that track record; they have not had time to build reputations of goodwill with constituents. In the end, the central challenge here—as Jeff Immelt is experiencing firsthand—is that memories of the great times under the previous leader are never far from people's minds. It thus takes very little in the form of disruption to cause people to yearn for "the good old days."

Returning to School for an MBA

Each year, tens of thousands of people around the world enroll in MBA programs. Although criticisms persist regarding the way the degree is delivered and suggestions abound about better ways to prepare for a business career today, the MBA remains seen by many as the "golden ticket" to career advancement. For now, let's stipulate that earning the degree is a good move. The question for the career game then revolves around two questions: When is it the right time, and does it matter where I go?[4]

Where to Go   There is a dizzying array of choices when it comes to MBA programs. Traditionally, most programs have required a twenty-one–month full-time commitment involving summer internships sandwiched in between two academic years of coursework. Stepping out of a career to pursue a degree in this way has high opportunity costs—including two years' missed salary, lost experience, and unawarded merit increases and promotions—and is thus not a decision to be made lightly. Evening and part-time programs have emerged in an effort to serve individuals who are not in a position to interrupt their careers for full-time study. Pricey executive MBA programs offer students white-glove treatment (such as no waiting in line at the bookstore and minimized bureaucracy) and weekend schedules in order to reduce time away from the office. Institutions with such programs are able to charge high tuitions based on a calculated cost advantage over full-time study, and the savings in cost and in uninterrupted careers tends to appeal to many candidates. In addition, universities have begun offering programs that require little or no time on a campus.

For the most part, students are cognizant of two features of the MBA product they are buying: purchase price and classroom time commitment. These are certainly relevant criteria to consider—and they have the added benefit of being easily and objectively quantified. Prospective students who are able to relocate in order to pursue their studies also pay careful attention to the myriad business school rankings, although it is unclear how rankings might guarantee an individual's success in the job market. In fact, a study by the Lubin School of Business at Pace University found that CEOs with degrees from prestigious schools did not outnumber those with less impressive pedigrees. It may be that the advantage of attending a highly ranked school lies in the prescreening benefit. Some employers may rationalize that candidates who had been accepted into prestigious schools must have something special to offer. Moreover, those who evaluate your candidacy for positions may use school rankings as a shortcut or proxy to judge your potential, thus choosing your place of study is a move that leaves evidence on your résumé for your entire career.

However, you should consider a number of other arguably more important criteria in order for this move to yield the best return. For example, some would argue that the most lasting takeaway from an MBA experience is membership in the alumni network. After all, much of the classroom learning will become outdated—and, for some students, large parts of the curriculum may never be core pieces in their leadership toolbox. The network effects, however, last indefinitely and can be leveraged as effectively thirty years after graduation as they can be for that first summer internship. Individuals vetting different programs are often not fully cognizant of the value of network access over the course of a career. Unlike tuition, it is difficult to quantify—but it undeniably represents unlimited value.

A second key to consider involves a program's track record in regard to career services and job placement. Some students pursue MBAs in order to prepare for future opportunities within their firms, while other students are quite deliberate about their desires to change careers, employers, or geographies. Nonetheless, even students who can articulate clear goals often fail to consider the likelihood of a particular program being able to take them where they want to go. As one insightful student told us, coming back to school for an MBA is "like jumping in a river . . . if you don't want to go where it ends, don't jump in." If you want to become an investment banker or a consultant with one of the big three firms, certain MBA programs are much more likely than others to take you there.

A third key consideration in this move—also often discounted or neglected entirely—concerns the value added by classmates. At most universities, the populations served by full-time, evening, and executive MBA programs are different in predictable ways. Given the number of hours spent in class—and given the popularity of out-of-class, team-based assignments across the curriculum—a great deal of attention should be devoted to considering just who occupies the seat next to you. As one student told us, "Reviewing the demographics of the executive program made it clear that the students were more accomplished than the students in the other program formats—I was sure I could learn as much from them as I would from the professors."

When to Go   The decision regarding the best time to make the move of returning to school for an MBA is a great example of the importance of understanding the time structure of the career game. For many students, it calls up images of the fairytale "Goldilocks and the Three Bears": there is a time that is "just right," and going either too soon or too late are poor strategies. Although obtaining an MBA quickly out of college has been the conventional practice, in fact, the ideal circumstances are in play when students can bring to the program enough experience to fully appreciate and understand the applications of the material being taught. Students with some real-world work experience also have more to offer their classmates in discussions and teamwork. Moreover, corporate recruiters looking to hire MBA graduates view those with experience and degrees as lower-risk hires than those with only degrees.

Delaying too long to obtain an MBA refers to the shorter postgraduation time frame available to earn a return on the investment made in earning the degree. That investment involves direct costs such as tuition and living expenses as well as the salary, raises, and other benefits that students must forgo when in school full time. Without a doubt, stepping out of a career is a potentially costly move, and assuring yourself that it will be worth it is an important front-end consideration. As one executive MBA student told us, "I have fifteen years of experience now—this is probably about as late in my career as I could go [back to school] and still have the degree benefit me at work." One tactic that reflects an understanding of this issue of timing can be discerned from the patterns of applications submitted to MBA programs in different phases of the business cycle. During periods of rapid economic growth, applications go down; when a slowdown looms or arrives, applications go up. This is evidence that potential students understand that the opportunity costs of stepping out are much lower when business slows down—graduate school can be a great place to ride out a recession. Of course, research has consistently shown that those who graduate during recessions never catch up from a salary standpoint with those who graduate in better economic times. Timing your labor market entry is not an easy thing to do, but it is one more factor that will impact every subsequent career game outcome.

In addition to those broad considerations, several personal elements also impact the timing of the move to return to school for an MBA. For many people, these are manifested as a recognition that pieces had fallen into place to create a "right time." Note how the expression "pieces falling in place" is paramount to an acknowledgement that *other players had made supporting moves*. Some examples from our conversations with MBA students are useful in order to illustrate this:

> "I am married, but we have no children—I have the time and money to commit to being a student. It helps that my husband is also in an MBA program and understands the demands."

> "I have wanted to for some time, but being a single parent didn't allow me the time ... shortly after I remarried, my wife indicated her full support."

> "My girlfriend and I decided to end our five-year relationship, so suddenly I had a lot of free time."

In other cases, it is the recognition that a ceiling of some sort has been hit at work—or that work circumstances may be changing, *signaling* to a candidate that it is the right time to make the move. For example:

> "At my company, anyone could lose their job at any time ... cuts are happening left and right with no rhyme or reason ... so I need the degree to be prepared, should this befall me."

> "My job had lost its challenge and I wasn't learning anything new ... I felt I was getting dumber each day I stayed in the position. . . . going back to school was a way to get my brain pumping."

> "My role in the company changed several times in the previous two years, and I was not happy with the position I now held."

> "I had no mentor at work to push me, so I thought going back to school would be a way to further my own development."

In some cases, the timing is right because elements are *pushing* an individual to make the move—dissatisfaction with the current job and a sense that a window of opportunity is closing for personal reasons (such as family circumstances) or professional reasons (such as limited time to earn a return on the investment) are prime examples. In other cases, elements in place are *pulling* the individual toward the move. The recognition that one's current experience *plus* the MBA will make a more marketable combination, for example, represents the sort of enticement that would convince someone to make the move of returning to school.

Big Pond Versus Small Pond

One way to think about job opportunities is to consider this question: Is it better to be a big fish in a small pond or a small fish in a big pond? And, not unpredictably, the answer is "it depends." Each circumstance contains threat and opportunity, and wise players will consider all of the options.

Benefits of the Small Pond   The most compelling characteristic of the "small pond" is greater individual visibility. This cuts both ways, of course. Both success and failure will be much more easily attributed to individuals in small ponds: there is no place to hide. The upside of this is that individuals working in small work environments have better opportunities to create reputations and build their personal brands. One executive we interviewed faced a choice like this early in his career, as a young man in his native Russia. After his undergraduate studies, he accepted a position with Maersk Line Shipping. The company offered him a choice between a position in the Moscow office and the office in Vladivostok—on the Sea of Japan and nearly six thousand miles from Moscow. He struggled to weigh the pros and cons of each opportunity. On the one hand, he could easily be forgotten in distant Vladivostok. On the other hand, because so few were willing to relocate to what some viewed as an unruly outpost, he knew he would have a chance to learn a great deal very quickly. Ultimately, that is what he chose to do, and it ended up being a great move because he found himself on the fast track. A similar career game strategy is reported in our conversation with Alex Vanselow, chief financial officer of BHP Billiton, in Chapter 6.

A close second in terms of the attractiveness of the small work environment is the opportunity to better understand the larger operation—this is the sort of understanding that can be leveraged over the course of a career. As one executive told us, "I can put my hands on lots of the levers that drive our business . . . and it is easier, as a result, to truly understand what makes things work around here." This breadth of exposure is, arguably, better preparation for higher-level positions than that obtained by someone buried deeper in the silo of a larger operation. In fact, our experience has been that executives with small-pond experience are seen as less prepared—and thus as a higher risk—than their big-pond counterparts. We counter, however, that as individuals work themselves into positions higher and higher in their organizations, breadth of experience is a much better predictor of success than "time served" in a big pond.

Benefits of the Big Pond   The greatest upside of the big pond is that it provides a great place to learn; time is largely spent "under the radar" because newcomers rarely are uniquely identified as owners of critical work. There are many examples of big ponds that provide world-class training and development opportunities that can be leveraged over the course of a career. Consider, for example, moves to join IBM to learn about sales, to join GE to learn about finance, to join Ritz-Carlton to learn about hospitality, or to join Nordstrom to learn about customer relationship management. This lower risk carries with it lower rewards, in that it can be very difficult to make a mark and build a case for further opportunities. This is the central trade-off that career game players need to wrestle with—how do you enjoy the benefits of the big pond while simultaneously making sure that you don't become invisible?

Catching a Rising Star

In some cases, the opportunity to latch onto a fast-rising executive presents itself. For this to work out well, several things must happen. First, it is important that there be a significant experience gap between the two individuals; otherwise, the junior player could easily end up being perceived as a competitive threat by the senior player. Our observation is that the best fit occurs with individuals who are three steps apart on an organizational chart. At this distance, the potential for a competitive threat is unlikely, yet there is enough proximity for each player to benefit from his or her relationship with the other—each can each impact the other's game in a meaningful and positive way. When the senior partner recognizes the gains from trade that are available from the junior partner, the latter experiences better opportunities for learning and development. Such was the case described in our conversation with Brian Humphries (see Chapter 4).

Opting Out

Sometimes the move a player decides to make is to exit the game. Recent work by Lisa Mainiero and Sherry Sullivan on what they call "kaleidoscope careers" highlights one example of such an exit strategy. Their research finds that women's career moves are discontinuous when compared to those made by men—hence, the kaleidoscope metaphor. Over the courses of their careers, women are often looking for work/life balance, the opportunities to stay home with their children, and the chance for career success. Balancing these desires will mean moves in and out—sometimes to stay out—of the career game. Adrienne Fontanella—former president of the girls division at Mattel—is an example of a fast-rising executive who opted out to raise a family. Of course, the magnitude of her severance package also helped make the move possible. It is not just women who opt out, but also men, such as Dan Palumbo, who served as chief marketing officer for Coca-Cola and as CEO of Rexel North America before he opted out—at least for the time being.

Entrepreneurship

Entrepreneurship provides players the opportunity—at least until investors are involved—to design their own games. While the strategy is risky and failure rates are high, it is a game in which failure is not punished nearly as severely as it is in a large company. In fact, failure is often viewed favorably; without some failure experience, players are often perceived as less ready. It is interesting to note how quickly failure is conceptualized as a learning opportunity and forgiven in that context. Our conversations with Chris Klaus, who dropped out of Georgia Tech and founded Internet Security Systems (which was ultimately sold to IBM for $1.3 billion), and Liz McCartney, a social entrepreneur, offer interesting insights on this career move.

Moving Down to Move Up

Some have found that the best way to move up is to first move down. This sort of move makes sense particularly when individuals determine that they are missing key experiences. A move down allows players to retool or round out their skill sets. The move is rational when it is clearly aimed at moving closer to a career goal, as opposed to simply running away from an undesirable current position. Jim Donald took a step backwards when he left the position of chairman and CEO of Pathmark Stores to become USA president of Starbucks. Ultimately, he had the opportunity to become COO and, later, to lead Starbucks.

"Giving Back" Careers

Our conversation with Brian Heese provides an example of a "giving back" career. Brian spent many years on Wall Street and has decided now to leverage that experience for the benefit of a Manhattan high school. In Brian's case, the move is a way to explore a new career game.

Quitting

Quitting is certainly a dramatic move. Although it may reflect nothing more than preparing the field for a chance at a more desirable opportunity, more often it reflects dissatisfaction with the current employer. The quitting move can be stigmatizing in the sense that it can greatly impact the number and nature of subsequent opportunities—less so when the dissatisfaction is deemed "normal" (after all, not everyone is cut out for every opportunity), and more so when the way the quitting occurs serves as an alarm to others. Whereas the career website monster.com offers suggestions on the best ways to quit, the Web is replete with anecdotes of worst ways to quit—including such ill-advised moves as setting a manager's car on fire or sending insulting or threatening mass e-mails to former coworkers.

Second Acts

The *New York Times* recently ran a story about executives appearing in their "second acts" in the executive suite; prominent examples include Michael Dell's return to run Dell Computer and Howard Schulz's return to run Starbucks.[5] Steven Jobs at Apple Computer is famously also in his second stint. The move to return to a previously held leadership position is undoubtedly rare, and the examples to date are too few from which to draw strong conclusions. It is likely a fair assertion that the greatest danger present in this sort of move would be a failure to properly assess what is *different* the second time around in terms of the competitive landscape, the nature and capabilities of the company's human resources, and other changed conditions. Furthermore, executives who return for second stints generally face strong expectations to restore the luster that somehow faded since their first times around.

SUMMARY

In this chapter, we introduced you to a typology of moves. Incidental moves are those that do little more than fulfill your obligation to take a turn. They require minimal attention and thus free you up to concentrate more carefully on your plans for later moves. The danger, of course, occurs when moves that you thought were incidental turn out, in retrospect, to have been of some consequence. Imagine, as an example, a newly hired employee who carelessly becomes involved in a quarrel over whose turn it is to use the copier, only to learn that the other player is the CEO's executive assistant.

Instrumental moves and blunders are types of moves that exert marked consequences on careers. Instrumental moves are "career refining" if they move you toward your career goals in an incremental manner. Such moves will allow you to sharpen a skill, remediate an experience deficiency, or improve your exposure in your field or company. By contrast, career-defining moves are disruptive, and they effectively leap you ahead in the game. Instrumental moves are "career defining" when they represent what Microsoft's Stephen Elop describes as opportunities to take a position for which you are "uniquely unqualified." Our earlier reported conversations with Charlene Begley and Ursula Burns provide useful examples of executives making refining moves over long careers inside their companies; our upcoming conversation with Muhtar Kent contains a great example of a career-defining move in his temporary exit from The Coca-Cola Company.

Finally, there are the blunders. Sometimes blunders are career limiting; sometimes they are career ending, and sometimes they are forgiven after some time in the "penalty box." In practice, an executive's reputation, situational characteristics, and the scale of the blunder work together to determine how much damage was caused by the bad move. It is also important to the career game to take away from this chapter an appreciation of the steps that you can take to recover when you have blundered. As former heavyweight champion Mike Tyson famously put it, "Everyone has a plan until they get hit." Blunders are effectively "hits" to your career game. How resilient you are as a player will determine the extent to which that hit leads to a knockout, the pursuit of a new game outcome, or dogged resistance to stay in the ring.

The chapter also describes elements of common moves in the career game. As noted at the chapter's outset, each player's game is quite personal, thus it is difficult to make definitive statements about what moves are good or bad, risky or not risky, and so on. Instead, the important takeaway is how important it is to be intentional around each move and to fully understand its consequence in reference to the career game. Questions to keep in mind when considering each and every move include:

How instrumental is this move in terms of my career objective?

Is the risk/reward associated with this move acceptable to me? If not, what might I do to make it a more attractive tradeoff?

Is the timing right for this move now?

How will other players interpret and respond to this move?

Who can help me be successful in executing this move?

How will this move help me tell a better story about my capabilities down the road?

What are the opportunity costs of this move, and are they acceptable?

Is this move reversible if I learn something suggesting that it is a mistake?

Do I understand the next sequence of moves—my own and those of others (what they are, how fast they should come)?

In the next chapter, we focus our attention on what we contend is a very important move—your exit from a position. The way you leave signals a great deal about you to other players in the career game. It also influences how well your successor will perform. Your last moves in a position are the best demonstration of how the way *you* play *your* career game impacts the games of others. But, first, we include our conversations with Brian Humphries, vice president of Investor Relations at Hewlett-Packard; Muhtar Kent, president and CEO of The Coca-Cola Company; and Marius Kloppers, CEO of BHP Billiton. Each executive's career story has useful insights specifically in reference to moves and, more broadly, in terms of the career game. In Humphries' case, he discusses the way he has made moves that were designed to help him develop his breadth of experience and company knowledge. He also warns you to be aware of career moves that are path limiting and thus take degrees of freedom away from your game. In our conversation with Muhtar Kent, he talks about his move away from The Coca-Cola Company and how it ultimately had the effect of preparing him to return to the company in a higher-level position. Marius Kloppers shared with us his efforts to build a strong foundation through formal education and how his time in consulting was a logical next move in his professional development. Like Pasha Fedorenko, Kloppers has been careful to consider how his different moves help him tell a good story about capabilities.

NOTES

1. http://fairwhistleblower.ca
2. J. Sonnenfeld and A. Ward, *Firing Back: How Great Leaders Rebound after Career Disasters* (Boston: Harvard Business Press, 2007).
3. Dean Foust," Breathing Life into HealthSouth," *BusinessWeek* (February 7, 2005).
4. Although we focus on the MBA degree in our discussion, we suggest that the same considerations apply to other further-education opportunities.
5. Steve Lohr and Damon Darlin, "2nd Acts in the Executive Suite," *New York Times*, February 3, 2007.

A CONVERSATION WITH BRIAN HUMPHRIES

SENIOR VICE PRESIDENT FOR STRATEGY AND CORPORATE DEVELOPMENT, HEWLETT-PACKARD COMPANY

Brian Humphries is responsible for leading Hewlett-Packard's corporate strategic initiatives and merger and acquisition activities. He previously served as vice president of Finance for HP Services and, prior to that, as vice president of Investor Relations. Before joining HP, he held a number of roles in finance with Compaq and Digital Equipment Corporation. Humphries assumed his current role with Hewlett-Packard in the summer of 2008.

AUTHORS: **Early in your career at Digital Equipment, you served in an internal audit role. How important was that experience to your overall career?**

HUMPHRIES: It was great both from a professional and personal point of view. I was part of a fast-track program for over three years, and internal audit was one of the roles I took in our Finance Development Program. It gave me a means to accelerate my learning of the business and the business controls. We would spend about four weeks on an audit, then come back to our home base for three or four days, and then go out for the next assignment. It was a valuable experience because it allowed me to get very deep into a number of different parts of the business, each of which had different business, financial, and competitive dynamics. In that position, you either sink or swim in terms of quickly learning the financial levers in play.

The main benefits to participating in this development program were getting a more worldly experience very early in my career and having the chance to test myself. At the subsidiary, our audit work didn't just drop off at the end of the four weeks. We didn't leave the subsidiary without negotiating with the management team about the audit findings, presenting our recommended fixes, and agreeing upon a timeline of when they would implement the fixes. So, there is an element in one form or another of strong communication skills being required, but also strong negotiation skills. I was doing this in my early twenties—going head-to-head with the CFO or the GM of a business or subsidiary about audit results. What a great opportunity to test your mettle. There aren't too many more challenging conversations than those that require getting people to admit that something of theirs is broken and agreeing to sign up and fix it by a given date.

AUTHORS: **What were other ways this development program impacted your career?**

HUMPHRIES: Digital Equipment picked ten high-performance people coming through the ranks each year. In my class, there were people from Russia, South Africa, all over the world. Although I am Irish, I was actually representing Belgium, which is where I had my home contract with the company.

Being pulled in to this program was great because it made you stand out in what was a very large organization. It would have been easy to get lost in a company of this size—a matrixed organization with independent business units, regional and subregional structures, and so on. Participating in the program made us easy to spot. It also gave those who were selected a sense of confidence as well as a sense of investment. Realizing that the company was investing time, energy, and resources in developing us couldn't help but be noticed and appreciated.

The rotational element of the program really suited me in terms of what I wanted for my career. I personally place a lot of value on breadth of experience rather than merely depth. The development program provided the structure to get around and through the company with a level of confidence and a level of management support. People were aware of the ten candidates, the hosting country, the sending country, the hiring manager, and so on. The hiring manager had confidence that, despite the fact they were putting an unknown person into a role, he or she would work around the clock and ramp up quickly to not only learn, but also add value.

The experience facilitated, in my mind, an approach to how you should join an organization, how you understand the environment, and how you view the players, the team you are joining, the dynamics within the team, and the dynamics between the team and management. It also shaped my actions about quickly learning a new environment so that I really understood the key business drivers, the sensitivities and politics, the strengths and weakness of the incumbent bench, how I leverage their skills, where I am weak, and how I can offset my weaknesses by surrounding myself with strong people.

Forcing early-career people to have lots of these development and onboard experiences builds their confidence for all sorts of challenges later in their careers. The key is going in with the kind of confidence, support, and visibility that our program created for us.

AUTHORS: **Effective leadership requires a global perspective. How has your international background helped your career?**

HUMPHRIES: I am European, but have only worked in American corporations: Digital Equipment Corporation, then Compaq after it acquired Digital, and HP, which acquired Compaq. As a European-based employee, there is a lot of finger-pointing—they feel that nobody at headquarters understands what is happening in their region. In large companies it gets more complicated—you have a subcountry or subregion model, and they all point fingers and tend to have a view that Americans don't understand their perspectives or challenges. The stereotype is that American executives have not worked in the field—in front of customers, in front of channel partners—but that lack of experience doesn't stop them from coming up with all sorts of rules of engagement, which seem disingenuous and are quickly discounted. So, in this regard, global experience is crucial for (at least) American leaders to establish legitimacy. Knowing other countries, regions, cultures, and how international dynamics work is critical. Not spending time on the other side of the fence can be a limiting factor.

Likewise, I have seen some salespeople who don't understand finance, and some finance people who don't understand the commercial side of the house. This limits their overall business acumen. Although global experience is critically important, so is an appreciation of the different functional and operational aspects of the business. If you have a broad set of skills and experiences, as opposed to just being really good at one job, then you end up in a great position to influence people.

AUTHORS: **Building breadth is one way to create a competitive advantage in your career. The flip side of that is rotating or moving too frequently in jobs and not sticking around long enough to see the influence you had. How do you recommend people use development roles?**

HUMPHRIES: Fast-track development, which ought to be viewed as a foundation of the pyramid for moving through the ranks, can only exist for a certain length of time. I distinguish between learning through accelerated roles or placements versus longer-term leadership and contributions in leadership capacities.

In the Finance Development Program, what we had was a bunch of young people who were earmarked to be the management team of the next decade. It worked out in part because you had a bunch of people who were willing to work twelve to eighteen hours a day, if needed, and travel around the world. This allowed them to immerse themselves into a new business with the expectation that they were being watched and developed. At the end of the three-year cycle, their first big role would be a function of how they performed in this development period. Digital had a formalized process whereby, at the end of each year, you were required to present to a board your dissertation about a specific program you had implemented. You had to show added value back to the organization.

Of course, the higher you rise in the pyramid, the shorter the tenure of these development roles. Invariably, high-potential talent is sometimes tapped on the shoulder and asked to change roles, but this shifting of gears is more acceptable while you are still developing. As you grow up through the ranks, your level of stability in a position is expected to change so that you can give back to the organization. The company can't afford to have you spend large parts of your career on a learning curve—at some point, you have to be counted on to produce a return on that investment.

AUTHORS: **What do you advise others about making early-career decisions?**

HUMPHRIES: In terms of planning career moves, I have always told people I am mentoring to avoid drifting. You have to be able to stand back periodically, and even if you don't have the precise answer as to where you want to be, have the directional knowledge of the next step and the next steps after that. As you go through the pyramid, your choices become restricted and you don't want to run the risk of developing a résumé that corners you in one form or another. Make moves that keep your later options open. Otherwise, you will always be faced with tough career decisions. When you make a move into a new business or model, it can be advisable to know where you can leverage your strengths while still allowing yourself to get immersed in a new business challenge.

AUTHORS: **What have been some of your significant mentor relationships?**

HUMPHRIES: There were three people who played key mentoring roles at different stages in my career. One was my first manager when I was in my twenties. I grew up in Dublin, Ireland, but my first corporate job was with Digital Equipment Corporation in Brussels, Belgium. I had a manager there named Harm Otter. He was a Dutchman, and you may not be aware of it, but there tends to be friction between the Dutch and the Belgians. I quickly began to see where there was a lot of back talk around him. He was an expatriate, and the local Belgians didn't appreciate that. They criticized how he operated in his marketing role. He saw me as an outsider coming into the Belgian organization and, like him, I was learning French and trying to integrate myself. From the start, he took me under his wing. Sometimes it involved sharing quick anecdotes that shed light on a challenge I was faced with. At other times, he might spend an entire afternoon with me. He would read through reports I had prepared and challenge me on what I had done. He would tell me what to expect and how to handle objections. After we had worked together awhile, he said to me one day on our way to a meeting, "I have a surprise for you—you are presenting for us today at the Belgian management meeting." He was throwing me in the deep end without any real warning—but he had spent all that time to that point preparing me for that push. He kept pushing me—while, at the same time, he kept training me. He taught me to be ready at all times to back him up—even if it was something a superior was expected to deliver.

The second key mentor I had was an up-and-comer in Digital Equipment Corporation by the name of Jeff Clark, who was an expatriate finance manager for DEC's French subsidiary. Our paths had crossed briefly when I was in my internal audit role because I audited his operation. When I moved to Geneva after the development program, I was in a financial planning and analysis role working in his organization. Invariably, over that year, it seemed whenever he was in town and in the office late, he would see me working late. We started striking up conversations. As time went by, he got to know something about my background, my reputation, and my ambition. Anyway, he started taking a greater interest in me. We laugh about it now because we have since become social friends. He loves to talk about his efforts then to persuade me to see things his way and how stubborn he thought I was in standing firm. He used to joke that it was my bad French that caused me to not understand, but I insisted my French was fine.

After Compaq acquired Digital, I went to South Africa. Jeff called me out of the blue and said he wanted me to come to the U.S. He really went out of his way, in my opinion, to pluck somebody from a small, relatively obscure subsidiary and try to fast-track me into roles that would in one form or another bring out my potential. After I came to the U.S.—my first time, by the way—he subsequently became an incredible mentor to me. He helped me become indoctrinated to the culture. For example, I had Thanksgiving and Christmas dinners with him and his wife and family. He always took a vested interest in me and my career. Still today, he will go out of his way to help me with any problem solving, but likewise, from working with him I learned a lot—his approach to numbers, his approach to not just knowing your current business, but also the rest of the company's business, knowing your competitors, making sure you see the big picture, knowing the people around you, and gaining breadth of experience versus just depth of experience.

After the HP merger, Jeff was instrumental in getting me a role back in Europe as a finance manager for one of the businesses. Then, about eighteen months later, he called me out of the blue again and said, "Brian, I want you to come here Thursday to interview for a role." I recall saying to him, "Well, I have just been promoted on Thursday in the European operations, and my manager and I believe that I should stay here and get more field experience." His response was, "I don't give damn. I reserve the right to pull you out of Europe and pull you back to corporate." It worked to my advantage to have an influential mentor and friend like Jeff.

Finally, there have been numerous times with [CEO] Mark Hurd where his leadership style in understanding the business, competitors, organizational effectiveness, etc. has been a remarkable learning experience for me. His energy and ambition is now permeating throughout HP, and I learn a lot from watching him and working beside him.

AUTHORS: **What should people look for in their mentors?**

HUMPHRIES: It should depend on the stage of their career and the ways in which they can select a mentor. Different times require different levels of access, skills, and influence needed in a mentor. Your mentors when you are in your twenties will differ from those you need to seek in your thirties, forties, and fifties. Sometimes you need prodding, sometimes you need visibility. The key is to find a mentor who can give you what you need at the time. Also, as you advance through the ranks, you start becoming more engaged in deciding who you want surrounding you. I often suggest seeking mentors who will link you to outside your current business environment, out of your current skill environment. So, later, if you want to build an alternative career path, you have a natural stepping-stone to people who recognize your name and your ambition. You almost want to have mentors who are clearly on a career path themselves and who will not be threatened by you. I also encourage choosing a mentor who is more than one level above you. Otherwise, there is sometimes tension or a conflict of interest whereby the manager isn't necessarily going to bend over backwards to facilitate his subordinate becoming his peer. Link to mentors who offer a diverse background and point of view, and who will view you as someone they can "bank on" and promote as their protégé. The goal is to engender their trust and respect, and to work hard—strategically and with a holistic and ambitious approach.

AUTHORS: **What about people you have mentored?**

HUMPHRIES: I am mentoring an individual now who just moved to our Industry Standard Servers business in Europe. ISS for HP is about a $10 billion business, and Europe is about 40 percent of that. We met recently, and I started to prod him to see if he knew the business and the market dynamics. Very often, you will get a sense of how holistic people are by asking them to explain cost structures. Cost structure is very clear to me; it is the difference between revenue and profit. Everything between revenue and profit is cost. A lot of young people do not get this. After a while, we started talking about his transition to his new role, his ambitions, what he thinks he can give to HP and ISS. He is high potential, and everyone swears by him. He said something to me which I thought was remarkable; he said, "Look, I just joined your team a few weeks ago, and I think I will be ready for a change in about nine months." I said to him, "Hmmm, interesting. Here is how I hear that as your mentor—and probably how your manager would hear it as well: 'I am a financial analyst for one of the biggest businesses within the biggest country within the biggest region within one of the biggest companies in the entire world, and I will be ready for a change in nine months.'" I was honest with him and said, "Don't you think it is a little ambitious to move so quickly? Your manager wants you to give back in this role, and don't you think you have more to learn than you will have picked up inside the first year?" He has to temper his expectations and make a measurable impact in his current role before considering another move.

AUTHORS: **What about the trade-offs you have had to make? You left a seat at the CEO table with your Investor Relations role to go into the business and** thus take the next step in your career, first as vice president of finance for HP Services and last year as senior vice president of Strategy and Corporate Development for HP. What have these transitions taught you?

HUMPHRIES: It has clearly been quite disruptive and quite a change. While working with Wall Street required tough hours and was difficult, given the lack of predictability about what will happen on any day, the services CFO role had more structure, and arguably, the hours are longer. The first year was mostly fifteen-hour days, six days a week. The devil is in the details in this job. You have to have a very good level of understanding of the business, the technology and service offerings, the financials of HP's entire portfolio, and our competitive positions via technology or solutions. Previous roles were much more externally focused and carried a higher level in terms of strategy, financials, products, technology, marketing, sales, and management team engagement. Now I am knee-deep and very tactical and operationally focused.

True, it is further away from the CEO than my IR role, and at times I felt more isolated from broader company initiatives. I became a leader in a business unit, but lost visibility in terms of the broader direction. I became more inwardly focused on business within HP. These transitions are a difficult adjustment, but worth it in the long run.

CAREER GAME OBSERVATIONS

- Like Charlene Begley at GE, Brian Humphries started in a leadership development program in internal audit. His participation in the Digital Corporation's Finance Development Program has clearly had a lasting impact on his career. The fact that membership in the program was select meant that it provided visibility in a large, complex company where, he notes, he easily could have become lost. It signaled to other players in his career game that he was someone to keep an eye on. Additionally, participation in the program meant that, after a fairly short period of time, he had acquired broad experience and a body of work that he could point to and leverage when seeking new opportunities.

- During his career, Humphries has made moves that have had the net effect of increasing his breadth of experience. He noted that the opinions and views of individuals without that breadth are often discounted because they are perceived by others as lacking a basis for strong opinions in areas in which they have little experience. Breadth of experience builds credibility; credibility provides voice that allows players to impact the game.

- Over the course of his career, Humphries has had very positive experiences with mentors and sponsors and was quite direct when noting that what individuals need from mentors and sponsors evolves along with their careers. His "invisible hand" mentor was Jeff Clark—not because Humphries asked Clark to serve as a mentor, but because Clark would see Humphries working late at the office, and they struck up a friendship. Humphries' reputation as someone who worked hard and delivered results was what convinced Clark that he was worth the investment.

A CONVERSATION WITH MUHTAR KENT

PRESIDENT AND CEO, THE COCA-COLA COMPANY

Muhtar Kent first joined The Coca-Cola Company in Atlanta in 1978 and has held a variety of marketing and operations roles throughout his career. In 1985, he was appointed general manager of Coca-Cola Turkey and Central Asia. From 1989 to 1995, he served as president of the company's East Central Europe division and senior vice president of Coca-Cola International, with responsibility for twenty-three countries. Between 1995 and 1998, Kent served as managing director of Coca-Cola Amatil-Europe, covering bottling operations in twelve countries.

From 1999 until his return to The Coca-Cola Company in May 2005, Kent served as president and CEO of the Efes Beverage Group, the majority shareholder of Turkish bottler Coca-Cola Icecek. Headquartered in Istanbul and listed on the London and Istanbul stock exchanges, Efes is a publicly traded beverage enterprise whose Coca-Cola and beer operations extend from the Adriatic to the Pacific Ocean. Under Kent's leadership, Efes experienced extraordinary growth, with triple-digit revenue growth and a 250 percent increase in market capitalization. During that time, in addition to taking Efes

Breweries International public on the London Stock Exchange, he also served as a board member of Coca-Cola Icecek.

Kent was named president and COO of The Coca-Cola Company's North Asia, Eurasia, and Middle East Group from 2005 until early 2006, where he was responsible for the operations across a broad and diverse geographic region that included China, Japan, and Russia. He served as president of Coca-Cola International through most of 2006, responsible for operations outside of North America, until his appointment as president and COO of The Coca-Cola Company, overseeing all operations of the business, including Bottling Investments. In July 2008, Kent succeeded Neville Isdell as CEO of the company. See also www.thecoca-colacompany.com/ourcompany/bios/bio_76.html.

AUTHORS: **You have spent the majority of your career at Coke, but you left for about six years to run Efes Beverage Group. How did that time outside of Coke benefit you as a leader?**

KENT: First, it was an important experience for me to run a public company. At the same time, though, I was still "inside the system" because one of our two principal businesses was Coca-Cola Bottling. I wholeheartedly believe that people who have been on both the bottling side and the company side are better off, more well rounded. Our leaders who have had bottling experience have learned how to succeed in a low-margin, high-volume business. By comparison, The Coca-Cola Company is a high-margin, high-volume business. So, learning how to run a low-margin business, getting used to dealing with customers at the point of sale, and understanding how consumers react to our products are all unique experiences that improve your effectiveness. Robert Woodruff, the patriarch of The Coca-Cola Company, used to always say, "We are in a high-margin business but we must run it like a low-margin business." He was right, and working for bottlers helps you learn how to do that and gives you a good perspective.

Secondly, going outside of the culture of The Coca-Cola Company to run Efes Bottling helped me develop respect for the importance of cash. When you run a smaller business, you must pay attention to cash—you have to ensure that you have enough money to pay salaries, suppliers, and so on. You need to be absolutely sure of how you finance your business in the very short term. You can't rely on selling paper or selling stock or debt. The bigger the company, the more you are distanced from cash. At Coke today, we never see cash. When I first came back to The Coca-Cola Company, I told my CFO that what I would love to see would be to convert this business into a just-cash business for one week. If everyone had to pay the airlines for tickets, pay the utility for the electricity bills, and pay for office supplies all in cash, it would help our people gain a respect for cash.

Another real benefit I discovered was a much better understanding of the balance sheet. The Coca-Cola Company is much more a P&L business than a balance sheet business, but understanding the balance sheet is getting so much more important these days.

Overall, I would say that leaving the company to have the experience of running another company in a different environment prepared me well to hold the position I have today.

AUTHORS: **There are challenges to surviving a long time in a single company when you have a history of decisions that follow you. Do you think that executives who move from company to company have it easier because the slate gets cleaned with each move?**

KENT: Leaders have to be willing to make tough decisions—it's unavoidable. I love to make decisions, and, while I don't look to make mistakes, I realize that they happen. What really matters over time is your batting average. If your batting average is okay, then you will be okay. The other piece is that, over time, you develop trusting relationships with people around you in the system—that is hard to repeat each time you change companies. When you stay with one company, those relationships help. I have been in the Coke system for thirty years, and my relationships inside the organization are invaluable. When you change employers, you may get a clean slate, but you also have a zero balance in terms of these relationships, so you would have to invest significant time building that relationship capital, but that is always a good thing to do anyway.

AUTHORS: **One advantage to working somewhere like The Coca-Cola Company is that it is a big enough place to provide a pretty rich career path. People who work at smaller companies may not have similar options unless they are willing to move from one employer to another.**

KENT: That's right. Our company has opportunities all over the world in every functional area—there is a great deal of variety of experience and challenge here.

AUTHORS: Most executives make a number of moves in their career. Some moves are incremental, while others are really game changing. What do you consider your most important game-changing career move?

KENT: The biggest break in my career was in 1987/88, when I was moved to run the East Central Europe division—twenty-three countries—for Coke. At the time, that region was still behind the Iron Curtain, but there was a view that the Berlin Wall may come down and that we needed to move very rapidly into these countries to create a Coke infrastructure. We also knew we would have to build this region differently than we had any other market previously.

I remember the day I came to Atlanta and requested the capital. We had never built factories. We always had bottlers build them, but we didn't have time to recruit them to our ideas and plan. We had to go out and create the infrastructure and gain leadership in that whole market of 400 million people—and we had to do it really fast.

In the end, we moved with a speed at which we had never moved before—we built twenty-seven factories in a matter of thirty months across the whole of East and Central Europe—from Poland all the way down to Albania.

It has been a very successful region—they have a leadership of more than three to one against our principal competitor there. It has been a great growth business ever since, and this influenced my career substantially.

AUTHORS: It gave you a chance to be entrepreneurial inside an established company.

KENT: Exactly. That kind of break-out growth was unique in The Coca-Cola Company up until that time. It was a game changer in many ways.

AUTHORS: What do you look for in the next generation of leadership at your company? What characteristics make you eager to invest in someone's development?

KENT: I look for courage, entrepreneurial flair, restlessness, and the ability to make a point of view clear. Those are traits that stand apart from integrity and accountability, which also make good leaders. I also value people who are humble and don't always need to take the credit.

AUTHORS: **Do you find any of these characteristics in short supply?**

KENT: If they are in short supply, it is our own mistake, because I believe that people have most of these traits in them. It is our responsibility to cultivate and leverage these unique traits in people.

AUTHORS: **On the one hand, if you haven't nurtured this kind of talent, you lack a suitable next generation of leadership. On the other hand, if you have a bunch of this kind of talent, you are challenged to keep them engaged so that they want to continue with the company.**

KENT: That is precisely why we ensure that we have an environment that constantly reads this for us—what talent we have, what talent we want to develop, and how to keep them increasingly stimulated and challenged. On top of that, we have built a structure that allows our talent to develop into successful leaders. Otherwise, we run the risk of people growing impatient and leaving the company.

AUTHORS: **How important are international assignments as preparation for leadership?**

KENT: They are an absolute must. The next generation of leadership needs to really understand the dichotomy between global and local elements of business. In a way, as our businesses get more global, understanding what goes on locally becomes even more important. Not every market is like your home country, and understanding how each is different is essential. I have moved from continent to continent, country to country, and city to city. Those experiences broadened my thinking and helped me in many areas, including building relationships, understanding our customers and global consumer trends, understanding how business partners think, negotiations, how to build a vision for the future, and how to allocate resources against that vision. It would be difficult to lead effectively in business today without a significant global understanding, and the best way to get that exposure is living and working in other countries.

AUTHORS: **Who have been the greatest influences on your career?**

KENT: There are three people in addition to Neville Isdell who have really influenced me in my career. My father, until his death six years ago, and my wife, who has been my partner for thirty years, have played enormous roles in my life. Also Don Keough, currently a Coca-Cola board member and formerly president and COO of the company, has been a great mentor to me and a great supporter and teacher.

AUTHORS: **Does the learning ever stop?**

KENT: No, it doesn't. I have worked very hard to keep learning and improving. One area I have worked hard on over the past several years is in communication skills. That should be a continual learning for everyone. I have also found it important to get into the marketplace at least two to three times a month. I go out and talk to people in restaurants, retail shops, cinemas, universities, and so on. I learn so much with every single conversation; I come back with many notes about the experience. I enjoy doing this, and in a business like ours, staying focused on the customers is key to success. It is also important to make sure you find the time to talk to people at all levels in your company, and really, it must go beyond just talking. You need to build relationships to truly understand their perspectives and to learn from them. When you have that level of understanding, you can go from a 30,000-foot perspective down to one foot to help them in the details, and then go back up to the 30,000 feet. You have to be able to do that to be effective leading a company.

CAREER GAME OBSERVATIONS

- Muhtar Kent made an interesting move away from The Coca-Cola Company to run a public company, Efes Beverage Group. The move allowed him to round out his experience by learning the bottling side of the business. He also learned how to lead a public company—albeit a smaller one than the one he leads today, and he learned the value of "cash" and cash management. At the same time, because of Efes' relationship to The Coca-Cola Company, his move never took Kent off the talent radar.

- Kent's comments comparing job performances to batting averages are important, as are his observations that his long career with The Coca-

Cola Company has allowed him to develop strong relationships with others in the company. The shared history he has with his colleagues means he enjoys what are called idiosyncrasy credits—effectively, past successes that provide a buffer against the consequences of a mistake. Decisiveness is important, and sometimes decisions result in mistakes. Thinking about "hitting for average" may help some executives avoid the trap of "paralysis by analysis."

- Kent offers a great example of a career-defining move in reference to the opportunity he took and excelled at with the chance to run Coca-Cola's East Central Europe division.

- One important takeaway from our conversation with Kent is his ongoing dedication to improving his capabilities. Kent is still developing his career agility even as he serves as chairman, president, and CEO of one of the world's largest companies. Although perhaps clichéd, this is his key message: learning is lifelong, and it's what you learn after you know it all that counts.

- Kent, like others we interviewed, is a strong believer in the importance of international experience as critical preparation for the next generation of leaders.

A CONVERSATION WITH CHRISTOPHER W. KLAUS

FOUNDER AND CEO, KANEVA

As CEO and founder of Kaneva, a 3-D online world and community, Chris Klaus is focused on driving the company's overall vision and strategy. At the core of Kaneva (Latin for "canvas") is the mission to extend the human spirit of creativity and connection to the Internet, bringing people together to socialize, create, and be rewarded in a 3-D community. Kaneva is also a "canvas" on which creative people can express themselves in an immersive, engaging, face-to-face experience. With Kaneva, people can build spaces, decorate homes, design fashions, host their own events, and even create their own interconnected 3-D experiences.

Prior to founding Kaneva, Klaus founded and served as the chief technology officer of Internet Security Systems Inc. (ISS), a company he created in 1994 and sold to IBM in 2006. A former student at Georgia Institute of Technology, Klaus donated $15 million in 1999 for the construction of a new building on the Georgia Tech campus—the Klaus Advanced Computing Building—representing the largest personal donation from anyone of his generation. Opened in 2006, the building was designed to inspire students to also give back and to accelerate future technology innovation, thereby making a positive, direct impact on our digital lifestyles and on the global online community. Klaus currently sits on the Georgia Film, Music & Digital Entertainment Advisory Commission. He is a game advisor to American Intercontinental University (AIU) and serves on the Savannah College of Art and Design (SCAD) board of visitors, as well as the boards of VerticalOne, the Georgia Game Developers Association (GGDA), Georgia Tech Advisory Board (GTAB), and the Georgia Tech College of Computing.

AUTHORS: Can you tell us what drew you to Georgia Tech for your undergraduate studies?

KLAUS: I grew up in Florida. Growing up, I was very interested in electronics and computers. It was fueled by my father who gave me a Commodore 64; I learned on my own to program with it. The emergence of the Internet was very exciting—it was something I was passionate about wanting to be involved with. I didn't begin with a clear idea of where I wanted to go—other than that I wanted to be somewhere with lots of smart people working with computers. I applied to universities in Florida and throughout the southeast. Georgia Tech was compelling from an engineering perspective, and I knew it would also provide a very in-depth knowledge around computers. My grandmother lived in Atlanta, too, so I guess having some family in the area provided the direct link to where I wanted to go. As it turned out, Tech gave me an answer to my application very quickly—that made my decision a bit easier.

AUTHORS: What had you done to get ready for college?

KLAUS: I had a great summer internship before I headed to Tech. It was the early days of the Internet. At the time, the only organizations with a real presence online were universities, the government and military, and a few very large companies. I was fascinated with the prospect of the Internet, and while looking for a summer job I found this internship called Super Kids. I wasn't exactly sure what a superkid was, but I knew that if I was able to land the position I would have a chance to work on supercomputers at the Department of Energy (DoE). It sounded like an awesome opportunity to make some money and work with some brilliant people. The program took one student from every state, and I represented Florida.

I had become interested in computer security. At the time, there wasn't much offered in terms of security beyond "change your password." The researchers at the DoE frequently complained about hackers trying to penetrate their systems to steal their research—so they were worried about security. And, because the Internet was starting to go outside the university/government setting, it was clear that security was only going to get to be a bigger challenge. I always have liked puzzles, and, to me, computer security presented the same sort of challenge. So, that is what I worked on.

AUTHORS: You ended up not staying at Tech very long. What led you away?

KLAUS: What led me out of Tech was that I developed some software that could look for vulnerabilities on a network and give the user a full report of what was open to attack. Once network administrators knew about these vulnerabilities, they could take actions to lock them down. I released a version and was quickly inundated with feedback from universities and government agencies and businesses around the world that were asking for updates and memberships and Internet classes. I remember sitting in class and trying to calculate the size of the opportunity—if I could charge a dollar for every vulnerability the software found, this could be a huge opportunity. I had a guy from one of the lead security institutions call me. He told me he was getting fifty calls a day regarding my software and told me I might want to commercialize it. I didn't know anything about commercializing or companies or anything, but it seemed like a great opportunity to learn.

AUTHORS: So, it really started not so much with you trying to find something around which to build a business. It started with you trying to understand a way to solve a problem in order to solve the puzzle. But it didn't take you long to recognize there was an opportunity there.

KLAUS: Yes—I didn't set out to start a company, I set out to solve a problem. I was very fortunate to have the experience with the Internet and the Department of Energy. Talking to people there helped me realize security was more than a great puzzle; it's a great problem that we're facing as a society. The more and more we become dependent on the Internet, the more security was going to be a challenge. And it's great validation when you have customers that are asking you to start working on it so they can pay you!

I worked on a commercial version of the software for another six months. During that time, I would get calls from people around the world asking how they can find a new copy. When I had it ready, my first customer—a research center in Italy—asked how much the software cost. I told them $1,000. A couple of weeks later, there was a check in my box at Tech for $1,000. Unbelievable.

AUTHORS: So, that is what capitalized your business?

KLAUS: That's what capitalized ISS. I had a lot to do. I had to talk to banks to help me get set up as a company, to work with lawyers to get the corporation formed, and all that kind of stuff.

AUTHORS: You went pretty quickly from sitting in class trying to figure out the opportunity, to being a global supplier! How did you develop fast enough so that the company didn't get ahead of you in terms of your ability?

KLAUS: In the beginning, there was really no "company." I was just a kid in a dorm room. My roommates were getting pretty frustrated. Remember, this was before cell phones. Three of us shared one landline; most of the calls were business calls for me. My roommates became my answering service. I realized there was no way I could really build a great company in a dorm at Georgia Tech. And I knew that meeting customer deadlines would inevitably interfere with my grades. I figured I needed to pick one thing to focus on.

At around that time, a company in Atlanta called and offered me $20,000 to sell them everything. That sure would have helped me with my school tuition—that's a lot of money for someone that age.

AUTHORS: **But you didn't take it.**

KLAUS: That's right. I remember them picking me up outside my dorm to take me to lunch. There, they offered me more money than I had ever seen. It got me thinking. I had already been mulling over starting a company. I figured that, if I did, it would provide a great education—just to go through the process—I would learn more than I could in any class. And, if I failed, there really was no risk. I would just go back to school. The fact that this company was willing to pay me what seemed like a ton of money was another validation that I had something real here, and it made me want to take it a bit further. To my way of thinking, I had already talked to the Department of Energy and other potential companies; one sent me a check for $1,000 when I wasn't even trying to sell the software. I had to ask myself what would happen if I went out there seriously and set up the company myself. Worst comes to worst, I could call that company up six months later and say I was willing to sell if they were still interested.

So, in my second year at Tech, I decided it was time to take a break from school to pursue this. I already had customers writing me checks. The Department of Energy and others were buying the software and were happy with it. So I called my grandmother and set up my headquarters in her spare guest bedroom. That's where the company started. There, I was able to set up a website for a real company.

AUTHORS: **Once you are at your grandmother's house and you've set up your corporate headquarters, what did you do to go about understanding how to run a company?**

KLAUS: I definitely learned on the job. Early on, I didn't have much in the way of employees. I did hire a part-time programmer to help develop some codes for me. I learned a lot from my customers, believe it or not. I remember, early on, a new customer called and told me I needed to send them an invoice. I had no idea what an invoice was.

AUTHORS: **Is it fair to say that your entrepreneurial adventure was a bit by accident? It sounds like your passion was really around working with the latest technology to solve problems—and that you might have been happy doing that in a big company or at a place like the Department of Energy.**

KLAUS: It's a good question, but it's hard to answer honestly with hindsight. I do think if ISS hadn't taken off, that I would have gone back to Tech and finished school. And, it is fair to say that my goal wasn't to become known as an entrepreneur. I think that is at least in part a function of the times. Fifteen years ago, there weren't as many entrepreneurial role models—there weren't as many incubators, advisors, and such to support entrepreneurs. What I was interested in was building something of value. That would have been my goal coming out of Tech, if ISS hadn't succeeded. As it turned out, growing ISS was a chance to do exactly that—to build something of value. The building of it is what I became passionate about. If money had been the goal, I probably would have taken the $20K. I didn't take the money then—or for a long time after—because I felt my vision for the company was bigger than what others saw in it. I could see the business growing faster than potential buyers thought it would and, as a result, I saw the business value as being much greater. If I had sold, that bigger vision wouldn't be pursued, and I didn't want that.

AUTHORS: **Can you tell us a bit about your thinking as you began to move out of the day-to-day leadership at ISS.**

KLAUS: One of the biggest decisions any entrepreneur faces is when to bring in outside partners. Fortunately, I was able to find trustworthy partners. Once you bring in venture capital, you basically give up control. Of course, you sacrifice control in order to get a piece of something that, hopefully, becomes a much more valuable business. I understood that if I didn't bring on these people, ISS might only grow a little. By bringing in investment, by giving up control, by getting the right people on the team, the idea can become much bigger. Whether or not you as the founder can make that work is a big question. Sometimes it works out and sometimes it doesn't.

AUTHORS: **How had your thinking about the opportunity evolved at the time of the sale to IBM?**

KLAUS: At that time, I had been in the Internet security business for over ten years. ISS had fulfilled any entrepreneurial dreams I could have had. We went from a start-up to a public company with employees in offices around the world. As I looked forward at the future of the security business, I felt it was likely to change. I thought it likely that security would become integrated with the infrastructure—not an add-on product or service. IBM was a natural choice as a partner for how I saw the future; they provide a ton of infrastructure and consulting around infrastructure. It seemed that's where the market was going. You know, the vision there is ultimately that security should be part of the routers, networks, operating systems, and so on. I think some stand-alone security companies will be successful, but I think ISS will be more successful with IBM. ISS was a great fit with IBM, too, because there was no overlap in what each company does. If a large competitor in the security business had acquired ISS, there would have been lots of overlap and then turmoil about which groups are going to stick around. To me, this felt like a great move to become part of an iconic American company.

AUTHORS: Was the sale to IBM something freeing for you—or was it intimidating in terms of what people expected from you as your next move?

KLAUS: I have tried to stay focused on being able to do work I am passionate about. It was good fortune that ISS provided that as it did. And now, it has provided me the chance to start something I am equally passionate about. As a kid, security was one really challenging area I explored. My other passion was video games. Games are what got me into programming in the first place. I can see now that there is a big transformation using video game technology and the Internet to fundamentally redefine video games. As social networking technology matures, as more and more machines with 3-D graphics come out, and as everybody is connected in faster and faster ways to the Internet, there is an opportunity to redefine what the video game can do. What we are trying to do with Kaneva is to pioneer a modern-day, online universe.

AUTHORS: If you were talking to a kid who was sitting in a dorm room today, thinking about starting a technology company, what advice would you offer?

KLAUS: I would definitely encourage young people to pursue their dreams. I would definitely encourage them, if they have a good idea, to put together an action list of what they need to do to get it done. The good thing, as I mentioned earlier, is that there are so many more resources for entrepreneurs these days. All you need in order to start is Google! The barriers to information are essentially nonexistent. You can probably even find help on invoicing! The other good news with information being so widely available is that, if you're building something valuable, the word would spread quickly.

AUTHORS: **What else?**

KLAUS: The next thing is to find the right team. That is always challenging, but probably easier now than it was twenty years ago. You want to get it right, though, because mistakes are expensive, disruptive, and hard to undo. Early on, you want to find people that complement your strengths and weaknesses and who can contribute as challenges emerge.

CAREER GAME OBSERVATIONS

- Chris Klaus provides a great example of a successful entrepreneur in that his early success was driven by his own deep interests and a clear focus on solving a problem that companies were increasingly experiencing.

- Klaus made early moves that had significant consequences for his game, particularly in the example of the Department of Energy internship he won while in high school.

- A number of players impacted his game over the course of his efforts to launch Internet Security Systems: his roommates, his grandmother, and even his early customers who helped him understand invoicing all helped him to develop and refine his career game.

- Klaus has made some timely moves that often trip up entrepreneurs—the ability to move away from the leadership position, to find others to push the company ahead, and to recognize the right time to make the move of selling his firm to IBM require an uncommon personal awareness. He demonstrated his career agility in taking these steps—and in returning to his other keen interest, computer gaming.

- Klaus's comments on the lack of entrepreneurial role models at the time he was launching his venture exemplify how a game becomes more challenging when the playing field is devoid of others who can support your efforts.

A CONVERSATION WITH MARIUS KLOPPERS

CEO, BHP BILLITON

Marius Kloppers is in charge of BHP Billiton, the world's largest diversified resources company. He holds a degree in chemical engineering from the University of Pretoria in South Africa, an MBA from INSEAD, and a PhD in Materials Science from the Massachusetts Institute of Technology. His career began in South Africa, working in petrochemicals with Sasol and in materials research with Mintek. After earning his MBA, he joined McKinsey & Co. in the Netherlands as a management consultant. He joined Billiton Group in 1993 as a core member of the team that created the company's aluminum business, assuming a variety of operating and functional positions that included general manager, Hillside Aluminum, and COO, Aluminum. Prior to the merger that created BHP Billiton, he served as CEO of Samancor Manganese and as Group Executive of Billiton Plc, where he was responsible for its coal and manganese businesses. Kloppers was appointed Group Executive and CEO Non-Ferrous in July 2007 and has been CEO of BHP Billiton since October 2007. See also www.cnn .com/2008/BUSINESS/05/29/kloppers.profile/index.html.

AUTHORS: You made it to the senior suite of a *Fortune* Global 20 company before the age of forty-five. What accelerated your career?

KLOPPERS: This is always such a difficult question for me to answer. Perhaps some of my success is because I didn't fret about what I wanted to do early on in my career. When I was in school, I studied chemical engineering because I had a scholarship from Sasol and that is the field of study they wanted from the people working for them. I also recognized that senior people at Sasol and leaders of similar holding companies elsewhere tended to come up through a chemical engineering route. During my schooling, I became fascinated by materials. But I really wasn't thinking about a long-term career then—I only knew what my interests were and I gravitated to my interests.

If I look back at the decisions that I made at the time, they tended to have an aspect of naïve optimism. I knew that a new experience was a good thing, yet I honestly never ever thought about building a career. That is a good way to frame my thinking at the time. Since I was never worried about the next job, I was able to fully commit to the current job. I have seen people doing a job just so they can check a box, and move on to what's next. I have avoided that. Honestly, I can think of only a few instances where I thought about vertical progression. Typically, I am not thinking, "if I do a good job, I will get promoted." Instead, I tend to do the jobs that interest and challenge me.

AUTHORS: Over time, though, you certainly were promoted—quickly and often. How do you explain that?

KLOPPERS: If your strategy is to hold a position simply so you can say you held it, then you are not likely to make any real impact. If you take a view more like the one I have tried to take—being 100 percent focused on the current job—then you will have an impact. Another way of thinking about career moves is that one approach builds a résumé that may be an impressive list of companies and titles; my approach builds a reputation for making a real difference in a company.

The advice I give to early-career people is to think about their résumés as more than a history of places visited. For each point on their journey, they should be able to point to something that truly is different today because they were part of it—something that, if they weren't there, wouldn't have happened in that way. It doesn't mean that you have to lead it or be the sole contributor, but there should be an undeniable case that you have contributed toward something that is lasting. That is extraordinarily important as you plan a career; yet, unfortunately, a lot of people think about what jobs they have occupied as a good enough story for their résumés.

Frankly, my experience has been that most people who jump from company to company rarely make it all the way to the top posts. They stall at a certain level. I suspect it is because the stories of their ability to impact a company don't necessarily translate or scale well.

AUTHORS: What are the most critical competencies for leaders today?

KLOPPERS: The first is that you have to have a demonstrated reputation as somebody who others are prepared to follow. But what explains that? What clearly matters is that others can sense you have a solid, core set of values that they can depend on. The key here—and it is the Achilles' heel of many who want to lead—is recognizing what is important to you, what you are good at, then building on it. When I was in high school, I was a good athlete and a good student, but I never was a leader in the traditional sense. In college, I didn't participate in any student organization or activity because I am too introverted. The students who were leaders were extroverts, and I assumed that my introversion precluded me from those sorts of opportunities. What I discovered later was that my introversion could really be a strength. As a leader, the higher you go, the more you have to rely on your inner strengths and the less you can draw on strengths from other people. What starts out as being a disadvantage in a leader becomes an advantage. That is my take on it.

Another trait of a good leader has to do with values and loyalty. We are accustomed to thinking about loyalty as something followers are supposed to offer their leaders, but I believe it must work in both directions. If you do not demonstrate loyalty, you cannot be followed. For me, the quid pro quo is absolute. I am deeply loyal to you as the person who wants to follow me. It doesn't mean that the loyalty extends to safeguarding someone at the company's expense if they make a terrible call, but loyalty means that you genuinely and deeply care for the person, and that impacts how you treat them even when they make mistakes. Loyalty is an underrated part of leadership. For me, personally, I am deeply loyal to the people who are prepared to follow. Without loyalty, there can be no true leadership.

AUTHORS: **What other skills are imperative for next-generation leadership?**

KLOPPERS: Practically speaking, basic management skills are key. I worry about the next generation of leaders on this dimension. Ultimately, management is about how well you understand a situation, your ability to run a meeting, your ability to make decisions, and your ability to follow up to make sure that the decisions are acted upon correctly. I am amazed by how many people have trouble with this, and I predict that the next generation of executives will be even worse at it! I have three kids in school now, and I am worried about how they are being taught. They do not learn how to abstract information, make notes, study notes, revise work over and over until it is excellent, and so on. Their study patterns are much more ill-disciplined, chaotic, and superficial because they have so much more information than we used to have. They aren't taught how to cope with all that information in a way that gets to root causes, for example. You cannot manage people by e-mail. You cannot manage others effectively if you are hanging around the watercooler, reading blogs, superficially touching every aspect of projects, and so on.

At a certain level in your career, if you do not have formal management skills, you will fail. And that means having the patience and diligence to put reports in place, possessing a real interest in the data, focusing on the trends, effectively managing meetings, following up on the details and actions, etc. These are the biggest deficits that we have in our organizations. We don't train for it; you don't see it in any business school curriculum, and so the next generation is going to come even more ill-equipped than the current one. What's ironic is that some of the smartest people are often the worst at these skills because they have been able to reach success despite being undisciplined in the way they think about, approach, and solve problems. Another competency I would encourage for up-and-coming leaders is to build their commercial sense—understanding the business, its customers, how it goes to market, the macro economics, and so on.

Cutting to the core of an issue quickly comes from experience. All of the jobs I have had helped me see things from different angles, and not that I planned it at the time, but ultimately—apart from leadership, apart from formal management skills—having a basic understanding of commerciality and its underpinnings and driving factors is more important than financial skills. If I look at the decisions that I have to make every day, they are around the commercial aspect of our business. I draw far more heavily on my commercial savvy than on financial skills such as reading the balance sheet, for example. Understanding the commercial side of a business is what builds careers.

CAREER GAME OBSERVATIONS

- Marius Kloppers built a solid foundation for his career game with degrees earned at some of the world's best-recognized schools.

- Kloppers emphasized the importance of working hard to demonstrate you are making a difference in whatever position you hold—and in considering your résumé as more than just a passport stamped with the various positions you have held.

- As proven by Kloppers, experience at one of the Tier I management consulting firms can be a tremendous second move after completing your formal education. These firms provide real-world MBAs, combined with accelerated personal development through the breadth of experience and accompanying feedback that result from performance. Additionally, they train you on how to problem solve and address both macro and micro issues using a set of tools and frameworks. Finally, you learn and practice client management and presentation skills that are incredibly beneficial throughout your career

- There is no doubt that experiences matter in your development. Kloppers has thought about different roles when looking through the lens of the experience that each provided. Passing through a position just to check off a box is not enough. Players should not allow themselves to become fixated on roles or titles—instead, they should devote themselves to evaluating the experiences that each role adds to the story that they can tell about their careers. Key to the story is the ability to show not just that you held a role, but that you had positive impact.

- As you become more senior inside a company, you must develop a thick skin and you let go of your need for external gratification. Along these lines, Kloppers discusses how his introversion may have been a weakness early on; in the most senior roles, however, he has found it to be a great strength because he does not depend on external forces for motivation and appreciation—instead, these come from within.

- Kloppers discusses the value of loyalty and fairness to people—important qualities that should, nonetheless, never override the goal of high performance. Too often, we see leaders for whom loyalty supersedes performance concerns. Loyalty is valuable, but when it comes at the expense of performance, leaders may be contributing to their own downfalls.

5

AS YOU MOVE ON:

BUILDING THE FOUNDATION FOR

YOUR SUCCESSOR

Moving on is a simple thing. What it leaves behind is hard.
Dave Mustaine, lyrics from "A Tout le Monde"[1]

As you experience success in your career game, you will inevitably leave behind positions for others to take on. When you begin to anticipate your next opportunity, it is natural to be tempted to give it too much of your attention. While this is only natural, we suggest that it is a temptation worth resisting because the moves you make on your way out matter. Last moves in a position are important because they signal a great deal about you to the others in your career game. How you leave says a great deal about you to your soon-to-be former employer, your new or potential employers, your former and new coworkers, other members of professional and social networks, and so on. Down the road, in one capacity or another, your career game may cross paths with people who you left behind. Your parting moves are also important because of the impact they have on another player in your career game—your successor—and on the company being left behind.

Our purpose in this chapter is to offer you guidance regarding your considerations involved in planning and executing your last moves with an employer. We frame the discussion around the concept of leadership transitions because, in effect, that is what these last moves often involve—as you exit, your successor arrives—and, during this time, the company and its people need to continue to work productively. Within that framework, we focus mainly on the motivations of the exiting executive, while also recognizing those being pursued by other key game players—the company and the successor. From this discussion, we hope it becomes clear to you that the metric against which last moves are measured is the degree to which they create a solid foundation for successors. Take, for example, the way observers such as *Good to Great* author Jim Collins views Jack Welch's ability as a leader. Sometime after Welch's departure from GE, Collins told a reporter with *Business-Week* that we cannot know whether Welch was a great leader until we see how his successor, Jeff Immelt, performs. Collins' logic is consistent with ours—much of the measure of a leader's effectiveness lies in the conditions left behind. Naturally, the way things were left for Immelt was in many ways determined by Welch's final moves.

ISSUES IN LEADERSHIP TRANSITIONS

Leadership transitions are complex to orchestrate because handing off responsibilities from one leader to the next is fraught with myriad organizational and interpersonal challenges. The military provides an example of one organization that recognizes why leadership changeovers (what they refer to as "relief in place" operations) can be dangerous for two reasons. First, short-timers display a tendency to focus on whatever next awaits them and, as a result, often take their eyes off the current situation and its challenges. Second, newcomers typically hold a false sense of confidence; it is false because it is based on naïve interpretations of the situations they are entering. The military has found that, during transitions, the rate of safety- and enemy-related incidents rises sharply while overall organizational effectiveness declines.

Leadership transitions in companies are also "relief in place" operations— they happen in real time with no pause in the action. Given the risk connected to transitions, it is not surprising that considerable effort has been made to provide the advice necessary to help new leaders start off on the right foot. Best-sellers such as *The First 90 Days: Critical Success Strategies for New Leaders at All Levels* by Michael Watkins and *The New Leader's 100-Day Action Plan* by George Bradt and his colleagues are examples of resources offering guidance to help new executives reduce the risks associated with beginning in a new position. The advice offered in these books is intended to help newcomers avoid the "perfect storm" that can derail their careers: a sense that their appointments carry a change mandate from above, combined with an insufficiently developed appreciation of both the company's culture and the position's challenges and constraints.

A striking contrast can be found in the dearth of similarly pragmatic counsel for the exiting executive. We see this as unfortunate. Both companies and newcomers can benefit from a consideration of the moves that exiting executives make as they leave their positions. As we see it, each party impacted by a leadership changeover is a player in a shared game. The players have a common interest in the changeover being well executed. Newcomers begin positions with enthusiasm and energy and are focused on making the best first moves possible. After all, their early performance sows seeds that they will nurture and hope to harvest later. Employers, having invested in either the development of an internal successor or the search and selection of an external one are eager to begin to see a return on that investment. Coworkers are curious to learn more about what the new hire brings to the table; subordinates are anxious to understand what it will be like to serve under the new boss. You, as the exiting executive, will benefit as others recognize the healthiness of the situation you have left behind. The payoffs in this game should be well aligned; clearly, opportunities exist for players to benefit from gains in trade. This will happen best when all of the players understand the game this way.

THE EXITING EXECUTIVE AS A PLAYER

It is clear from our observation of dozens of leadership transitions that a departing executive can have a considerable and positive influence on his or her successor's performance, and, as such, is a key player in the successor's career game. In fact, playing off the title of Michael Watkins' book, we contend that the moves made during last ninety days of the outgoing executive's tenure may be more critical to the successor and the company than the successor's moves during his or her first ninety days. The value of the exiting player is too often overlooked by other players in the game. Former Starbucks CEO Jim Donald shared with us that, over the course of his career, he has taken on four new jobs as an outsider and in each case his entry was different. In one instance, Donald relates, "the message clearly was 'Here is the job—good luck with it,'" whereas, in other instances, he benefited from others at the company who put a foundation in place and helped get him started.

Donald's experience points to the most common—and most easily remedied—missed opportunity in the exiting executive's career game: the opportunity for the exiting and incoming executives to spend sufficient time together.

In spite of the fact that departing executives possess a vast amount of information about the companies and the positions they occupied, the norm in leadership transitions is for a "clean break" between the outgoing and incoming executive. Herein lies a paradox—typically, managers and consultants alike have labored to create systems, processes, and cultures that, by design, facilitate knowledge sharing. Yet, at this critical "handing-over/taking-over" stage, the opportunity to allow exiting and entering executives to work together is too often thought to be too uncomfortable, too inconvenient, or too unimportant to be given priority. When a company is able to create a productive exchange between the two executives—something that requires each to recognize the importance of the handing-over/taking-over process—the factors that lead to poor performance during the transition are minimized.

For these reasons, we think it is justifiable to conclude that, as an outgoing executive, you have an interest both in the way you are remembered and in the shape of the company you leave behind. And, it is also the case that you have the ability to take actions that clear the path for your successor. Finally, it is apparent that companies have a considerable vested interest in your last moves. Unfortunately, too often, we see companies create situations in which the exiting executive feels poorly treated. When this happens, it breeds the sort of resentment that in turn creates the "let them figure it out for themselves" reception that many newcomers report facing from their predecessors.

MOTIVES OF THE EXITING EXECUTIVE

We have made a case that when you exit a position you have the ability to impact your successor's career game—and that the impact becomes a part of your own game. What, then, are the likely motives behind your moves? Like your employer and your successor, you should have an interest in the company's ongoing performance. Your interest may be driven by the fact that you expect deferred compensation based on the company's performance. Alternatively, your interest may result simply from your acknowledgment that you have a reputational stake that survives your formal employment relationship—your later game will be influenced by the *way* you leave and by *what* you leave behind.

Before beginning to discuss how, as outgoing executive, you can best exit effectively, one caveat should be mentioned. Individuals leave organizations for many reasons—some quite abrupt, most less so. It is certainly true that, in some of these cases, the opportunity for a deliberately choreographed handing-over/taking-over process is slight at best. We contend, however, that you have a responsibility to make your operation's readiness to continue without you an ongoing cause. When your moves take this into account, then even in cases of an abrupt departure you contribute to a situation in which a newcomer can succeed. When there is a meaningful period of time between your decision to leave (regardless of whether this decision has been shared with others) and your last day at work, there are a number of ways to facilitate the "onboarding" of your successor, to protect the company's performance, and to create a positive legacy. When we had the chance to speak about this with Jim Donald, he shared with us his view that "Managers have a responsibility from day one to begin looking for their eventual replacement. The people who work with you need to have something to shoot for, and the company has a right to expect that you are doing what it takes so that it can operate after you leave." In fact, while he was at Starbucks, Donald required each of his managers to have a "two-deep" succession plan. His logic for this requirement was that his best employees were often targets of search firms and, by creating greater depth, the company was better positioned to survive the departure of talented individuals.

MOVES FOR EXITING EXECUTIVES

Three broad classes of recommendations will serve you when you are in the role of exiting executive. First are the fundamental "dos and don'ts" that originate in common sense—which essentially boil down to an encouragement to "mind your manners and watch your ego" on your way out the door. Although these reminders are hardly revolutionary, they are important to mention explicitly because everyone can appreciate that common sense is increasingly uncommon. The second recommendation refers to the efforts that you should undertake to prepare the platform for your successor. Finally, we recognize that your move to exit a company may also be the last one in your career game.

In this instance, this move effectively ends a relationship that may have been among the most defining in your life, and you will undoubtedly experience a range of emotions. As has been true throughout your career, you will manage more effectively and, as a result, perform better in your waning days if you are prepared.

The Basic Moves: "Do unto Others"

A Web search quickly returns dozens of articles from sources ranging from Vault.com to Money.CNN.com to Quityourjobday.com that discuss the right way to leave a job. Typically, these articles stress the importance of (1) not burning bridges with superiors and coworkers whom you might later rely on, (2) working hard to make clear quite literally where projects and other ongoing work have physically been left, (3) resisting being labeled as a "lame duck" by continuing to execute your obligations with diligence until the final day of work, and (4) continuing to treat others with respect. This advice is consistent with ours. Taken together, the points above have the net effect of emphasizing the importance of recognizing that the people you are leaving behind may still be important players in your career game.

Whereas these are simple tactics to understand, they might be difficult to execute. Much of the challenge comes from one of two factors. First, if your departure was the company's decision, not yours, avoiding feelings of resentment can be difficult. Second, as one executive told us, "companies need to remember that when someone exits for what they consider a better opportunity, leaving a capable successor behind isn't likely to be high on their list of priorities." This sentiment is likely whether the departure was the individual's idea or the company's. People who are excited about pending opportunities may struggle to work up the resolve necessary to stay focused on their current positions. It may simply be more enticing to envision the opportunities ahead. In anticipation of just these sorts of situations, companies often minimize the time that someone is expected to "soldier on" because it is only natural for even the most disciplined executive to begin to mentally "check out" of a role. At the same time, colleagues will likely struggle to continue to be fully invested in following a "lame duck" leader.

The Harder Moves: Build a Platform for Your Successor

Understanding what the newcomer needs for success is the right place to begin understanding your role in the process. *The First 90 Days*, a book by Michael Watkins that we have previously referenced, provides a useful framework for considering how exiting executives can put things in place to increase their successors' performance prospects. The first key for newcomers is to *mentally promote themselves* into their new roles. In order to make a clean break with the past, newcomers must internalize their new roles and responsibilities and take deliberate care not to continue operating as if they were still in their previous positions. Too many incoming executives are slow to catch on to this. The failure to internalize a new job is often driven by the false belief on the part of newcomers that doing *more* of what led them to the new position is what is required. In other cases, the new position contains a slew of uncomfortable uncertainties—it just feels safer to newcomers to stick to what they know. These strategies inevitably lead to early derailment or outright failure. An additional challenge confronts internally promoted executives and concerns the habits that others in the company have developed in relation to them. Many coworkers will remember the help that their newly promoted colleague provided in his or her old role, and they may have a difficult time adjusting to the change. This reluctance can affect the newly promoted executive, as well. When a newcomer has not mentally accepted his or her promotion, it is unlikely that others will.

Most important of all for the outgoing executive is to provide sufficient space and latitude for the newcomer to assume the full responsibilities of the new role. This takes great personal discipline—particularly when the outgoing executive has an ongoing role with the company. The quicker everyone realizes that the new sheriff in town is really in charge, the better. Each episode of second-guessing, whether outright or on the grapevine, erodes the newcomer's authority as surely as each crashing wave erodes a beach. Another common outgoing executive error—hovering—signals a lack of confidence that similarly diminishes the newcomer.

One might conclude that the best tactic that an outgoing executive can employ in order to ensure the newcomer's success is to leave as quickly and as permanently as possible. Indeed, this might be best for all involved. Yet many key tasks confronted by newcomers are much better accomplished with the help of the outgoing executive. Thus, while ideally avoiding the growth of a toxic situation between incoming and outgoing executives, the best case is one in which the outgoing executive is able to both create and maintain a proper distance between him- or herself and the newcomer. Finding that point is quite an art, but, when achieved, it pays certain dividends to both parties.

Six essential areas require a carefully choreographed partnership between the newcomer and the outgoing executive. First, newcomers must *achieve alignment*—to the extent that their roles allow and require efforts to create alignment among managers in terms of skills, strategies, systems, and structure. Second, newcomers are encouraged to move quickly to *build their own teams*—a focus that has been sharpened by Jim Collins' popular metaphor stressing how important it is to "get the right people on the bus." Third, newcomers must *expedite everyone*—by establishing relationships with their new subordinates and focusing their efforts on making the ongoing development of everyone a part of the normal organizational routine. This element of the role benefits from the energy surge that newcomers possess, but it cannot be done well by someone with only a surface understanding of each individual's potential for growth. Fourth, newcomers must *create coalitions*—doing this well requires the ability to quickly diagnose and understand power relationships among members of the company and, essentially, to understand the "chart behind the organizational chart." Fifth, newcomers are advised to *accelerate their learning*—this involves deliberate efforts to instigate conversations that will help develop an understanding of relevant elements of the past, present, and likely future of the company. And sixth, it is critical to *match strategy to the situation*—new executives must understand the situational nature of their positions and of leadership in general. Personal strategy has to be crafted accordingly.

It is clear that the key to effective pursuit of each of the six recommendations above is a simultaneously deep and nuanced understanding of the company and its people. Such an understanding likely does *not* reside in the newcomer, even when he or she has a history with the company, because the new position likely changes the nature of many of the relationships involved in ways that the newcomer just cannot yet appreciate. Thus it falls to outgoing executives to make some critically important moves—if they can do so in a healthy manner. When well executed, these moves help the newcomer quickly come to grips with the new position, the company, its people, its culture, and its strategy.

In many companies, procedures to hand over tangibles are well developed. One executive shared with us his company's formal handing-over/taking-over policy. It specifies in detail the way that documents, other materials, supplies, petty cash, and the like were to be transferred. It also requires departing and incoming executives to document their attendance at meetings that take place as a part of the transition process. Unfortunately, much of what has to be "handed over" is intangible—it would be difficult for a company to design a form or a checklist guaranteeing that the outgoing executive has been able to transmit culture, norms, experience, and other informal or intangible elements of the organization that are important for executive success. Short of achieving the sort of "mind meld" portrayed in *Star Trek*, a successful transition can happen only to the degree that the exiting executive has internalized the view that the successor's performance is his or her responsibility.

Outgoing executives are the holders of tacit institutional knowledge. To the extent they are able and motivated, they have the opportunity to transfer to newcomers knowledge about how things really get done. Additionally, because they also have held the newcomer position, they can facilitate connections between newcomers and the hubs of power and influence. Similarly, the outgoing executive can discuss strategy with the newcomer and simultaneously help the newcomer identify places where it makes sense to begin to formulate and express his or her own thoughts about best paths forward for the team and the company. Finally, although outgoing executives understandably have ties and feelings of ownership regarding "their" team, they also have a higher responsibility to the newcomer to provide a dispassionate review of team members. Newcomers will be supported by an unflinching review of just who on the bus is "right" and who can be "made right" through development.

Unfortunately, not everyone is capable of this sort of honest brokering. We spoke with a disappointingly large number of newcomers who told us that the message from each of their predecessors was, effectively, "No one helped me figure out how to do this job, and I did fine. Why should I take time to help you when I am worried about my new position (or my retirement or my health, and so forth)? You'll have to figure it out on your own."

Three final success factors center upon the efforts that newcomers ought to take in order to support their own career games. First, the need to *secure early wins* in order to help build momentum is noted. Outgoing executives can help newcomers identify the projects, initiatives, and other efforts that offer the best chances for early successes. Further, they can highlight the situations that might serve as flashpoints or quagmires—the issues that newcomers should approach cautiously, and then only at risk of their own peril. Finally, newcomers often arrive with forceful action imperatives and are ready to undertake major change initiatives right "out of the gate" as a way of demonstrating their bold leadership. Effective outgoing executives can provide sage counsel with regard to how quickly and at what scale the culture might support change and other initiatives. By incorporating this wisdom into their thinking, new executives can better resist the temptation to attempt too much too soon.

Second, newcomers need to actively *negotiate success*. They must be able to set the bar in a realistic manner with regard to performance expectations. The outgoing executive has a complete understanding of the position's constituents and their expectations. Sharing this knowledge with newcomers so that they have a basis from which to begin their own negotiations is a critical step. In addition to information about the level and reasonableness of performance expectations, insight around workplace norms—such as the right way to express disagreement with the boss, the way conflict is addressed, and how decision making is approached—can help newcomers manage themselves in ways that avoid personal embarrassment. Finally, the newcomer is in a limited position to negotiate his or her own successes without a thorough understanding of the quality of the team of subordinates he or she has inherited and the team of managers on whom to depend for success. As noted above, outgoing executives should openly and honestly outline the strengths and weaknesses of their teams so that newcomers can understand how any limitations are likely to impact their abilities to meet expectations.

Finally, newcomers must find ways to *stay balanced.* Transitions to new jobs are stressful; newcomers should work deliberately to avoid letting their new responsibilities become all-consuming. The outgoing executive can help by engaging in expectation setting—for example, establishing what is reasonable in regard to early levels of performance for someone in the newcomer's position. Similarly, outgoing executives can relate strategies that they employed to create a proper balance between work and other responsibilities. Anything that the outgoing executive can do to assist the newcomer's efforts to understand workload, work flow, seasonal demands, and senior management expectations will help.

Taken together, it is evident that outgoing executives play key roles in building the platforms from which newcomers begin their tenures. The most difficult—and perhaps the most useful—work that the exiting executive can do involves efforts to help the newcomer understand the many subtleties of the company, its people, and its operation. Additionally, using Watkins' evocations as a framework reveals that there are many reasonable and tangible ways that exiting executives can help prepare newcomers for success.

The Hardest Moves: Coping with Exits

Easily, the most fascinating look at the psychology of exits from executive positions is reported in Jeffrey Sonnenfeld's 1988 book, *The Hero's Farewell.* Although he focuses specifically on CEOs, much of his advice can reasonably be applied more broadly. The psychology that underlies the behavior of outgoing executives draws its power from what Sonnenfeld labels a loss of both heroic stature and heroic mission. The former refers simply to the fact that positions come with a variety of trappings and perks. The possession of these often serves as a signal—to oneself and to others—and as confirmation of an individual's importance. As people leave positions, voids are created because many of these perks must be left behind. The latter, heroic mission, is quite literally that—growing the business in one sense or another has been the exiting executive's quest for some time. Progress toward business-related goals has likely become a critical part of the way outgoing executives measure and understand their success. At exit, questions as to whether they "did enough" are certain to surface, and any equivocal data that might speak to that question merely feeds their insecurities. Similarly, the frustration and near-rudderless feeling that many former executives experience who are left without a next "hill to climb" is well understood.

From the interviews he conducted in the course of writing his book, Sonnenfeld identifies four types of CEOs, defined by their manner of exit from their companies: monarchs, generals, ambassadors, and governors. Each type is defined by predictable patterns of behaviors around their exits from organizations. Our suggestion is that these CEO types provide insight into what level of help heirs might expect and what companies might need to do in response. Even more potential value, however, lies in departing executives' abilities to understand which of these types describes them. That insight, combined with the willingness to play "against type," if necessary, provides a great service to the heirs.

Monarchs and generals have in common the fact that they have been forced out of their positions. The difference between the two is that, whereas monarchs have indeed been dethroned, never to return, generals are confident they will be asked back at some later point in order to save the company. In contrast, ambassadors are the group most able to leave gracefully. Unthreatened by the company's ability to succeed without them, ambassadors are likely to be comfortable playing an ongoing role as mentors to their heirs. Finally, governors—exiting at the end of their "terms"—though also graceful in their exit, are unlikely to pursue any sort of ongoing relationship with the company.

Clearly, ambassadors, and then governors, are the types that might be expected to be the most willing to invest in building platforms from which newcomers can launch their own success. Monarchs and generals, however, are going to be tough for their heirs to follow. In fact, these types fully expect their places of business to fall apart without them—thus they would rationalize that anything they might contribute toward their heirs' success would merely be wasted effort, serving only to delay the inevitable. Continuing with Sonnenfeld's metaphor, monarchs tend to leave the figurative castle on fire. The situation for someone following a general is hardly better. At best, generals might be expected to be waiting quietly in the wings—either for disasters that call them back or for their supporters to rise up and beg for his or her return. At worst, the general (and the allies left behind) may actually be actively plotting the moves required to create the call for their return.

A sense of how the outgoing executive fits within this typology will, at a minimum, help a newcomer assess the risk associated with the new position. Such knowledge would be useful in determining what indicates success in the role. For employers, the primary implication of Sonnenfeld's work is clear: cultures in which the selection and reward systems are favorable to the hiring, nurturing, and promotion of monarchs and generals do not bode well for the company's ability to handle leadership transitions. Further, some thought about minimizing the sense of loss around the outgoing executive's stature and mission will likely increase the support that she or he makes available to the newcomer. Finally, for outgoing executives, the strongest implication may be that "forewarned is forearmed." The importance of performing honest inventories of their situations and the way that today's actions can set in motion tomorrow's possibilities is critical. Outgoing executives who succumb to the insecurities of the loss of heroic stature and mission are constrained in their abilities to take the necessary steps to shore up their successors' platforms.

SUMMARY

Our goal in this chapter is to help you understand just how important last moves are because of how they impact your game and your successor's game. Our experience suggests that, too often, the players involved in transitions minimize or ignore the impact that departing executives can have on the outcomes produced by successors. For that reason, a genuine and meaningful opportunity exists for career game players and companies to experience better outcomes through improved game play.

The experiences of two prominent companies—Microsoft and Apple—offer a timely example. Throughout 2009, a great deal of speculation circulated on blogs and in traditional media outlets about the possible departure of Steven Jobs from Apple Computer. Leadership transitions at high-flying companies such as Apple are something that people love to talk about. Moreover, this case of leadership transition is all the more dramatic because of what happened at Apple the last time Jobs left. In contrast—not that Apple Computer would want to take a page from the Microsoft playbook—based on results to date, Bill Gates has done a careful job of transitioning leadership to Steve Ballmer. Originally brought on as second in command, Ballmer was given an independent voice in the company, access to a public stage, and real decision-making authority. These steps have allowed him to develop good relationships with important constituents and to demonstrate his legitimacy as the heir. Of course, his onboarding has been facilitated because he was an internal successor who had the opportunity to participate with Gates in a transition over a long period of time.

The first time Jobs left Apple, he had no opportunity to engage in a deliberate process of making moves that would favorably position his successor. The situation effectively represented a clean break, and the results were not good. Recently, Jobs has made moves that reflect his engagement in a much more deliberate process of transitioning leadership. Currently, Timothy Cook, the well-regarded COO who has been given center stage many times during the past several months, may be in the best position to succeed Jobs. Regardless of who ends up in the successor role, it will be important for Jobs to continue to make moves to help build the foundation for his eventual heir. For example, opportunities should be created for the heir to establish credibility as the eventual CEO and in terms of guaranteeing that the successor really knows Apple Computer—something that is very hard to do when adhering to a "clean break" transition model. Finally, Jobs should engage in some expectation setting; his heir will be following an executive who seems to be able to do no wrong. One of Jobs' last moves should be to take the leadership of a process to design a game plan for his heir in which the heir can "win." This is the outcome that ultimately best measures the way a leader serves the company, its employees, and its shareholders.

In the next chapter, we introduce you to what we hold is the key individual characteristic that describes a strong career game player—career agility. We will argue that you can improve your play by investing in activities that develop your career agility. First, however, we present four of our conversations. We had the opportunity to speak with New York Life CEO Ted Mathas. Mathas' advancement in the company provides an example of career agility. His efforts, along with those of key mentors, prepared him for positions with increasing responsibility. Second, we spoke with Liz McCartney—cofounder of The St.

Bernard Project. Shortly after Hurricane Katrina devastated much of the Gulf region, McCartney left her position as the executive director of a Washington, DC, nonprofit to move to St. Bernard Parish, just east of New Orleans. The organization she cofounded has grown dramatically and has leveraged the efforts of over eight thousand volunteers to rebuild homes and help over 120 families move back to the area. She was honored recently as CNN's Hero of the Year. Next, you will find our conversation with Dan Palumbo. During his career, Palumbo has held a number of key positions at Proctor & Gamble, Kodak, and The Coca-Cola Company. In 2007 he led Rexel Inc. through a successful initial public offering. We spoke when he served on the board of The Huber Corporation. Finally, we spoke with Bill Perez, the first CEO of the William Wrigley Jr. Company who is not a member of the founding family. Perez's career is interesting because he has spent so much of it in family- or founder-controlled companies—SC Johnson, Nike, and then Wrigley. In that kind of situation, the career game takes on some interesting elements because the controlling family has an inevitable and potentially dramatic influence on the company, its culture, and its top management team.

NOTE

1. Lyrics by Dave Mustaine; music and lyrics copyright by Dave Mustaine/Marty Friedman/David Ellefson/Nick Menza.

A CONVERSATION WITH TED MATHAS

PRESIDENT & CHIEF EXECUTIVE OFFICER, NEW YORK LIFE INSURANCE COMPANY

As CEO of the nation's largest mutual life insurer, Ted Mathas is responsible for running all domestic and international business operations—the domestic business includes life insurance, retirement income, investment management, long-term care insurance, and related businesses, as well as the company's career agency system; the international business includes operations in eight markets located in Asia and Latin America. In July 2007, Mathas was named president by the board of directors. He became CEO in July 2008, while retaining the title of president. Mathas has been a director of the company since July 2006. He also serves on the boards of Haier New York Life Insurance Ltd., the company's joint venture in China, and the American Council of Life Insurers. He first joined New York Life in June 1995 in the Asset Management operation. Since then, he has held positions of increasing responsibility, including president of NYLIFE Securities LLC, a retail broker-dealer subsidiary; COO for Agency Distribution; COO for Life and Annuity; and executive vice president and co-head of U.S. Insurance Operations. Effective July 2006, Mathas became the company's COO and was elected vice chairman of the board.

Mathas graduated with an AB from Stanford University, with distinction, in 1989. He received a JD from the University of Virginia in 1992, where he was a member of the Virginia Law Review and the Order of the Coif.

AUTHORS: How has your career evolved at New York Life?

MATHAS: My first job at New York Life was chief of staff for the person running the asset management business. It was a tremendous learning experience; it provided me with plenty of exposure to the business and access to many top executives. It's an incredible role if that's what you're looking for in a career— but it's also one of those positions where the longer you stay, the longer people will want you to stay. And, that wasn't for me. I wanted to run an operation, a business, of my own. So, I kept my eyes open for an opportunity, and eventually I was able to take a job no one else really wanted: running NYLIFE Securities and Eagle Strategies, which were then the company's struggling securities and broker-dealer areas. This was, essentially, a small, self-contained company that, at the time, was so far outside of New York Life's core businesses, more than one of my colleagues called to tell me that I might be making a big mistake. But from my perspective, the job offered everything I was looking for—a chance to build something the way I wanted.

It turned out to be a rare opportunity. When I arrived, there was no chief marketing officer or CFO—I was really on my own. This experience was great training to be a CEO, where you have to be able to change hats quickly and understand all aspects of the operation. And the fact that this subsidiary was more or less off the radar screen gave me the chance to try my ideas and develop my leadership skills without much pressure. I looked at it this way: you wouldn't have much of shot hitting a pitch in Yankee Stadium if you didn't spend the time taking a bunch of swings (and misses) in Little League with just your parents in the stands. NYLIFE Securities was my chance to take a bunch of swings.

Over a two-year period, I was able to turn things around and grow this operation. I assembled a strong team, hiring a CFO, CMO, and other key staff positions. I really was at the point where I was able to step back and watch the business run itself. Sy Sternberg, the chairman and CEO of New York Life, also recognized this, and I don't think more than a month passed by before I got a call from him, saying, "We have a new assignment for you. We want you to work in the Agency Department." This, initially, was a difficult move for me. It meant going from being the person in charge of something to being someone else's right-hand man. But I knew that if I wanted to continue to develop and advance in New York Life's organization, I would have to integrate myself back into the company's core business. In hindsight, I realize that my success with the securities operation showed Sy that I could run a business—putting me in Agency was his way of finding out whether I could learn "the" business. After Agency, I was assigned to other positions in our life insurance and annuity operation, every step being another chapter in my development and all culminating in being named president and CEO of New York Life.

AUTHORS: Can you reflect on the chief of staff role? Though some companies still use it, it seems to have gone by the wayside.

MATHAS: It was a phenomenal, phenomenal opportunity for me. I think more companies should consider this role. But people in this role have to be very careful how they manage it.

The job is essentially about helping the person you're working for work more efficiently and effectively. That means a chief of staff has tremendous access. You get to read every single thing coming across your executive's desk. You get to attend the vast majority of senior-level meetings and observe how business is done, how people interact, the interpersonal dynamics at the table. It's an incredible learning experience.

But, as chief of staff, you also have a lot of influence—and other people in the organization cannot help but recognize that. So, you have to be very mindful of how you carry yourself and how you handle your responsibilities. Relationship building is key to getting the role right. You have to work hard at building trust with other executives and making sure they understand you are not there to tell them what to do—you are there to help them work with the executive you support. In many ways, when working with others, it's often not what you do or say as chief of staff, it's what you don't do or say. You do not want to come across as someone who is there to impose the direction of your manager—you have to position yourself as a partner. And, when you do that successfully, people in the organization will welcome your phone calls, rather than roll their eyes and worry about "what's coming next."

AUTHORS: **Did you have a mentor during your career development?**
MATHAS: I have never had a formal mentor in my career. That is to say, I never had someone sit down and say, even informally, "We should spend time together for your development." Indirectly, however, I learned so much from so many others.

Watching and listening is critically important, particularly early in your career. You can grow a lot just by paying attention, by watching what people do and by gut checking your own sense of what the right thing to do is against what they are doing. It sounds very basic, but I think it's important not to simply take what is said only at face value. When people made a decision, I wanted to understand the framework of that decision—why are they doing what they are doing. You may not always agree with what's going on, but understanding the "whys" of decisions helps you evaluate how you would do or not do something.

The many insights I learned from Sy were clearly a result of watching him, listening to him, paying attention, and looking for the broader implications of his decisions. In other words, it was pushing to understand not only the actual specifics of the issue at hand, but also the broader lessons to be learned.

If there's one thing I believe people should keep in mind when it comes to learning from others—especially those you admire and respect—it's that advice is always free, and therefore listening doesn't cost you anything. You would be surprised how even the simplest of tips can go a long way. I remember a senior-level guy sent me an e-mail that said "You really should be careful in your e-mails to say, 'hello so-and-so' and 'thank you so-and-so' at the end." And, when

I looked at my correspondence, I realized that I was, indeed, being too direct in my communications and had to soften the edges a little bit. I never would have seen that on my own—it took someone I respected bringing it to my attention.

AUTHORS: **You have led a lot of change in your career at New York Life. How do you manage change in an organization that has been around for so long?**

MATHAS: I think, in corporate America today, there is this sense that people will say anything they need to say, and that undermines your credibility and it undermines your ability to connect with people. That can be a big problem when you're trying to implement change. From my perspective, genuineness is the key. If people don't believe you are genuine, they may follow your direction because they have to. But as soon as they are given a choice, they'll go in the opposite direction. When people believe in you, it goes beyond simply taking direction—it becomes a buy-in to what you're trying to achieve. But being genuine means showing some vulnerability, and that's not easy for many people.

When it comes to change—especially at established companies—I think it is also important to remember that corporate cultures are strong. They constantly evolve . . . and they can handle change. The key to being successful when implementing change is balancing your passion with some patience. When I have a new initiative in mind, I have a tendency to get very energized and excited when I convey it to others—and that's important . . . you need people to know how personal and serious you take your work. But you then have to slow it down a bit. I'm not saying you have to turn down your passion—just the opposite; it's very important that you don't lose it. But you can't expect to impose your passion on others . . . you have to give the organization time to absorb it. When you achieve that balance, change can come relatively easy—even in a company more than 160 years old.

AUTHORS: **Your family influence on your approach to work is interesting. How have you applied lessons learned throughout your career?**

MATHAS: I feel I got different things from key people in my life. My grandmother was someone special. Her husband died when he was in his forties and she was in her thirties. She wore a black dress every day from that day forward. She took care of her three daughters—my mother and her sisters.

My grandmother worked hard every day of her life. She eventually came to live with us—and she was incredible to watch. Every single day, she got up, she cooked, baked pies, caught fish, swept the patios, ran errands, washed clothes, and cleaned. And she genuinely felt *fortunate* to be able to do so. How can you watch that every day and feel any sort of entitlement—how could you not develop a healthy work ethic?

My dad was all about principles, orientation to the world, and values. He didn't get bogged down in details. He was the person who instilled in me the belief that there is always a right thing to do, and the right thing should be based upon both your intuition and your logic. For example, he owned his own business, but he didn't think he could afford to offer his employees a health insurance plan. So when people got sick, my dad would just pay them and pay for their hospital bills. He felt it was the right thing to do. His view of business was that we have to make money, but it is also a phenomenal opportunity to help people and take care of the community. That had a big impact on me.

My dad was also interested in politics and history, and we had great dinner-time conversations. He nurtured my interests in these areas and challenged me without injuring my confidence. For example, at the dinner table, he gave me room to share my ideas; teaching me that my voice counted. But at the same time he provided a structured framework that allowed me to learn from each discussion. He didn't dominate the conversation, but in retrospect I see that it was absolutely directed by him.

My mom emphasized completely different things from my dad. What mattered to her is how you treat people. As a kid, I would have arguments with my mom where I would insist I was right but she would insist I wasn't—and it was because of *how* I delivered my argument. From her perspective, message delivery was equally important—if not more important—than having the right answer. That was a tough lesson for me to get my mind around. But now, I deeply appreciate the wisdom of what she taught me. When you're a company leader, you will undoubtedly have to make tough decisions—decisions that are right for the organization from virtually any logical perspective, but ones that will make some people unhappy. In those instances, it becomes very clear that how you communicate the decision is critical to how it will be received and how successful it will be implemented.

AUTHORS: How has your law school education helped you in business?

MATHAS: I loved law school because I love concepts, principles, the integration of ideas and trying to find connections. In many ways, the study of law is training in pattern identification to solve problems.

The law also teaches you how to frame an argument. It forces you to question the assumptions you are making behind your point of view. Not only does this strengthen your argument, it can help you communicate your position in a compelling way. I don't think enough business people take the time to go through this type of "proofing" exercise.

AUTHORS: Which do you think is better for your career—assignments where you needed to turn things around, or assignments where you were guiding a steady ship?

MATHAS: Early on in one's career, it is absolutely better to have the turnaround role. By definition, the organization is more open to fresh thinking since what they have been doing clearly hasn't been working. In addition, when you take on assignments where things are already working very well, people might say, "Yes, so and so is doing a good job . . . but that business has never been a problem." Turn a loss into a win, however, and you quickly get noticed for a job well done.

However, if you want to be trusted with a core part of the franchise, you have to show that you can manage the "steady ship." It is the rare manager who finds the way to innovate without rocking the boat. For example, consider the business mantra of identifying and using "best practices." How did best practices come into existence? Someone took the initiative to challenge the way something was done and do it differently. That means tomorrow's best practices won't emerge until someone decides to challenge the conventional. So, whereas in a turnaround assignment the challenge is obvious, really good managers will dig deeply even when they are running an already successful operation, and they will find ways to materially improve it.

AUTHORS: What advice would you share with someone who is looking to find opportunities inside his or her company?

MATHAS: When you're in a large organization, one challenge is having access to the decision makers and getting noticed. There's no question that there are bright individuals with tremendous potential in the lower ranks of every company. From a practical standpoint, a management team cannot invite hundreds of people to offer their input at a meeting. And often when you're the junior person sitting at the table, you probably won't have a chance to say anything . . . and even if you do, someone else will likely jump in before you can get ten to twelve words out of your mouth.

If you want to have meaningful input in your company, a really good way early in your career is via the written word. In fact, this is how I was first noticed by Sy Sternberg. He read something that I wrote and was impressed by it—and as a result, he wanted to meet with me. It was that simple.

And when you prepare a memo or a business plan or a position paper, you have the advantage of time—you can be more thoughtful; you can polish and perfect your message; you can demonstrate your logic and thought process. That's something you can never do in a fifteen-second window during a meeting.

CAREER GAME OBSERVATIONS

- Entering New York Life in the chief of staff role was a great first move for Ted Mathas because it meant that he was noticed early on by the most senior executives, including chairman and CEO Sy Sternberg. Sternberg would later become Mathas' invisible hand, impacting his career inside the company.

- The position also gave Mathas a direct working relationship with a senior leader in the company who helped him quickly get the lay of the land inside the company. This is, as we have argued, the most important role that early-career mentors can play in your career game.

- Finally, the position exposed Mathas to all the information he could possibly absorb about goings-on at the company, which ultimately produced tangible results. Mathas demonstrated, time and time again, that he was a "go to" person who would, in a timely manner, deliver solutions that were well thought out.

- Mathas feels he was noticed initially through what he wrote. In today's world of "management by Blackberry," many do not invest enough time and care regarding communication. Each communication episode is an opportunity to be recognized—Mathas leveraged those opportunities to support his game.

- Mathas revealed that Sy Sternberg let him know that he could stop by any time just to chat. He resolved not to take Sternberg up on that offer because he did not want others in the organization to think that he had special access. This rationalization is a demonstration of one characteristic of career agility—the ability to recognize the broader implications of a move before making it. Projecting the image of a favored person might have strained working relationships with his peers and his immediate supervisor. In other words, Mathas anticipated how other players in his career game would react to his move of taking advantage of the offer that Sternberg had made to him.

- Mathas shared some useful observations on the best moves for individuals at different career stages. He advises you to look for situations, early on, that you can "fix" and to build your reputation from that experience. He notes that, later in your career, you must demonstrate the ability to get the most out of operations that are already effective.

A CONVERSATION WITH LIZ MCCARTNEY

DIRECTOR AND COFOUNDER, THE ST. BERNARD PROJECT

Liz McCartney is the director of the St. Bernard Project, a nonprofit organization she cofounded with her boyfriend, Zack Rosenburg. The organization's purpose is to rebuild homes in St. Bernard Parish, New Orleans, for those who have not been able to return to the area after the devastation along the U.S. Gulf Coast that was caused by Hurricane Katrina in 2005. After graduating from Boston College, she worked as a Peace Corps volunteer in the African nation of Lesotho, taught in a middle school, and earned a master's degree in curriculum and instruction at George Washington University. Before moving to Louisiana, Liz worked for a community-based nonprofit organization in Washington, DC. She was recognized for her efforts as CNN's 2008 Hero of the Year.

AUTHORS: What were you doing around the time Hurricane Katrina hit New Orleans?

MCCARTNEY: I was living in Washington, DC, going to graduate school at George Washington University, and serving as the executive director of a community-based nonprofit. I was working on my master's degree in education with a focus on curriculum and instruction.

AUTHORS: What had you intended to do with that degree upon graduation?

MCCARTNEY: I wasn't exactly sure, but I was leaning toward getting back into public education and more specifically to working with programs designed to help high-risk kids be more successful.

AUTHORS: Your first trip to the New Orleans area after Katrina hit was as a volunteer, right? Can you tell us about that experience? How did you end up in St. Bernard Parish?

MCCARTNEY: That's right. I finished my master's and graduated in December of 2005. We came down—Zack, my mom, and me—in February of 2006. That would have been about six months after Katrina hit. We ended up in St. Bernard for a simple reason—I had sent e-mails to many organizations to see how we might help, and the only one I heard back from was based in St. Bernard. The group, Emergency Communities, was operating out of a tent on Judge Perez Boulevard. So, really we ended up there just by luck. We worked alongside people from the community offering food, some clothing, and a chance to use an Internet connection.

AUTHORS: Since you ended up leaving DC and moving down to St. Bernard Parish, the place must have really made an impression on you.

MCCARTNEY: Absolutely. When we visited, it was shocking how much work there still was to be done. Six months after the storm, and people were still waiting in line for food. The storm made virtually every home in the parish uninhabitable. People had no way to realistically plan to get back in their homes. At the same time, the people here are incredible. Before Katrina, St. Bernard Parish was a vibrant place. Unemployment was low, home ownership was high, and people had a lot of pride in the community. These were people like us—they worked hard; they raised their families. After the storm, they had hardly anything. These are people who never had to ask for help—they didn't think they would ever need to ask for help.

AUTHORS: So, a few months later, you and Zack packed up in DC and moved here to start the St. Bernard Project. Can you share with us a bit about it and how it has grown?

MCCARTNEY: When we started, it was me, Zack, and a handful of volunteers. Now we have around forty-five people involved full time. Most of the full-time people come to us from AmeriCorps. Beyond that, we rely on volunteers—over twelve thousand people have volunteered, to this point. Over the years, we have learned a lot about how to rebuild a home. Now we can make a gutted house ready for the homeowner's return in eight to twelve weeks for a cost of about $15,000.

AUTHORS: What in your formal education—at Boston College and at George Washington—best prepared you for this work in St. Bernard?

MCCARTNEY: There were two things those programs stressed that helped me here. First, I learned how important it is to make sure the clients you serve—and the larger community—understand that you want to be their partner. People will respond much more positively to your efforts if they see how they have a role and that they aren't simply recipients of your charity. If you can show them how you want their engagement in the process, that you want them to be an integral part of it, then things work more smoothly. Second, I learned that it's necessary to make people the priority, rather than some process.

AUTHORS: What have you learned from the experience that might help others who want to be effective in a position like yours?

MCCARTNEY: One of the things we were fortunate to recognize early on was how important it is to listen. It is easy for an outsider to come in with opinions about what is best for the people who have been impacted by something like this. But that outsider can't really know what it is like for people caught in crises. You can't be effective if you are stuck on your preconceived ideas about what is needed. When we arrived in St. Bernard, we had all sorts of plans for what we thought would be needed. Thankfully, we were able to listen and to realize that lots of the things we thought people would need were not what they needed at all.

Another piece of what we have tried to do is educate our volunteers about the community. We let them know that we never, ever, tell a resident that "we understand" what the people in St. Bernard have been through. We can't. We can't understand what it means to lose all your possessions, to feel powerless about how to move forward, to be dislocated for years, to miss your friends, your family, and your community. But what we can do to help is listen.

Before volunteers go to a job site, we do an orientation for them. During that orientation, we share with them what St. Bernard Parish was like before the storm. When it is possible, we like them to meet the family they are helping. Volunteering means a great deal more when the help you are giving is less abstract. It also helps the people of St. Bernard to have the chance to tell the volunteers "thank you for not forgetting us." The personal element just makes it a better experience all around. And I think it helps people stay connected. It also helps that, by the end of a week, a volunteer can see very clearly how much closer they have taken things to bring the family home.

AUTHORS: As you reflect back, is there anything you would do over or do in a different way?

MCCARTNEY: There is a lot I would try to do differently, but at the same time we learned from many of our mistakes. We made a lot of mistakes, but they helped us. Some of the things that come to mind are that we probably could have been quicker to streamline our construction process; we probably could have hired more people earlier. Of course, the problem is that sometimes you just have no way to know until after you have the experience.

One thing that I have learned is how to get out of my own way. There have been many things that I agonized over when a decision could have been made more quickly. It is difficult, but you have to find a way to balance things. It would be dangerous to be too cavalier, but on the other hand, speed matters in what we are doing so that we can bring people back home to St. Bernard. When agonizing won't lead to a better decision, it's best to just make a decision. So, finding a way to worry less and do more is something I would share with others.

AUTHORS: In many ways, St. Bernard Parish was a bit of a frontier, and you headed out there basically on your own. Who do you turn to for help and support when you have these worries? Who is mentoring you as you grow the organization?

MCCARTNEY: At this point, we have lots of friends and supporters. Zack and I are really very lucky because we get thanked all the time. I actually wish it was the other way around—that our staff were in a position to hear more of the thanks. But no, positive reinforcement is not lacking. In the beginning, we had each other. That made a big difference, of course. What I would point out is that doing something like this probably wouldn't have been possible if we had not been in a relationship. The work was very much all-consuming. I don't think it would have been possible for both of us to make it through if we had just been business partners. The fact that there are two of us helps, too, because we are very different people and have very different work styles. We complement each other—and the staff gets a break from one or the other of us.

AUTHORS: What are your plans for the St. Bernard Project?

MCCARTNEY: Right now, we are able to rebuild about a hundred homes a year. We want to grow so that we can do a thousand. As we get bigger, we want to preserve the culture of the project and we don't want to threaten the quality of the services we provide. So, one challenge is to figure out how to scale the operation up to where that is possible. We have a partnership with KPMG. A number of their senior consultants are helping us figure out how to get it done.

AUTHORS: Scaling the operation is a classic entrepreneurial challenge.

MCCARTNEY: Yes, it isn't easy. The people from KPMG have been a tremendous help already. Without their experience, it would be very hard. We are learning a lot—the phrase "supply chain" didn't mean much to me until last month, for example. Additionally, we need to recruit more office staff to go after the larger grants that will be necessary to do more homes. And, the larger grants mean that we will need people in place to oversee all the reporting that is required.

Additionally, we are going to begin working in Orleans Parish. A smaller percentage of the homes there were damaged by the storm [than in St. Bernard Parish], but the parish is so much larger that the number of homes needing repair is very significant.

The vision we have is to become a housing triage center for people who lost their homes in the storm. We are starting a program called "Good Work, Good Pay." We are going to train people, mostly veterans, in the construction trades and then hire them to work on homes. We also are putting together what we are calling the "Fair Rate Plan" that is intended to provide people references to contractors who agree to provide services for a set fee per square foot. Right now, many residents are hesitant to get involved with contractors because of the stories they hear of people being taken advantage of. When all this is in place, a displaced family could come in to the triage center and explain their circumstance. If they have some money available, but not enough to do the whole job, we can serve them with the Good Work, Good Pay program. If they have enough money, but are unsure how to proceed, we can serve them with the Fair Rate Plan. And, if they do not have money, we can serve them in the way we are helping people now—with our volunteers.

AUTHORS: **You have really taken the project a long way.**

MCCARTNEY: It is amazing to look back on how it all started; hopefully, each year, it becomes a better version of itself.

AUTHORS: **What have you learned about work from this experience?**

MCCARTNEY: I am fortunate that I am doing something that really is important to me. So much satisfaction comes from that. I know a lot of people my age have jobs they just really don't like. Maybe they took them because it was what their parents wanted for them or because it was what their friends were doing. But it is so much easier to keep going when you are involved in something that matters personally to you.

CAREER GAME OBSERVATIONS

- Liz McCartney had a career game plan to leverage her education at Boston College and George Washington University, as well as her volunteer experiences, in public education. What she observed in New Orleans after

Hurricane Katrina led her in a different direction, but it was one in which her capabilities translated well.

- McCartney makes an interesting observation about moves—notably, that learning how to get out of your own way is sometimes an important move to make. In her work in St. Bernard Parish, she has had to learn to assess when further thinking would yield a better result versus simply cause things to move too slowly.

- Other players have been critical to her career game. As she notes, the enormity of the undertaking with the St. Bernard Project would have overwhelmed her had she not been able to take it on with her boyfriend Zach. The residents of St. Bernard have played an important role in helping her understand how to be effective in her job.

A CONVERSATION WITH DAN PALUMBO

FORMERLY CHIEF MARKETING OFFICER, THE COCA-COLA COMPANY

After serving in key domestic and international roles at Procter & Gamble, Dan Palumbo became president of the $7 billion Global Consumer Imaging Group at Eastman Kodak. He later was named the worldwide chief marketing officer at The Coca-Cola Company. Most recently, Palumbo was a major investor in and CEO of the U.S. arm of Rexel Inc., the worldwide leading distributor of electrical and datacom supplies. He led Rexel through a successful IPO in April 2007. Palumbo left the company later that year.

Palumbo learned world-class marketing, innovation, and strategy as he helped to grow some well-known domestic and global brands, including Duncan Hines, Pringles, Folgers, Pantene, Oil of Olay, Head & Shoulders, Vidal Sassoon, Vick's, Kodak, Coca-Cola, Sprite, Fanta, Powerade, Dasani, and Minute Maid.

Palumbo credits his parents with helping him to always "respect the individual" in both his personal and professional life. Palumbo is the middle of five children born to Angela and Gus, both of whom grew up in a small town in Southern Italy before emigrating to Toronto, Canada. He grew up playing multiple sports and was active in theater arts in high school. He then played soccer professionally in the National Soccer League and represented Canada in the World University Games, while earning a business degree at the University of Toronto. He later earned an MBA from Penn State, and taught undergraduate corporate finance at Penn State and Bucknell University. In between, he coached Penn State Women's Soccer.

AUTHORS: **What has driven your various career moves?**

PALUMBO: A lot of people make career moves in a way that they think is opportunistic. Of course, the art is in understanding just what *truly* represents opportunity. I had a boss who taught me, a long time ago, to never run *from* something in terms of job opportunities. He said you should be sure you were always running *toward* something. It can be much easier to run from something—you can always find ways to focus on what is bothering you about your current position. But you will make better career decisions if you focus on what you are heading for.

The Kodak opportunity emerged at a time when I was looking around a bit. I had just returned from an international assignment with Procter and Gamble, and I was more sensitive to outside opportunities. The main reason was that I had enjoyed a tremendous experience and I wasn't sure I was going to be able to apply it over the next ten or twenty years at P&G. There is no one to blame for this—it is just the way their process was at the time. The Kodak role presented two things for me to move toward. First of all, it was an opportunity to move into an enormous responsibility in a company that I felt I understood. Second, I saw great potential in spite of the fact that it was arguably in a very tough situation.

AUTHORS: **Are these the same drivers you always consider when evaluating opportunities?**

PALUMBO: I certainly wouldn't force these rules on everybody, but for me, a common theme on every move was the sense that I could contribute more in the next opportunity than I could in my current role. Also, I have always felt that, in order to make that bigger contribution, you had to feel you had a pretty deep understanding of the company you were considering. Finally, knowing something about the company could help you quickly identify the missed opportunities, the crises that needed attention—essentially, getting an early start on making a positive impact. So, considering the company's pain points and how you could apply your capabilities to make a bigger contribution than you presently are will help you decide whether you should move toward the opportunity.

AUTHORS: **What were Kodak's challenges when you arrived?**

PALUMBO: Kodak was being assaulted by Fuji. Their market share was being threatened and they had sort of lost their way. Later, the Coca-Cola opportunity presented itself similarly, but in that case, Coke had been calling me for quite some time, and I initially had no interest whatsoever.

AUTHORS: **What happened to change that?**

PALUMBO: Although I had been identified as the leading internal candidate for the CEO position at Kodak, the decision was made to bring in someone from the outside. Antonio Perez from Hewlett-Packard came on board as CEO—he had been passed over there when Carly Fiorina was named HP's CEO.

I can see why the board was interested in Antonio—he had digital world experience and the film business was going away. So the calculations around my chance to make a difference at Kodak and my chance to make a difference at Coke changed. Coke was struggling from a marketing standpoint. They didn't appear to really know where they wanted to go in terms of marketing directions and, more broadly, with their brand portfolio management. Our discussions rekindled at some point, and it was clear to me that I could dramatically contribute to their situation. This is a good way to evaluate the moves you should make and the moves you should skip.

AUTHORS: **So, it is important to factor your ability to contribute into your decision-making process. How about what the next job offers you in terms of the opportunity to learn?**

PALUMBO: That's an important point, too. Moving to do the same work in a different venue never really made much sense to me. This is especially important to people earlier in their careers. They should still be thinking about how they can have an impact, but they are also at a stage where they are building their capabilities. Going somewhere that will let you learn is great for that purpose.

This is also part of what helped me become excited about the world of private equity. It was an industry I had long been interested in, and I knew that running a private equity–backed firm would be a different dynamic in terms of managing the day-to-day operations—and, certainly, in regard to the allocation of capital. There was unbelievable pressure to dive into every element of operational detail. It was an opportunity to be hands-on in completely new ways for me.

AUTHORS: So, just what did you want to learn in that opportunity?

PALUMBO: I wanted to absolutely demonstrate that I could helicopter up as high as ever needed, but also helicopter down into the most precise details. In each job, I have thought about how my work could help demonstrate my capabilities for the next job. Your résumé becomes a portfolio of work—thinking about how to build an attractive portfolio is an important thing to do. Take a step back every once in a while to ask, "What profile am I creating for myself in this job?" In the private equity case, my view was that it would demonstrate that I wasn't purely a "packaged goods guy," but that I could adapt from manufacturing to service. Also, in this position I had to be absolutely careful about how I managed cash—that was much different from what I had to demonstrate at P&G, Kodak, or Coke.

AUTHORS: What has allowed you to be agile as you have gone from company to company, industry to industry, public company to private equity–backed firm?

PALUMBO: That is a tough question—I can better share with you what others have told me in terms of why they thought I could make these transitions. I have been told—and I agree—that I am a very process-focused person. I am fascinated by trying to understand the best process for getting the work done. If you are really into that, I think you have a pretty transferable skill. Just about everything is, after all, a process of one sort or another. I can see why people would view that as a very core, transferable skill. The second thing I have been told is that I am good at understanding how to operationalize a plan. Of course, this may just be another way of leveraging interest in processes.

Beyond those two factors, there are a handful of things that are more personal traits than anything else. For example, I think being a consistent and fair dealer in both easy times and tough times is important. I have worked hard at this, and of course it is much easier in good times! I have talked with my teams about intellectual honesty. What I mean by that is a reliance on fact-based leadership. I try to set an example by making decisions on things that are real—not on wishes. Finally, having and leveraging a sense of humor goes a long way. In leadership positions, you spend a lot of stressful hours with overburdened and worried people—the ability to lighten a moment here and there is so useful. With the right light line, you can reduce stress in the environment without causing people to lose focus. Anybody can stand there and tell the team that "margins are down"—that isn't hard to do. Finding ways to help people cope with the stress associated with that fact is useful.

AUTHORS: **An important career decision for people is the company they choose to join for that first job. What kinds of companies would you recommend to someone early in his or her career?**

PALUMBO: I strongly believe that people should first and foremost go to a learning institution. Procter & Gamble is a learning institution. In my first year there, at least 50 percent of my time was spent learning, versus growing the business. I can't begin to count the number of courses they provided me or the number of times executives pulled me into their office to just coach me for an hour on new skill sets that you just can't learn in school. It was unbelievable. Friends would ask me how I liked my job—and not just in the first year or two, but for seven or eight years, I always had the same reply: "I can't believe they are paying me to learn."

So, individuals should pursue a learning institution for their early-career experiences. The company does not have to be big to be a learning institution. The larger organizations have cache and deep pockets—but I am sure there are smaller companies that provide key formal and informal learning opportunities for their employees. That is part of what appealed to me in the beginning at Procter & Gamble. True, P&G is certainly marketable on your résumé, but what really made the opportunity there great was that it emphasized learning and management, and P&G was willing to invest in me.

AUTHORS: How long do you think people need to stay at a new job before the return on investing more time begins to fade?

PALUMBO: They should focus on moving toward opportunity, not away from it. If you can still have impact after three, five, ten years, then nothing is wrong with staying. The way you have impact after ten years is that you accept the role of the seasoned executive who pulls others into the office for coaching. Preparing the next generation is a critical way to add value to your company.

Here is another way to think about it: The person calling you for a new position had better be able to convince you that you would learn more with them than you could in the next five years in your present company. If they can faithfully deliver that, then it is time to move—whether that is after one, three, or ten years.

AUTHORS: How important are international assignments to people with high career aspirations?

PALUMBO: It absolutely helps. Let's be honest—most international assignments don't really "teach you the world." What they do that is truly valuable is teach you that you are culturally flexible—that you can not only survive, but produce somewhere foreign to you—where the customs, language, and culture are not your own. The feeling that you can successfully run a European meeting, including country managers from the Eastern Bloc, is a confidence builder. If you can read body language and understand a little bit of why that body language is the way it is, you also will actually have better radar when you get home for how people, even in this country, are behaving. So, I would highly recommend international assignments, but I don't think it is a mandatory requirement. It absolutely and positively helped me, though. Put it this way—I am certain that Kodak would have had no interest in me had I not had any international experience. The job at Kodak required that I be responsible for operations in 150 countries.

AUTHORS: What are attributes that you are looking for in people that get you excited about investing time to mentor and coach them?

PALUMBO: The first thing that I want to see is that the person has a really strong moral center. I don't really care if someone is aggressive or passive, outgoing or introverted, and so on. I absolutely do care that I can trust they are principled and sincere. That is a deal breaker. If that is in place, then there are a couple of other things I look for. I seek people who have demonstrated the ability to make a courageous move. Another way to say it is that I look for people who have "created a discontinuity" in a situation that made it better. It might have been something when they were a teenager or in college or at work—but something where they had the courage to take a measured risk for a chance to make a change for the better.

AUTHORS: **When people take risks like that, there is a chance they may not recover. What separates the people who recover from the people who don't?**

PALUMBO: Well, I certainly could start with me. I probably made about a hundred mistakes at Procter & Gamble. Recovery begins with personal honesty and accountability. One thing I have done is that I deliberately keep track of mistakes, and I revisit them regularly. I kept all of my mistakes written down in the left drawer of my desk. Every time I reach into that drawer to grab a pencil or a calculator, I am confronted by them. I have found it to be a great way to sort of remind myself of my fallibility every few days, simply by opening the left drawer of my desk. Of course, recognizing the mistakes is just one step—you have to then take action. I use these lists to remind myself to get out from behind my desk to do something positive. Sometimes it involves sitting with a subordinate to talk about what we are doing and to see how I can help them succeed.

When there are things about you and your leadership that people have not felt so great about, you just attack it to get better. It may involve formally writing down a plan that helps you clarify what you are going to do. If, in each successive position, you identify a few things that people have pointed out as weaknesses of yours, and then develop a plan to attack them, you are going to protect yourself from committing another major sort of mistake. Sometimes, you can turn a weakness into strength—sometimes, you have to settle for just getting "good enough" so that the weakness is no longer a dangerous liability.

AUTHORS: It is really about playing offense, not defense.

PALUMBO: That's right. In the end, only you can be in charge of your career.

CAREER GAME OBSERVATIONS

- Dan Palumbo is among those who started their careers at big companies—in his case, Proctor & Gamble. His advice is that a strong first move in the career game is to find a position at what he calls a "learning company."

- Many recommendations around how long to stay in a role have been offered; Palumbo's view is eloquent. It is time to move when you are convinced that you can contribute more in the next role than you can in your current role.

- Palumbo is an advocate of making sure, with each move, that you are "running toward" a great opportunity, not "running from" something. His suggestion is that better decisions (that is, moves) are made regarding careers when they are made with a destination in mind.

- The recommendation to consider your résumé as a portfolio of your work is a strong idea that others have noted, as well. As he states, it is important to step back and ask how your past accomplishments have prepared you for what might come next. You should regularly examine your résumé for compatibility with your endgame and round it out with experiences that fill in gaps or that simply accurately describe what you have done to get ready for the next move.

- In Palumbo's mind, the most portable executive skill is strong process orientation. Career agility would, arguably, be enhanced through the development of strong process skills and a reputation for such.

- In thinking about the move having to do with developing international experience, Palumbo explains that what he thinks you learn by working abroad is really *not* so much about other cultures, economies, and so on—instead, you learn about *yourself*. Specifically, you will learn whether you can survive in a place that is foreign to you. Framed that way, the move makes sense. If you think a year overseas will make you nearly native, you will be disappointed. Go with the goal of learning about yourself and, in doing so, improving your ability to play the career game.

A CONVERSATION WITH WILLIAM D. PEREZ

DIRECTOR, CAMPBELL SOUP COMPANY; DIRECTOR, JOHNSON & JOHNSON

Prior to his current position, Bill Perez led the William Wrigley Jr. Company as president and CEO from October 2006 until December 2008, shortly after it was acquired by Mars. As a leading global confectioner and the world's largest manufacturer and marketer of chewing gum, Wrigley's annual sales under Perez were in excess of $5 billion. With manufacturing facilities in a dozen countries and wholly owned subsidiaries and offices in more than three dozen countries, the Wrigley Company markets its products to consumers in more than 180 nations around the world.

Perez was the first person from outside the Wrigley family to serve as president and CEO of the company. Before joining the company, he served as president and CEO of Nike, Inc. Previously, he spent thirty-four years with SC Johnson, a multibillion-dollar privately held global consumer product company, including eight years as president and CEO.

In addition to his present duties as director of Campbell Soup and of Johnson & Johnson, Perez serves on the boards of directors of The Grocery Manufacturers Association, Cornell University Council, Boys and Girls Club of Chicago, and Northwestern Memorial Hospital.

Perez was born in Akron, Ohio. He received his BA in Government from Cornell University and a graduate degree from the Thunderbird School of Global Management. This interview was conducted while he was still active at Wrigley.

AUTHORS: You have spent your career in family-owned firms—or at least firms where the founder had a tremendous presence—SC Johnson, Nike, Wrigley. Was this a deliberate strategy?

PEREZ: I ended up in my first family-owned company by chance. At that time, I would not have even claimed to have a firm sense of the differences between private and public. The story begins in the days when my family was living in Argentina. My dad worked for Goodyear, and SC Johnson was in the same suburb of Buenos Aires. Over the years, I met a number of SC Johnson people

I found I liked. As I was finishing up grad school, I sent a letter to the corporate office of SC Johnson, saying, "I know all these people in Argentina and I would like to work for you," and so on. Somehow or another, it worked—they actually sent a telex down to Argentina to the general manager and he telexed back saying, "I don't remember Bill, but his old man is a good chap. Why don't you hire him and send him here for a year for us to train him as a salesman, and we'll see what happens." That's how I got my job at SC Johnson. Ironically, after about fifteen years with the company, our records system had evolved to where you could access your human resources file—so I did. Believe it or not, the original letter and telex were there. I read them and thought, "I never would have hired this guy!"

AUTHORS: Were you considering other options out of graduate school?

PEREZ: I had four offers coming out of Thunderbird [Thunderbird Global School of Management]—and, actually, the SC Johnson offer had the lowest salary. It was the people that drew me to Johnson. It was a great experience because I believe so much of work is about relationships and people. I ended up in the right company—it was a great place to work.

AUTHORS: How did that experience prepare you for your role at Nike?

PEREZ: To understand Nike you need to know a bit more background about my time at SC Johnson. I had the opportunity to be the CEO there for eight years. For the first four years, I had the good fortune of working for a giant of a man named Sam Johnson. After he retired as chairman, I worked for his son, Fisk, for another four years. So, although my time at SC Johnson had been a great experience, it was also really time for a change. Phil Knight at Nike had been after me for quite some time, and the search firm, Heidrick & Struggles, had also been calling on the opportunity. Their senior chairman, Gerry Roche, called my house every night for probably twenty-five consecutive nights. If I was out, he would chat with my wife for half an hour. My wife thinks she knows him pretty well even though she has never seen him!

I was and am a big Nike fan. I run a lot and have used their products for years. It was an opportunity of a lifetime. Looking back, it was interesting that the recruiting was handled by Phil Knight, Gerry Roche, and one board member. I didn't meet any of the other board members until basically the meeting at which I was elected.

Interestingly, I had one point of negotiation with them, which was to lower my base pay. I wanted to make less than Phil Knight was making because I knew he was far more experienced and knowledgeable than I was in the business. I also wanted to make less than I was making at SC Johnson because I wanted the Johnson family to know that I didn't leave for money.

AUTHORS: How did Phil Knight and the board frame your role there? That is, what did they expect you to accomplish?

PEREZ: The guidance I received with that first board meeting where I met everybody was, "Hey Bill, don't change anything. For the first six months just learn the business, meet the people, and see how it goes," and that's what I did. I attended meeting after meeting, tried to learn as much as I could about the business, and met as many people and learned as much about them as possible. At the next board meeting, Phil Knight told the board that, on a scale of one to ten, I had been an eleven. But I knew it would get interesting because I had some ideas about parts of the business I wanted to change. This foreshadowed my most important lesson from Nike—you have to pace change to fit the culture where you are working. In some ways, I felt I was moving at a snail's pace relative to the culture at SC Johnson.

AUTHORS: What led to your departure from Nike?

PEREZ: There was a lot to Nike that was untouchable—marketing, for example; their marketing is brilliant. There were a number of areas, however, where I thought we could change for the better, but I moved too fast. On top of that, Phil did not signal me that he thought I was moving too fast until the very end. Part of the challenge was keeping on the same page with Phil. Our plan was to meet weekly, but by the time calendars were sorted out, once a week turned into once a month. For me, I saw things moving in the right direction, but from Phil's perspective, things were getting progressively worse. It finally came to a climax a few days before a significant reorganization was going to be announced. Phil said, "Bill, you can either leave amicably or you can go fight it with the board." I did appeal to the board because I thought I was right, but since he controlled 75 percent of the company's voting stock, I realized there wasn't much of a chance of me staying. But I hold no grudge against Nike—I still run, I still use their products. It is a great company.

AUTHORS: **What did you take from that experience to Wrigley, where, again, the founding family is a big part of the company?**

PEREZ: The most obvious lessons I took from Nike were the importance of communication and pacing change. When I came to Wrigley, you can rest assured that the pace at which I instigated change was one I felt could be handled by the organization. Throughout the process of each change, I consulted, time and time again, with the "veterans" there who understood what pace of change would be appropriate without hindering productivity.

Also, Bill Wrigley and I communicated all the time. We were also able to find a good rhythm to working together. We called it "divide and conquer." He did some things, I did some things, he would go to one country, I would go to another country. He did the things he enjoyed doing, and I worked around that with the other things that needed to be done. We just set out with such a great teaming effort that it was apparent to the whole team at Wrigley. Teaming together at the top is a great concept.

I'm going to miss working with Bill a lot. He is a great person, a wonderful leader, a visionary. He deserves a lot of credit for what this company is today and obviously deserves the real credit for the great deal that was won through the merger with Mars.

AUTHORS: **What is your next move?**

PEREZ: I don't want to leave the people here, but postmerger, my role amounts to general manager of a business unit, which is something I did thirty-five years ago for SC Johnson in Spain. We shall see what happens next. I'm leaving at peace, which makes thinking about the next step easier. I didn't leave Nike at peace, which made it a much tougher transition.

AUTHORS: **What would you tell early-career executives about the pros and cons of working in a family-controlled business?**

PEREZ: There is absolutely nothing better than a family-run business. It is easier to have a long-term perspective about the company; you don't have to be distracted by what analysts are saying about the company—both of those things help reinforce a clear vision for the company, and that keeps everyone working together. You are able to just keep on doing what's right for the people and the brands.

Of course, this requires that the family controlling the business be the right family! By that, I mean a family that respects your values and ideas, complements your working style, wants you to grow professionally with the business, and is always focused on the long term. Otherwise, it may be the worst situation.

I would also suggest that you make sure you are comfortable with the culture you are entering, particularly with the values that the controlling family holds dear. Because those are unlikely to change, and if you can't internalize them you will be miserable.

Of course, this is all true for public companies too. Culture matters. Credible leadership matters. But, in family-controlled companies, I think values are more enduring, so if you join, you really need to be comfortable with them.

AUTHORS: How have mentors played a role in your development?

PEREZ: I would not have ever been CEO of anything if I hadn't had a mentor early on in my career. When I was in Spain, I was a product manager, and, frankly, there are a lot of product managers out there. A new marketing director came in who had worked for SC Johnson for a number of years. For whatever reason, this guy really believed in me, and he gave me opportunity after opportunity. I went from product manager to group product manager to marketing director, and then, in 1977, when I was twenty-nine, I was made general manager. At the time, I think the next-youngest major company general manager was in his mid-forties. Anyway, the new marketing director who was by then an area director, said to me, "You know, Bill, the guys and others had some doubts about giving you this opportunity, but I know you are going to do well." He went on to say, "If you screw up the first year, do not worry about it because anything that goes wrong the first year, I will say it wasn't your decision; it was my decision. But after the first year, you are on your own." In the beginning, he was coming to check on me every couple of weeks. He was running half of Europe and I was running Spain. Finally, I told him, "You have to decide whether you want to be the general manager here, or if you want me to be general manager, because if you keep coming in every two weeks, people won't know who is in charge." He pulled back, and let me run Spain, and that was what propelled me in my career. That was the opportunity that separated me from other people.

Mentors are valuable, but you also need one who will sponsor you as well. My boss mentored me, gave me some ideas, gave me feedback, and he taught me some basics about business. Even more importantly, he made sure my name was on the table when opportunities surfaced.

We had a wonderful mentoring program at SC Johnson that worked extremely well. Every high-potential employee had a mentor/sponsor.

AUTHORS: **What do you look for when you are deciding whom to mentor?**

PEREZ: Chemistry, capability, energy, and—quite frankly—diversity. I haven't gone back and done a demographic breakdown of people I have worked with, but I would guess that well over half were either women or minorities.

Often, I will have a relationship or encounters with people for six months or more before we embark on a mentoring relationship. During that period of time, I can hear what other people have to say about them and I can see what they have done to impact the business, their area of responsibility. This ensures that the decision is not made on the basis of a single interview.

AUTHORS: **What skills do executives need to excel at today if they want to progress quickly in their careers?**

PEREZ: Analytic skills are essential, whether you are working in finance, manufacturing, marketing, or sales. More subjectively, you need to have communication and people skills. You also have to fit "chemically" in the company culture to succeed. Whether it is at SJ Johnson, Nike, Wrigley, or any other company—you need to fit in. Finally, demonstrations of success are critical. In the end, all businesses are results-oriented enterprises.

AUTHORS: **Who mentors CEOs?**

PEREZ: Actually, I think CEOs need to be open to learning from those they mentor. This can be true for anyone, because the people you mentor will come from a diversity of backgrounds and will have different views on things. Perhaps it isn't mentoring, but it is learning. Whether it is spending time out in the field with the sales team, working with marketing people, or interacting with your direct reports, you can learn what is working, what isn't, and so on about your leadership. If you do it right, it is basically an ongoing, 360-degree appraisal. I can't say how many countries I have visited or how many people I have met, but I have always been eager to hear what they thought we could do better or differently.

As CEO, the board can also be helpful in providing a sort of mentorship, but the board only sees you once every two or three months in a board meeting. They can see the numbers, they see what your priorities are and what your strategy is, but they don't necessarily know how well the day-in and day-out encounters are going at the business.

I had a big advantage with Bill Wrigley during my tenure at Wrigley. I could talk to Bill about absolutely anything, and I got advice from someone who knew the company and industry inside and out. Bill and I were always able to be candid with one another. At the end of every meeting, he would say, "You are the CEO; you make the decision." Bill allowed me to get advice from him, but it was always nonbinding—it was never a direct order. So, where a board of directors might not understand enough about the day-to-day to really be helpful, someone like Bill certainly was. He could give advice on the issues around the daily blocking and tackling that had to get done—it would be hard for a typical board member to do that.

CAREER GAME OBSERVATIONS

- Bill Perez worked his network hard for his first job opportunity at SC Johnson. Further, he picked his first job based on the people, not the money. He was more concerned with the other players and how well he thought he fit than he was about maximizing his income.

- His move to Nike and, with it, his request that he be paid less than offered (the same amount he had been earning at his previous position) is a demonstration of signaling. In this case, he took care to signal to his former employer that he was not moving because of the money. This is an interesting example of an executive paying attention to what were, in effect, his last moves at SC Johnson and to the way others might remember him.

- In terms of the time structure of the game, an important observation is that, from Perez's perspective, the primary difference in leading a family-controlled company versus a publicly held one is that the former offers a longer-term focus of various business decisions.

- Along the lines of understanding family-controlled companies—the cultural fit is very important. Essentially, the controlling family dominates this element of the playing field, and players should carefully consider the degree to which they will be comfortable playing by those ground rules.

- Perez points out the importance of developing the ability—and the willingness—to learn from people below you in the organizational hierarchy. This is a theme that also arises in our conversations with Stephen Elop and Keith Wyche. Other company players are often given short shrift, but it is clear that they can impact a player's game in substantial ways—for better or for worse.

6 CAREER AGILITY

No matter how good you get, you can always get better.
Tiger Woods

Numerous authors, academics, and executives have offered a plethora of executive competencies regarding "what it takes" to be successful. Our intent in introducing the concept of career agility is *not* to add to the list. Rather, our aim is to help you understand that what ultimately matters is not what you have, but how you use it. Merely possessing one or more of the most coveted competencies is meaningless without the ability to develop and then deploy those skills strategically. Just as effective business strategy involves leveraging a company's sustainable and unique competitive advantage, so too does effective career strategy. It is also true that there simply is no single "it" regarding any key competency that might unlock the door to career success. We suggest that what ultimately determines success in your career game is your *ability to leverage your competencies in a manner that exploits career opportunities*. Another way to think about this is to remember what Stephen Elop shared in our conversation—that disruptive opportunities are the ones that have the most potential to accelerate a career. In our view, career agility is the key to staying aboard when forces are acting to disrupt your career. As the chapter-opening quote from Tiger Woods indicates, we hold that career agility means finding ways to continually get better, no matter how good you are. Woods is an example of an athlete who, many have observed, is tireless in his efforts to understand how to continually build and then leverage his competitive advantages. In the business world, Microsoft CEO Steve Ballmer is one of many who have highlighted the critical need for leaders to be able to develop ways to adapt to new situations.[1] *Wall Street Journal* reporter Carol Hymowitz has written about the importance, with each promotion, of managers learning how to act their new parts because successfully doing so is a demonstration of agility.[2]

And, prolific author Marshall Goldsmith has devoted an entire book to making the point, which is aptly titled *What Got You Here Won't Get You There.* Goldsmith's argument is that—even if there were an "it" tied to success—what has worked up to this point in your career climb is not likely to be what you need for the next step. Moving up the organizational chart is a climb, and agility is critical to the success of a climber.

Just as was true in our discussion of career moves, your career game circumstances are unique, and it would be impossible for us to name the capability that offers the greatest potential in your game. Instead, our goal in the pages that follow is to present a sample of the capabilities that others have advanced and to discuss how they might impact a player's career game. We also consider, in the same manner, elements of agility that were raised by the executives in our conversations. Your task, as you read the chapter, is to focus on two things: first, which capabilities are most likely to provide an advantage to you, given the unique circumstances of your own career game, and second, how you would go about developing and strategically deploying them.

SOCIAL LEARNING

Learning is the obvious key to initial development and long-term effectiveness in any position. Even after the fundamentals of a position are mastered, most job holders find that, in order to achieve the highest levels of excellence, they must continually adapt to changing market environments, deal with innovative competitors, and find creative solutions to unforeseen problems. From our perspective, social learning theory provides the most fundamental and straightforward recommendations for how individuals can improve their career game. Social learning theory traces its origin back to work published by Albert Bandura in 1977.[3] Simply put, the theory proposes that "vicarious observation" is a powerful way to learn behavior. In Bandura's words, such observation allows us to "organize and rehearse modeled behavior symbolically, then enact it overtly." In the career game, social learning theory has its most obvious application when the role of mentoring in reference to career success is considered. For example, in our conversation, Carol Tomé described how one of her mentors provided a model of how a woman could be successful in an industry that was dominated by men. Mentoring was also a very important element in our conversation with Ted Mathas. To the extent that career game players are open to social learning, they have opportunities to learn from the efforts, successes, and mistakes of others. As players look for mentors, an understanding of their own career objectives is critical in narrowing down the choices. When mentoring programs are formal, employers will have the best results in terms of making assignments when they consider who best displays the behaviors they want learned.

Social learning theory is also consistent with the issues brought up by several executives in our conversations. Alex Vanselow and Charlene Begley are among the executives who talked about the trade-off between depth and breadth of experience. The downside of some moves to build breadth, or a varied set of experiences, is that they are often made at the expense of depth of understanding, thus the learning that takes place is too superficial to provide any opportunity for leverage. Tomé spoke about learning, as well, indicating that the proper way to approach it in new positions is to begin by understanding the business, then the people, and then, lastly, one's functional area of responsibility. The implication of her comments is that developing a deep knowledge of only one functional area, disconnected from an understanding of the business, is just as hard to leverage as knowledge that is broad but shallow.

EMOTIONAL INTELLIGENCE

Emotional intelligence (EI) has recently become a catchall for a variety of competing theories and models that attempt to explain executive success. Fundamentally, individuals who are high in EI can effectively realize their own emotional state and, subsequently, use that insight to make decisions about the ways in which they approach people and problems. Emotional intelligence also includes the ability to read the emotions and unspoken feelings of others, leading to an increased awareness of interpersonal relationships that can be leveraged in negotiations and employee management, as well as both internal and external selling and influencing. How EI is acquired and developed—as an inherent trait, as a developed ability, or as a competency that lies somewhere in between—remains the subject of debate. One Achilles' heel for the EI construct regards whether it can be effectively assessed. More broadly, some have commented that, when it comes to understanding EI, the "ratio of hyperbole to hard evidence is high."[4]

While the jury is out on just how to best understand the EI construct, it clearly has a great deal of intuitive appeal. Although academics have not yet become comfortable with it, the term has become quite common in business vernacular, and companies seek it in their employees. In the career game, players high in EI could be expected to have quite an advantage. The heightened ability to assess the unspoken thoughts of other players, for example, could be quite powerful in its consequences for play. So, too, would be the ability to discern the instrumentality of different career moves in the context of the larger game. EI is thought to be critical to effectively understanding and navigating complex environments—such as those confronting most executives. Finally, individuals with high EI levels are less likely to be "knocked off their game," as Marius Kloppers stressed was a critical success factor.

SOCIAL INTELLIGENCE

Social intelligence (SI), a close sibling of social learning and emotional intelligence, refers quite simply to an individual's ability to function effectively in social environments. Like EI, SI encompasses the ability to evaluate and judge the thoughts and emotions of others. But social intelligence goes beyond that definition to include other underlying elements of social situations such as motives, intentions, and prevailing attitudes—basically, SI refers to an individual's ability to accurately assess intangible features of social situations. Measurements of social intelligence attempt to capture not only the capacity to understand the behavior of others, but also the ability to effectively deal with that behavior. In essence, to be fully socially intelligent, one must first be impelled to consider the status of one's counterparts, then successfully translate whatever information is available into the proper conclusion regarding that status, and finally, act in a manner that is reflective of that conclusion. In the career game, it is readily apparent that individuals high in social intelligence will enjoy advantages in many aspects of play—for example, such individuals would be expected to have an enhanced ability to make predictions in terms of the moves of other players and to take actions necessary to influence others' moves.

CULTURAL INTELLIGENCE

Today's top executives face more cultural demands than ever before. Business is truly global. For all its benefits, global business brings with it several potential pitfalls for business leaders. Therein lies the obvious need for cultural intelligence: knowing what makes business partners from disparate backgrounds tick, what to say, and what not to say. A leader must know how to approach the unfamiliar and have an innate sense of what can be attributed directly to people's personalities, as opposed to traits that derive from people's upbringings and environments.

But the definition of culture, in this case, is not limited to differences in geography and lifestyle. Cultures also exist within large organizations; different peer groups—the IT department, for example—may have their own internal cultures with their own peculiarities. Understanding those quirks and integrating that knowledge into day-to-day internal dealings can help make a leader more effective and influential within the organization.

Cultural intelligence is learned through exposure; many of the executives to whom we spoke reinforced the importance to you, as a player in the career game, of engineering the sorts of experiences that can provide you with such exposure.

SELF-MONITORING

Self-monitoring refers to the ability of individuals to adapt their behavior in order to fit their perceptions of role expectations. According to the theory, *high self-monitors* are attuned to the interpersonal and cultural cues in situations, and they adapt their behavior to conform to role and social expectations. *Low self-monitors* respond less to interpersonal and cultural cues of appropriate role behavior; people who demonstrate this characteristic desire to be themselves despite social expectations. High self-monitors tend to have high concern for the appropriateness of their actions, use social comparison information skillfully, and monitor their own behavior continually. As leaders, they are capable—as Warren Bennis and Robert Thomas describe—of being "geniuses at noticing context" and adapting their behavior accordingly.[5] Ursula Burns provided a wonderful example of how this characteristic has worked for her at Xerox. She credits the company for not asking her to be someone she is not, but she acknowledged that she learned from the company how to "round off some corners" in terms of the way she worked with others. Those two things—the ability to see the environmental cues that suggest a need to round off corners and to then succeed at doing it—provide a great example of someone who is an effective self-monitor.

INFLUENCING UP

Even the greatest ideas and the greatest strategies are destined to die on the vine if their protagonists cannot sell them. Having the ability to gain first the attention, and then the respect of managers and other superiors within an organization is critical both to success in a given role and to career advancement. The basis of effective influencing lies in knowing the audience. Regarding superiors, it is important to know what *they* value. This does not mean being a yes-man/ yes-woman or telling higher-ups what they want to hear; rather, it means understanding how to provide them with the support they need—and doing it reliably. Your ability to influence others is a function of the degree to which you are trusted. Social learning and the various intelligences mentioned earlier are clearly connected to this ability. "Influencing up" is connected to the career game concept of understanding how you can encourage other players—here, your organizational superiors—to take interest in your game. Players accomplish this goal by showing their leaders that they want to help *them* win at *their* game.

RESILIENCE

A great deal is made of how successful executives deal with adversity. The prevailing view is a reasonable one—having to do with how people learn from crucible experiences and the degree to which they then bounce back—and it provides strong insight into individual character. Basketball great Michael Jordan has often spoken about the fact that he missed more that nine thousand shots in his career—twenty-six of those were times his teammates trusted him to take the game-winning shot. Reflecting on his career, he notes, "I've failed over and over and over again in my life. And that is why I succeed." Most who follow basketball would want Jordan to have the ball in his hands at critical times in the game for just this reason—he has demonstrated that he can handle adversity, will often win, and, when he can't win, he will bounce back in time for the next challenge. In the business press, Warren G. Bennis and Robert J. Thomas argue for the value of adaptivity in leaders.[6] The capacity to recognize change, whether long term or instantaneous, leads to opportunities for growth. The realization that nothing is constant or certain opens the opportunity for continued learning. Adversity can arise at any point; the most effective leaders will attack that adversity with equal shares of resolve and optimism. Adversity can be a golden opportunity to develop new competencies or refine existing ones. And, as Ursula Burns pointed out, it is important not to let others use your mistakes to define you.

When assessing leaders, we have found that those who have been through difficult times—personally, in business, or both—offer a clearer view into just how they might react in the inevitable down business cycles. Those who have been in the trenches, taken on the most difficult tasks in the most difficult times, and emerged successfully have a clear experience edge on their counterparts who have chiefly overseen growth and prosperity. Business is clearly cyclical; in the competitive business environment, even the best-run companies will face difficult decisions. Handling those decisions—fighting the small battles (and losing some) while keeping sight of the larger, longer-term war— is held by many as the telltale marker of a true leader. In the career game, this capacity reinforces the role of understanding not just how to build a résumé, but also how to build a narrative that shows how this ability to bounce back is a part of your game.

A number of the executives we interviewed had stories that reflected the concept of resilience. Bryan Bell and Pasha Fedorenko are both at the early stages of their career games, and both landed desired positions because they were able to demonstrate resilience. In Bell's case, early on, he had to overcome difficulties in finding a fit between what his credentials signaled he was prepared to do and what he really wanted to do. Fedorenko had to find a way to tell a better story—he was told directly that he was unqualified to do what he wanted to do. Instead of giving up, he worked to find a way to address what others pointed to as a deficiency. Finally, Ken Frazier's experiences with Merck, including his experience working through the 2004 recall of what had been a blockbuster drug for the company—Vioxx—and his pro bono legal work tell memorable stories about the value of resilience.

EMPATHY

An empathetic person is able to imagine what life in someone else's shoes is like. Similar to social and emotional intelligence, empathy allows for heightened awareness of one's surroundings. Being able to correctly empathize provides individuals with the needed background to recognize how others are feeling, to anticipate their next moves or greatest needs, and to act accordingly. For top executives, achieving empathy is often most difficult—and most appreciated—when dealing with employees who are multiple levels below them in the organizational hierarchy. A genuine display of empathy can help executives gain both credibility and emotional support among subordinates. Likewise, by projecting empathy upward in the organization, leaders can demonstrate that they understand the stresses and demands placed on top executives. Doing so proves the ability to "think like an executive," which can go a long way toward attaining the credibility so important for career advancement.

AUTHENTICITY

Many of the concepts mentioned in this section deal with leaders' abilities to put forth an image of themselves, to sell both themselves and their ideas, and to conform their thinking to a way that meets the needs of the audience. The notion of *authentic leadership* is driven by the need for employees to see organizational leaders as truly sharing the same mission and ideals for the business that they do. Bill George, former CEO of Medtronic, champions authentic leadership in a book by that title.[7] George argues that leaders must espouse and adhere to values that conform to business ethics and values. And, as the term explicitly suggests, the leader must be truthful and transparent in doing so, or risk setting a dangerous precedent for the organization.

DECISION-MAKING STYLE

Leader decisions are often highly visible and are frequently scrutinized at all levels of a company. Because of this, leaders must be cognizant not only of the end decision that is made, but also of the process used to arrive at the decision. Who should be included in the decision-making process? How much weight should be given to each participant's opinion? When is consensus necessary, preferred, or unimportant? When do we have to get the decision right—and when is "good enough," in fact, good enough? These are all process questions that must be considered; in many cases, the means used to arrive at a conclusion or action plan can be just as impactful on the end result as the decision itself.

As leaders move onward in their career games, decision making is one of the many competencies that has to evolve in order to support efforts to merit additional opportunities. Kenneth Brousseau and his colleagues studied a sample of executives at various levels, and found that the successful ones were indeed able to do just that.[8] Their framework described four decision-making styles, based on how much information needed to be considered in the process and on how many options needed to be generated from the process. The *decisive* style is the most direct and is appropriate when dealing with a single option requiring that only a small amount of information be processed. A *hierarchic* style is described as appropriate when only one option is required, yet a greater amount of information must be considered in reaching it. This would be preferred, for example, over the decisive style when the decision is one the company will have to live with for some time. The *flexible* style describes a situation in which only a small amount of information needs consideration, although a number of options are required in order to provide flexibility in a shifting situation. Finally, the *integrative* style involves the processing of large amounts of information in an effort to generate many courses of action. Effectively engaging in this style requires executives to think differently—to eschew conventional thinking techniques, such as breaking the complex down in to simple parts to be handled one at a time—that is, it requires them to develop the ability to see the problem as a whole.[9] Brousseau and his colleagues find that effective first-line supervisors demonstrate primarily the decisive style of decision making, whereas effective senior managers engage primarily in integrative decision making. This research suggests that one important way to demonstrate agility is to develop and then properly deploy these different decision-making styles. Executives who fail to do so will find their approach to be a mismatch with their new responsibilities and, as a result, they may face a risk of derailment.

POLITICAL SKILL

Seemingly, any notion that includes the "political" label will almost invariably carry a negative connotation. But, in terms of career advancement, the ability to navigate the political waters that invariably exist in any large organization is vital. Political savvy can often be confused with outright self-aggrandizement; actually, it is more a matter of establishing oneself as a key player *in* the group, worthy of the attention and consideration of leadership.

In fact, truly effective leaders and the ideas and initiatives they champion *deserve* the attention of the most influential members of the organization. Often, employees erring on the side of humility or lacking the social or professional network to have their voices heard within the company, are left without the exposure they have earned. As a result, they can be passed over for significant assignments or promotions. In such cases, the entire organization suffers.

Building political skill is largely a social process. Exposure to top leadership is crucial and must often be demanded when it is not easily attained. But politics must also be utilized laterally in the organization; winning favor strictly upward rings hollow without the respect and support of peers and lower-ranking individuals.

SUMMARY

When examining the career derailment of a promising executive, we often find the root cause is that individual's inability to understand how to respectfully disagree, to effectively influence others, and to show savvy in the way battles are picked and prioritized. Career agility is the key capability that one must develop in order to avoid such derailment. When agility is not developed or deployed, career game players run the risk of falling into a frustrating career "middlescence."[10] This term was coined to refer to employees between the ages of 35 and 54—in the midst of their career games—who are "burned out, bottlenecked, and bored." Fewer than half report having any amount of passion for their jobs; more than a third say they face a dead end in their careers. Not surprisingly, these individuals present a management challenge to their employers, who are rightly concerned about how these frustrated employees are or are not contributing. These are career game players who cannot afford to walk away from the game, but no longer have real passion about playing.

The next and final chapter summarizes what we hope you will take away from this book. Before we wrap up this chapter, however, you will find the last three of our executive conversations; they are with Carol Tomé, Alex Vanselow, and Keith Wyche. Tomé was the second woman and one of the first outsiders to earn a position in the C-suite at The Home Depot. Not only was she from outside The Home Depot's founding family, but she also lacked retail experience. Her early moves at The Home Depot reflected her sensitivity to these issues and, because they were good moves, they set the stage for her success in the role. Like Tomé, Alex Vanselow is also a chief financial officer. He is with BHP Billiton, a global leader in natural resources based in Melbourne, Australia, and London, England. He very successfully made a move that many make—from a consulting firm (Andersen) to its client (BHP Billiton). While at BHP Billiton, he has made a number of interesting and less common moves. Finally, Keith Wyche has had a remarkable career in his own right with Pitney Bowes. We sought him out because we were interested in his recently published book *Good Is Not Enough*. In our conversation, he offered some useful recommendations based on his book research, as well as his career-long work as a mentor to minorities in the workplace.

NOTES

1. Knowledge@Wharton interview series, January 10, 2007.
2. C. Hymowitz, "As Managers Climb, They Have to Learn How to Act the Parts," *Wall Street Journal*, November 14, 2005, B1.
3. A. Bandura, *Social Learning Theory* (Englewood Cliffs, NJ: Prentice-Hall, 1977).
4. M. Zeidner, G. Matthews, and P. D. Roberts, "Emotional Intelligence in the Workplace: A Critical Review," *Applied Psychology: An International Review* 53, no. 3 (2004), 371–99.
5. W. G. Bennis and R. J. Thomas *Geeks and Geezers: How Era, Values, and Defining Moments Shape Leaders* (Boston: Harvard Business School Press, 2002).
6. Ibid.
7. W. George, *Authentic Leadership* (San Francisco: Jossey-Bass, 2004).
8. K. R. Brousseau, M. J. Driver, G. Hourihan, and R. Larsson, "The Seasoned Executive's Decision-Making Style," *Harvard Business Review* (February 2006).
9. R. Martin, "How Successful Leaders Think," *Harvard Business Review* (June 2007).
10. R. Morison, T. Erickson, and K. Dychtwald, "Managing Middlescence," *Harvard Business Review* (March 2006).

A CONVERSATION WITH CAROL TOMÉ

CHIEF FINANCIAL OFFICER AND EXECUTIVE VICE PRESIDENT OF CORPORATE SERVICES,
THE HOME DEPOT

Carol Tomé joined The Home Depot in 1995 as vice president and treasurer. At that time, the company's fewer than five hundred stores reported revenues of less than $16 billion. In 2007, the company reported revenues of over $77 billion, placing it twenty-second on the Fortune 500 list. Tomé serves on the board of directors and as the chair of the audit committee for another Atlanta, Georgia–based Fortune 500 company, United Parcel Service, Inc., and is the deputy chair of the board of directors for the Atlanta Federal Reserve Bank.

Tomé received a BA in Communication from the University of Wyoming and an MBA in Finance from the University of Denver. After completing her degrees, she was employed as a commercial lender with United Bank of Denver (now Wells Fargo). She later joined the Johns Manville Corporation as the director of banking. From 1992 to 1995, Tomé was employed by Riverwood International Corporation as the company's vice president and treasurer. At The Home Depot, Tomé served as treasurer for six years before becoming the company's CFO.

Tomé is also known for being focused on the needs of her community. She devotes a significant amount of time to local nonprofit organizations, including the Atlanta Botanical Garden, the High Museum of Art, and the Metropolitan Atlanta Arts Fund, which she serves as advisory board chair. Additionally, Tomé is a member of The Committee of 200 and the Women's Forum of Georgia and has served on the national board of directors for Girls Incorporated.

AUTHORS: Can you begin by telling us a bit about the role mentors have played in your career? Specifically, how have you found that what you needed from mentors changed as you matured as an executive?

TOMÉ: I have been extraordinarily blessed in that I have had a number of mentors through the years. Most of these were informal mentoring relationships. Although I have participated in a few formal mentoring programs, my experience has been that the relationships that develop naturally are more valuable than those that are arranged. The informal programs tend to be much more beneficial because you are naturally bringing together people who have common interests and who can really leverage each other's strengths.

Early in my career, these relationships were very important to me. When I first started my career as a banker, I was one of just a handful of women in the industry. I was looking for help on how to survive—I wanted to be authentic to myself. I didn't want to suffer because I don't like to play golf, for example. I was really fortunate that there was a senior executive at the United Bank of Denver who basically took me under her wing and gave me confidence to be that authentic leader. She was always looking out for me in a way, kind of blocking and tackling for me as I continued to grow. She was fabulous.

AUTHORS: **As you pointed out, this works best when it is voluntary on both parts. What do you think it is that she saw in you that caused her to be willing to make that investment in you?**

TOMÉ: She was a very interesting person. Her first name was Mary Louise, but she would not go by it. She went by "ML." She had really assimilated into the male culture of banking. She was a scotch-drinking, smoking woman. Outwardly, she was really tough, but I think, inside, she was uncomfortable with having been forced to put on that sort of a mask. I think she wanted to help me find a way to succeed without having to make those kinds of compromises. She really helped me develop my confidence.

She helped me find a way to be authentic, rather than to assimilate. As I moved on, she made sure to point out blind spots that could derail me in the end. Mentors are great for this—they can raise these things with you in a way that is less threatening and more open than, perhaps, a direct supervisor can. Mentors can afford to be more frank sometimes than your official boss—they can really get in your face and make it impossible for you to not hear their message!

AUTHORS: **So now, later in your career, what role have mentors played for you?**

TOMÉ: I came to The Home Depot more than thirteen years ago. I was just the second woman officer and was one of the first officers hired into the company from the outside. I was immediately grabbed onto by one of the directors. If

I hadn't been, I am not sure whether or not I would have made it. The Home Depot is a fabulous company, but it is a tough one to come into from the outside. This board member was excellent—she put her arms around me and said, "You are going to make it."

AUTHORS: **Which was the tougher challenge to overcome, being one of the first outsiders or one of the first women to be named an officer?**

TOMÉ: The outsider. At that time, the company was only sixteen years old—it was a really young company, and everybody had grown up within the stores. I joined as an officer without that experience, without a retail background. This key board member encouraged me to put on an apron and work in the stores, so that is what I did. I learned the business from the ground up, and she spent a lot of time with me teaching me about the business. She had been with the company from the start and was a great source of information about the company, its people, and its culture. People are very passionate about this place. So, I owe her so much. She was really terrific to me.

Before I came to The Home Depot, I was working for a highly leveraged company, Riverwood International, based here in Atlanta. I had been part of the IPO team. Riverwood was taken public in the early 1990s—it was the first IPO that JP Morgan had done. From that experience, I got to know a lot of great people at JP Morgan; one in particular was David Ellis. Anyway, I came away from my first job interview with The Home Depot convinced that the job wasn't for me. I talked with my friend David about it, and he told me I was crazy to not give it my full consideration. With his encouragement, I went back for an interview with then-CFO and cofounder Arthur Blank. Arthur sold me. He said, "Carol, we don't know how high 'up' is for you; that's for you to show us, but we will give you every opportunity to reach your highest potential." He has been right—I have had every opportunity to reach my highest potential— and I have never been bored. Thank goodness I had David's influence as a mentor. That was more than a decade ago, and he still helps me now. Once, after an earnings call, he sent me an e-mail letting me know how I could have done better with the analysts on the call. He gave me pointed feedback as only a mentor can. After the next earnings call, he sent me a note to let me know how much better I had done. It was tremendously useful feedback.

AUTHORS: Can you tell us a bit about your move from banking to retail? What led you to make that change in industry, and what did you find was difficult in terms of the portability of your skills and experiences from one to the other?

TOMÉ: I have learned that leadership is the ultimate portable skill. If you can lead, you can make a difference anywhere. There are still many things for me to learn in terms of how to lead, but I am happy to share what led me to where I am today.

I started out as a banker simply because I always thought I would be one. I grew up in Jackson, Wyoming, and my father owned a bank there. I worked for him every summer, and I always intended to go back and work for him and eventually take over, one day. That was my career goal. In my last year of graduate school, though, my father called me and told me he was selling the bank. At that point, I felt pretty committed to the banking path, but I no longer had a place to do it! I took one interview when I was in graduate school with the United Bank of Denver, and I got hired. I was naïve to take a job after interviewing with just one company, but it turned out to be a blessing that I was hired.

I loved the work, but after seven years it was clear to me that if I really wanted to challenge myself, I was going to have to leave Denver for the banking centers on one of the coasts. Around the same time I was thinking about moving, one of my clients, the Johns Manville Corporation, called with an opportunity. They said, "We would like you to help us." They were in Chapter 11 at the time. I thought that if I really wanted to grow, this would be a fabulous way to do it, and I called my dad to ask him about it. He thought I was crazy to even be considering leaving the stability of banking for a company in bankruptcy protection. I assured him I wasn't crazy and that I wanted to learn from the experience. So, I moved, and what an incredible experience it was. I learned so much that prepared me for so many things. We immediately started growing through acquisitions, and I was deeply involved in all of the merger and acquisition activity. In addition to the finance side of the deal, I was exposed to human resources. There were lots of lessons there, too. Our company had to downsize. I had to meet people in my office and tell them that their jobs had been eliminated, and then help them think about what they needed to do next. I was doing this at a very young age. But these are great life lessons, to learn the people side of the business and not just how to do deals, because at the end of the day, if you understand how to lead people and how to surround yourself with the best people, you can do anything. So, after Johns Manville emerged from Chapter 11, we took one of its subsidiary companies public, and that was Riverwood. Riverwood was a small company, but I had a very senior role, so I learned about all of the aspects of the operation. After Johns Manville and Riverwood, I was well prepared for my move to The Home Depot.

AUTHORS: **What are some of the important career lessons to come out of your various experiences?**

TOMÉ: That having an appreciation for how important it is to really understand the business is necessary before you can lead effectively. Although my positions were all in finance, I have come to recognize how important it is to know the business first, the people second, and then the finance. So, with Riverwood, I spent a lot of time out in the field. I worked for days at our plants in Louisiana, for example. I continued to learn about not just the dynamics of running the business and how to make money, but how to lead people. That has been critical at The Home Depot because of the number of people I have the opportunity to touch. It has been interesting here because I have been able to observe a number of leadership styles, having worked for our founders, Arthur Blank and Bernie Marcus, for our former CEO, Bob Nardelli, and now for our CEO, Frank Blake, who has been leading a significant change effort. Also, The Home Depot has had some difficult periods, and that provides some good lessons. During one tough stretch, I was working long hours and woke up one day, looked in the mirror, and wondered what my tombstone was going to say. I was pretty afraid it was going to say, "She worked hard." I realized that was not what I wanted it to say. I wanted it to say, "She made a difference"— for my family, the people I work with, and for my community. That epiphany of sorts helped me refocus on what was important. It helped me determine that I mostly wanted to make a difference in my life. After that realization, I felt extraordinarily free and my life became less complicated in a way because I approached everything as making a difference—to the people I worked with, to my family, and in my work for the community. These have been some of the critical career lessons I have learned so far.

AUTHORS: Can you speak to the importance of experience, depth, and breadth with respect to building a résumé?

TOMÉ: It is an interesting point—some people grow up and become experts, yet their experience is a mile deep and an inch wide. One advantage of smaller companies is that it is less likely you will get pigeonholed. There are too many things to do and never enough people, so you may get exposed to a broader range of the business. But, by and large, people work within their function, in their immediate group or business unit. As you build your career, if you don't have the opportunity to understand the business more broadly, it is critical that you surround yourself with good people who can fill in your blind spots. I have been in a number of situations where I wasn't an expert, but I understood where to ask questions and when to get the expertise. For example, I am not a CPA, so I have surrounded myself with the very best CPAs.

AUTHORS: How have you helped your people develop their breadth?

TOMÉ: What I have done for my team is that, wherever personal situations allow, we move people around. I don't let them stay in their jobs for too long unless there is a family situation or some circumstance outside of the business environment that would preclude them from moving. Moving people into different roles, situations, regions, and so forth allows them to continue adding tools to their tool kit, which I believe is very important.

AUTHORS: It seems that the trend is for people to make moves from one company or role to another at an increasing rate. Can you ever really demonstrate your value or really learn a business if you move all the time?

TOMÉ: Spending six or so years in my first job out of school certainly worked well for me. The first two years were a training program. It would have been foolhardy for me to leave that training program, because the bank was making a major investment in me and it was a learning experience I couldn't get elsewhere. After that training, I went into a commercial lending role and was given some very interesting and challenging assignments. Again, it would have been foolhardy for me to move—and it was smart of the bank to make sure they put me in a position where I would want to stay. After all, they had just invested two years of training in me. So, to answer your question, ideally, it would be a collaborative effort of sorts between the company and the employee to decide together how long each role would last and what the expectations are to learn from that role—and closely measure the value added from the employee, because that is also an indicator of job satisfaction and personal growth. We are all justifying our investments, right? Mine in you and yours in me. Unfortunately, I do see people very willing to make a move for a few more dollars or what they see as a more impressive title. I often wonder if they aren't being a bit shortsighted. Because it may very well be, in many cases, that better long-term—and personally rewarding—opportunities are possible just by leveraging the relationship and experience you already have.

AUTHORS: **How has your role as a board member at UPS helped you develop?**

TOMÉ: It has been a fantastic experience. First of all, UPS is a terrific company with great leadership and business practices. I have learned a lot. I chair the audit committee, and that's been a good experience for me because it allows me to appreciate how to help the chair of The Home Depot's audit committee. Overall, I am a better CFO and a better communicator to our audit committee because of my board roles at UPS.

On the other hand, it is a very time-consuming opportunity. The decision to join a board is obviously not one to be taken lightly.

AUTHORS: **In addition to all these demanding roles, you find time to be very active in the Atlanta arts community. How have volunteer experiences helped you develop?**

TOMÉ: Working in the Atlanta arts community has been incredible. I feel so blessed to be able to give back to the community and to meet many wonderful people. It makes you feel connected. We are headquartered in Atlanta, so we want to support our local community, in addition to having a meaningful presence in all the communities we serve worldwide. Through this work, I have learned a great deal about leadership in such a different context. Leading a group of artists is a bit different from leading a team of executives! It is neat to see how differently people with these backgrounds approach things. It helps me reflect on how to bring people along—the leverage points are completely different. I would strongly encourage others who are building their careers to seek out these wonderful learning experiences.

CAREER GAME OBSERVATIONS

- Carol Tomé's father—a key player in her career game—made a game-changing move for her when he announced he was selling the family business, thereby disrupting her plan to take it over one day.

- Tomé benefitted from early mentors who "blocked" for her. This was particularly important because she was one of only a few women working in the banking industry at the time. Like many others, she has found naturally emerging informal mentoring relationships to be the most useful.

- Further, she has benefitted from different sorts of mentoring at different stages in her career—from her early advocate, ML, to later in her career, when she was mentored by executives and one of the founders at The Home Depot.

- Tomé, like Ursula Burns at Xerox, comments on the ability to remain authentic—rather than assimilating—as important to her confidence as an executive.

- Leadership is the ultimate portable skill. Certainly, leadership ability is a critical competency for someone desirous of career agility. Everyone—at every level in a company—should work on developing it.

- From a moves standpoint, Tomé's assessment that she could not remain in her first job if she really wanted to succeed at banking is important. She recognized that literally moving—to either the East or the West Coast—was necessary as a career move if she wanted to continue to excel at that game.

- Her comment that it is harder to be pigeonholed in a small company is important from the standpoint of how players understand the playing field. In conversations with Charlene Begley, Dan Palumbo, and Ursula Burns, for example, it was clear that a big-company benefit is the ability to work on career-refining moves inside its confines. But here, in Tomé's story, is an example of a small-company advantage: gaining the skills of a generalist by not being forced into a specialized skill set that is a "mile deep and an inch wide."

A CONVERSATION WITH ALEX VANSELOW

CHIEF FINANCIAL OFFICER, BHP BILLITON

Alex Vanselow has served as the chief financial officer of BHP Billiton since March of 2006. He previously served as CFO and then president of the aluminum business. Prior to those experiences, he was vice president and CFO of Orinoco Iron, as well as the manager for accounting and control at BHP Iron Ore. Before joining BHP Billiton, he was with Arthur Andersen.

AUTHORS: You are CFO of one of the largest companies in the world. How did you get where you are today?

VANSELOW: I suppose part of it is that I learned the value of hard work early on. I started my career by carrying bags in a bus terminal in Rio de Janeiro while in college. My father passed away early in my life—so, a lot of what I learned about work ethic comes from watching my grandfather and his work practices. He and my father were both tireless workers. One of the things that I picked up from watching is that, when you get a job, in order to justify your employment, you must do more than the minimum. You really need to do more than people expect—no matter what the job.

When I was carrying bags at the bus terminal, there were times when there were no buses, no people. I could have just sat and waited, but instead I would just look around for things I could do to make sure that my time was valuable for the employer. If there was nothing to do, I would sweep the floor, clean the place. My employer had an interesting system of recording luggage and keeping track of charges and fees and all of that. It was full of flaws. It wasn't really something that provided a lot of security. So, in my free time, I started to play with the system to create one that would allow for better controls. When I presented my work to them, they said, "Oh, why didn't we think of this?" It gave me confidence.

At university, a professor of mine said I had a good aptitude for balance sheet interpretation. He was mentoring me about my career and suggested I look at one of the CPA firms. He pushed me to interview with Andersen.

When I did interview, after a battery of tests, of course, the interviewer asked me what work experience I had. I wasn't ashamed to say that I was working in the bus terminal. I went on to fill him in about the whole job—sweeping, carrying bags, and the new luggage control system I developed—and he just started laughing. I said to him that I wanted to do more and that my professor said I was pretty good at accounting. I was hoping to show my interviewer that I would take initiative and that I would work to exceed what was expected of me. He saw it the same way, and offered me a professional job.

AUTHORS: **Some might attribute your position at Andersen to luck.**

VANSELOW: Luck favors the prepared! So, again, thinking about my time at Andersen—we would have slow times. Instead of sitting and coasting during the slow time or having chats with guys in the office, I volunteered myself to work in tax and consulting, because I don't believe I'm being paid to sit around and also because I had an interest in broadening my knowledge. Had I not done that, I would not have come across BHP at all. I could have just sat around, picked up the phone, or played around with my coworkers, because in the off-peaks nobody really cared what you did. But I felt extreme guilt if I was not adding something and justifying being there. Doing the minimum or what is expected is not enough.

AUTHORS: **How was the transition from consulting firm to client?**

VANSELOW: It was very painful. It was exciting in a way, but the decision was painful because my loyalty was totally with Andersen. They paid my school tuition and they put me to work with great clients. I had one of the quickest careers anybody ever had in the group in Brazil. I was put in a privileged position with Andersen. I was part of the technical team that looked at new standard releases. I was part of the training team that would go to the educational center near Chicago every few months to train a new group of rookie auditors. Andersen had rolled out the red carpet for me, and I felt very bad when BHP approached me. BHP first approached me two years before I accepted, and I rejected joining them then. Their second approach was something that had the characteristics of a temporary position—I would go to San Francisco for a year, just to help set up the international arm of the internal audit group because they really didn't understand how to audit in the developing world. I thought, well, that's okay because I can add this experience and then come back. Andersen said, "Look, we would love for you to go and get that experience, and you will have your place here when you come back." So I left for BHP.

International audit was my area of expertise. When I got to that arm of BHP, I was surprised that things were not well controlled and that people really didn't have a good understanding of practices in foreign countries or of the role that they played in the context of finance and controls. I thought to myself, "My god, there are rich pickings here." I started soaking up information like a sponge and tried to gain their respect by going beyond what was expected. For example, in BHP's operations in Japan, they were using Symphony as their accounting system. The Japan office was the only office in all of BHP that had Symphony, so not many people in the company understood it. I knew how to use Symphony quite well because of the consulting business in Andersen.

Overnight, the local financial controller quit. I was the only person who could go and close those books and make sure things were working well. They pulled me out of audit and sent me to Japan to hire a new controller and to keep things moving until he/she was in place. So, again, being curious in system applications and about how controls worked played a role in my early career at BHP. It also gave me exposure to a lot of new people. To some, I was viewed as someone who could contribute in many different ways. When I was in Japan, I didn't stay still. Within a few months, more people from headquarters in Australia started seeing that there was a guy in Japan who had some different ideas. That's when the Australian option came through.

AUTHORS: And that is when you decided to leave Andersen for good?

VANSELOW: Yes. This was back in 1990. I made that decision not to go back to Andersen, and that was a tough decision. I went back to Brazil and talked to the partners. They fully supported the decision when I explained to them that what I saw in front of me at BHP was very different from what I saw would be waiting for me at Andersen. I still talk to all my former partners, because they could have really played hardball, but didn't. They made me feel very comfortable in making the decision. Back at BHP in San Francisco, I was interviewed by two senior finance managers—the CFO for the coal business and the CFO for iron ore. I think my style helped—they liked how I talked and that I was Brazilian. There were no foreigners that I knew of in finance in BHP Australia. They considered me for three jobs, one in Queensland and two in Western Australia.

AUTHORS: How did you choose among the three?

VANSELOW: I intentionally picked the worst one. It was in a group that had had no finance manager for eighteen months, and the leader there didn't want any finance manager at all. He gave me a five-minute interview, and I thought to myself that, if I make this one work, that will really be something. I knew the boss would be hard to win over and that the job would be a challenge. The location wasn't highly desirable, either. I can admit now that I kept the details of this position from my wife a little bit. Instead of taking her on the trip with me to see Port Hedland, I just made a video. You don't see the flies and you don't feel the intense heat on a video! She hopped on the plane with me.

But I figured if I had gone to a role where things were working well, it would have been hard to make a difference in a short period of time. I assured my wife it was important for me to get the hands-on experience, and that I would either do really well here or it would break us, but it wouldn't take too long. Fortunately, the leader there gave me more and more responsibilities over time—to the point that when he went on leave one year, he put me in charge of the site.

AUTHORS: How did your relationship with that boss develop?

VANSELOW: In the end, he was one of my best mentors. The way he developed me gave me an interest beyond finance. I wanted to learn the depths of the operation. I wanted to know what he knew. He would pick me up at home, sometimes at five o'clock in the morning, and we would go until late at night doing plant inspections. He would teach me about the whole plant, but also about how he operates, how he works, what to look for, etc. We developed a solid relationship, and I was able to help him as well. My growing interest and his approach to teaching me created a bond between us—a trust where he would come to me with problems and we solved problems together. It was good. He backed me up. Sometimes I did things differently than the rest of his management team. My ideas for the transformations he wanted to do were different, and he grew to respect my opinions.

AUTHORS: **What came after that position?**

VANSELOW: The next job took me to Perth. People in the company saw how I grew in Port Hedland, and they relocated me to this beautiful city to the role of manager finance & control Iron Ore. This was at the same time as the unsuccessful start of the HBI [Hot Briquetted Iron] plant. I was not clear where the company was heading—and it was the first time I wondered if I wanted to stay at BHP. I was seeing things that I didn't agree with but decided to stick around and see what played out. A few months after I moved to Perth, the whole thing fell apart. The person who was my supervisor was made the scapegoat for some of it, but the whole senior management team basically disappeared. Then I thought about my duty to BHP and how to react in a moment of crisis, and ultimately I decided to stay. I ended up creating a managers forum. We got all the managers together and would discuss significant issues and how to operate in a leadership vacuum. It took a while for the company to appoint a new CEO and senior management team for our group. They finally sent John Hannah to lead our group. I knew him from my early days at BHP and the audit work I had done for our Escondida asset. He respected the work I did for them and knew me well, and he eventually became another mentor for me.

One thing I learned from this role was the importance of investing to build trust with others—it isn't enough to just work harder. I started by offering sandwich lunches to the managers group, because I knew those guys liked to eat and it was a good way to get them all together. I designed the content of those discussions to get them involved and to get them aligned to the objectives of the company, and tried to not let them get too emotional about what was happening with BHP's leadership. The managers group was positive and productive, and they all appreciated it in the end. For me, it gave me confidence that I could step into a leadership role and make a difference. Previously, my influence was due more to hierarchy, because I was the manager and people worked for me. But the managers group was the first time that I had experienced building trust and influencing peers.

AUTHORS: **What was it like when you took your first CFO role?**

VANSELOW: Given all the challenges BHP was facing at the time around HBI and Magma Copper, I was ready to leave BHP. The complexity of the work was one thing, but how it affected my private life was another. I voiced my intention to leave BHP. Right at this time, our merger with Billiton was announced, and they asked me to interview for three senior finance positions, two of which were being formed from the merger. With one of those positions, the leader was a real difficult personality and didn't necessarily want anyone from BHP on his team. But I interviewed with him, and we hit it off. He said, "Come to London, and you can lead the team. Just make sure that you understand that I don't have to hire you. I am hiring you because I like your style." I really wanted that job. It was the hardest one to get and yet I knew it would be one where I could learn many new things. My new boss understood that I knew a lot about BHP at the time, and asked me what I knew about aluminum. I said, "I know it is good to wrap up sandwiches, but if you ask me whether it should be the shiny side out or in, I wouldn't know the answer." He said that was fine, because I knew BHP and could facilitate bringing the two finance processes together. We did good work together, then his successor eventually came in and he gave me more and more responsibility, recognizing that I could contribute more than just on financial matters. We spent hours and hours discussing technology, strategy, and the business overall. I knew my boss had a very full plate, and I wanted to learn so that I could make his life easier.

The CFO position interested me for about a year. That was the learning part. After I got the functional expertise and systems that I wanted in place, I felt the urge to branch out. What I started doing was meddling in other parts of the business, pushing new managerial processes into the rest of the organization. I started intervening in areas outside the finance area to try to get people to understand that I wanted to be considered for an operational role. From there, I became CEO of the aluminum business. It was a P&L of about $400 million with ten thousand direct and contract employees.

AUTHORS: **How was the transition from CFO to CEO of this business unit?**

VANSELOW: Frankly, I was surprised when I was offered the CEO job because I had been asking for something more sensible. I presented a ten-year plan to become CEO of one of our customer sector groups. It turned out to be a ten-minute plan, because they decided to skip my idea to put me into a senior operations role in South Africa as an intermediary step. The hardest part was letting go of finance, which meant letting go of my comfort zone and areas that I had depended on and dealt with for years. My boss coached me on this and how to focus on other areas such as talent development and strategic work.

Finance is a short-term and precise discipline where everything is certain. Now, in a CEO role, I had to become more emotional and really understand the key levers of the business, especially the people lever. That was one of those "click" moments. I could not rise to that level if I was still concerned about finance. So, I had to put somebody in the finance role who knew it through and through, because I did not have time to guide him/her. I chose someone who complemented my style, and we worked well together.

AUTHORS: **From there, you transitioned to the top CFO post of BHP Billiton.**

VANSELOW: Again, it was another big change for me, and choosing the team was key. It is important to have the right team in place, and to make sure your team understands how to behave like a team. Setting the tone from the start, having conversations as a group, behaving in a different way—this is imperative when you are trying to make some big changes. It is engaging. I treat everybody with a great deal of respect, and that is what I ask back. I intentionally picked a team that would infuse the best of the old way of thinking with the new way, and have worked hard to develop each team member to their potential. I try to be very supporting of them all and to look after their views, and I put a lot of enthusiasm around their progress.

CAREER GAME OBSERVATIONS

- Alex Vanselow acknowledges that luck favors the prepared. It is clear that he has long tried to be sure he was contributing far beyond the minimum. This additional effort is commonly displayed by successful executives. From a game theory perspective, this effort is important because of what it signals: a dedication to the current responsibilities and a work ethic that will carry over to future responsibilities. It also has the result of lowering your personal risk in your career game—how often is the hardest-working player the one who is dismissed or forgotten?

• At one point in his career, Vanselow was given three opportunities—he picked the worst option and then worked hard to sell it to another key player, his wife. His sense was that success or failure would become apparent quickly (reflecting his understanding of the time structure of the game around the move), thus it was unlikely they would need to be there long.

• Over his career, he has made it a habit, when new to a position, to clearly display that he wants to help others—particularly the boss—do well. Moves of this manner signal cooperation, as well as working to enlist other players to your cause.

• Vanselow's comments about the move from CFO to CEO are consistent with our recommendations regarding last moves. He related the importance of "letting go" of the CFO role and the challenge associated with promoting himself to the new role and the new habits it required.

A CONVERSATION WITH KEITH WYCHE

PRESIDENT, U.S. OPERATIONS, PITNEY BOWES MANAGEMENT SERVICES

Keith Wyche joined Pitney Bowes in 2003 as area vice president–Western Operations for Mailstream–The Americas, where he focused on driving customer acquisition and retention strategies to achieve accelerated growth in the company's western region. His impressive performance in that role earned him the added responsibility of managing the Pitney Bowes Employee Development & Performance training facility at Aberdeen Woods in Georgia. His work there led to the creation of several leadership development programs. Prior to joining Pitney Bowes, Wyche was group vice president for Wireless Sales at Convergys Corporation. He was the lead executive for Convergys' largest vertical market and was a key architect in developing the company's call center operations in India and Canada. Wyche's previous experience includes a variety of senior-level positions at Ameritech, AT&T, and IBM.

Wyche has been recognized for his leadership by *Black Enterprise* and *Ebony* magazines and was also named "MBA of the Year" by the National Black MBA Association's Cleveland chapter. He is a member of the Executive Leadership Council (ELC), a professional organization consisting of the top 250 African American senior corporate executives in the U.S. He was also recently recognized by the National Urban League as an "African American Man of Distinction." He is the author of the 2008 book *Good Is Not Enough and Other Unwritten Rules for Minority Professionals.* See also www.keithwyche.com/corporate.html.

AUTHORS: **How have mentors been influential in your career?**

WYCHE: Mentors and sponsors are invaluable. In my life, I have always had four or five mentors. How frequently we meet depends on what I am dealing with in my career. I suggest to others to have their own "board of directors" to serve as mentors. Many professionals believe they just need one mentor, but I am not convinced that that approach works. Mentors should arise out of specific needs you have. For example, if you struggle with understanding the financial space, then one of your mentors should be able to help you in that realm.

Mentors will also change as your career changes. For example, what I needed from mentors earlier in my career was help in developing leadership abilities and understanding personal relationships. Later, my mentors helped me understand how to manage in a group where I was once a peer, and then became the boss. I also needed mentors who helped me deal with difficult and different personalities. As you climb the corporate ladder, mentors can prove invaluable as they help you understand what is required at each level.

It is also valuable to have mentors who provide "diversity of thought." By looking at issues from various and diverse perspectives, you will ultimately find that "true" diversity will fall into place.

AUTHORS: **Have you ever had to "fire" a mentor?**

WYCHE: One time I had to fire a mentor because the person violated a trust. Another time was early in my career, when I was in a forced mentoring program of a company. This person was assigned to me as my mentor, but we had no chemistry and there was no desire on his end to really invest much in me. After about three months of meeting with him and him seeming disinterested, I just said, "This probably isn't working for you and it's not working for me." We were both relieved to dissolve the relationship. I would be surprised if the success rate is better than 50 percent on formal, forced mentoring relationships.

But typically, the mentor relationship ends more naturally. For example, I reached a point with one mentor where I had learned everything I needed to learn from him. He recognized it was time to part ways, too, and he went from mentor to cheerleader and good friend.

AUTHORS: **What do you see in the young people you mentor and coach?**

WYCHE: Gen X and Gen Y embrace technology because they were raised in a world where the classroom was a multimedia environment. They look at the world differently, and they bring a whole different level of creativity. For example, I run outsourcing for an organization of about eight thousand people. Many of our employees work on other customer sites where they typically don't have access to e-mail because of firewall issues, and our voice mail doesn't integrate with customer systems. I was struggling with how to communicate with these employees if I can't send an e-mail or leave a voice mail, and mailing eight thousand letters each month is cost prohibitive. My team (of baby boomers) was kicking this around when one of our interns overheard us, and said, "All you need to do is create a YouTube URL, put your video message on the Web, and they can download you." That solution would not have occurred to us.

Gen-Xers and Gen-Yers also have a totally different sense of work/life balance—it is more like a European version. They value working to live, not living to work, and so work/life balance is very important to them. Also, whereas baby boomers tend to be competitive, the younger generation struggles with being stack-ranked. Consider this: when boomers were growing up and there was a track meet, the fastest kids would compete and the top three won a ribbon. Today, everyone gets to play, and all eight kids competing in the race will get a ribbon. But, in reality—in career games, for example—this does not happen.

AUTHORS: **You highlight in your book** Good Is Not Enough **how difficult it can be to be among the first of a minority to join a company. What would signal a risky opportunity?**

WYCHE: I encourage people to look for an indication that the company "gets it"—even if they haven't yet had success attracting large numbers of women or minorities, there can be signs that their commitment to doing so is real. As companies come to realize that diversity is not just the nice thing to do, but the right thing to do, you will see very visible efforts to make it clear that they understand and respect a diverse workforce. I'll use Disney as an example. About two years ago, I started hearing Disney on urban radio stations selling timeshares and inviting families of color to Disney. To me, this was a signal of an organization that realized minorities buy time-shares, too. They are demonstrating openness and respect. Microsoft, for instance, gave away three hundred copies of my book at a recent Black Enterprise Golf and Tennis Challenge. They hired me to go speak to the Alpha Phi Alpha convention in Kansas City to underscore Microsoft's interest in building a diverse workforce. Companies that value diversity participate in forums such as National Black and Hispanic MBA events, and make other visible efforts.

AUTHORS: **What are some risks that minorities face over the course of their careers?**

WYCHE: In some cases, there is a question that implicitly follows minorities around: "Are they a diversity hire?" This erodes credibility. Then, when they make a mistake, others may be too quick to attribute it to a lack of ability. Also, when a derailing event happens, you may or may not be given the chance to recover, or at least may not get many chances to recover. This is why it is important for women and people of color to make sure that they have credibility from doing a great job.

AUTHORS: **How important is it to learn about a company's culture before joining?**

WYCHE: I coach people to focus on three things. The first is checking sources on the Internet. From a diversity standpoint, it is useful to go to the company's website and see what the board of directors and senior management looks like. Also, on the site, does the company talk about its mission and ambitions? Do you see words or phrases regarding valuing people? Also, check other published sources such as magazines and newspaper articles. Is the company listed in *Diversity Inc.* magazine as one of the top fifty companies for diversity? Are they listed in *Black Enterprise* as one of the best top-fifty companies to work for? Are they listed in *Latino Style* magazine?

Second, for public companies, I recommend getting a copy of the most recent annual report and reading the CEO's (and/or chairman's) comments. In the beginning of the report, he or she will be defining what is valuable to the organization, what the mission is, what the goals are for the upcoming year, and where the failings may have been for the previous years.

Finally, I encourage people to check their network. We live in a world of "six degrees of separation," and the likelihood is that you can get to someone who can give you insight on what it is like to work at your target companies. If you can, reach into your network and try to get a sense of the source of any rumblings at the company. Each of these steps provides a data point, and you can use them to get some idea of what you are stepping into.

AUTHORS: One of the pieces of advice you share in your book concerns career exit strategies. How important is it to have an exit strategy?

WYCHE: The whole premise of exit strategy is that we are no longer in a "stay in the same company or role forever" environment, so I view exit strategies from a couple of vantage points. The first is that I believe you need to have one, not just from a company perspective, but from a role perspective. There is something you are looking to gain from the experience that each opportunity provides, so at some point during that experience—you need to gauge whether it's after two years, three years, or maybe just six months—you may conclude that you are not getting what you need from it, that you are not a good fit with the position, or that you have learned all you can. You need to have a plan in place ahead of time that helps you know what to do next. It can be something as simple as "I am a salesperson today, but I want to really broaden my experience so I will be open to a customer service role." Going into that role, you should have a plan that says, "I'm going to do this customer service role for two to three years, learn what I can, and try to parlay that into more of a general manager role."

I recently asked a group of about sixty executives, "How many of you today are doing what you did coming out of college?" Only three hands went up. I then asked, "How many of you today are working for the same company you worked for when you came out of college?" Not a single hand went up. This is reality. This means everyone has to reinvent themselves throughout their careers.

It is important to think of your career as a stream of learning experiences where you have to move around to gain valuable skills. As such, going in to each experience, it will be key to know what your expectation is from a time perspective, what your expectation is from a goal perspective, and how you will get out of the role when the time is right.

CAREER GAME OBSERVATIONS

- Keith Wyche advocates always having an exit plan—a next move—ready. As individuals realize they are approaching the ceiling in their current positions, they need to cultivate a next opportunity so that they continue to learn and be challenged. Very few successful executives today are in jobs that reflect where they started—being prepared for the moves that create such careers requires that individuals never stop learning.

- Wyche offers some actionable advice for players who want to understand more about the condition of the playing field. Research using the Web, company annual reports, and the like can provide insight into what a company says matters and to how its culture might impact the way the career game is played there.

- The "board of directors" approach to mentoring is a useful metaphor. Assembling a team of valued advisors, each leveraging his or her unique strengths and experiences to help you navigate your career, is a savvy move.

- Like Tammy Erickson, Wyche has noticed systematic differences in the way members of different generations approach the career game.

CONCLUSION

One day Alice came to a fork in the road and saw a Cheshire cat in a tree. "Which road do I take?" she asked. "Where do you want to go?" was his response. "I don't know," Alice answered. "Then," said the cat, "it doesn't matter."

Lewis Carroll, *Alice's Adventures in Wonderland*

If you have read this far, it is a safe bet that you are more certain about where you want to go than Alice. Understanding where you want to go, where you are now, and how you came this far all matter in the career game—as does understanding where to start. Our purpose in this book is to share our thoughts on how you can use game theory concepts to better understand your career, to evaluate the impact that others might have as supporters or competitors, and to make moves that are more effective as you pursue your objective. Our contention is that game theory provides a useful framework for these purposes because, like the other situations in which it has been fruitfully applied, your career game involves interdependent players with varied motives, complex reward systems, and evolving playing conditions.

In several places, we note that your career game is highly personal. Your goals, your talents, your predilection to risk, your game history to date, and characteristics of your fellow players are unique to your situation. Based on this uniqueness, what we offer in conclusion is a bit different from what is commonly found in business books. We don't have a precise set of laws, habits, or rules that can be simply adopted in an effort to increase your odds of getting from where you are to where you want to go. Instead, we pose a number of questions—you must provide the individual answers that characterize your own career game. We think that, if you can do that well, the moves you need to make will become apparent to you.

- *Where do you want to take your career?* If, like Alice in Wonderland, you don't know, then you need not address any of the questions that follow. If, however, like Dave Barry, you have observed that many others are competing with you for opportunities, then we hope you will consider the issues that these questions raise.

- *Who are the other players that I need to consider, and how can they impact my game?* Depending on your career goals, a wide cast of characters will at one point or another have the ability to support or frustrate your efforts. Family members, coworkers, bosses, fellow students, and competitors for positions all may play roles in your career game. In each case, our recommendation is that you carefully consider other players' motives, the degree to which they can make credible commitments to you, and where you might find opportunities for gains in cooperation with them. From this analysis, you will be in a position to better understand their likely moves— and, particularly, their probable reactions to your moves. By investing in building this understanding, you create a situation in which you can more accurately evaluate the utility of the various moves open to you.

- *What other game elements, such as information asymmetries and time structure, should I consider?* In addition to investing in understanding the impact that other players might have on your game, we encourage you to also analyze the potential impact of other elements. The most critical game elements to consider are information asymmetries and time structure. Information asymmetries exist when one player is disadvantaged in terms of what he or she knows about the game. In some cases, your career game will be accelerated by your ability to leverage an asymmetry to your advantage. In salary negotiations, for example, your knowledge of your best alternative to a negotiated agreement provides you with an advantage. If you know that you have an attractive "plan B," you can negotiate much more aggressively than you might otherwise. In other cases, you will find yourself on the short end of the asymmetry, and your task thus becomes one of acquiring information that reduces or removes the asymmetry.

The game's time structure is another element that deserves your consideration. Understanding when play begins, when play ends, and how much time is available to consider planning each move are all important strategies in developing your own career game strategy. Time also plays a role in what it signals about the motives of players. Quick moves may reflect confidence or desperation; slow moves may reflect indifference or careful deliberation. Whether considering the importance of time to the rules of play or the way that time signals something about other players, you make yourself a better player by explicitly thinking about time in your preparation to make moves.

- *What is the condition of the playing field?* At different times in your career game, you may find yourself competing in a variety of conditions. We described how an understanding of both the internal and external labor markets provides players with important information about the way the career game might play out. Similarly, we described how the permeable and interconnected nature of the labor market could impact play. For example, permeable markets offer easier entry to players than impermeable ones. They may also be more forgiving of sloppy moves. In loosely interconnected labor markets, players need to pay special attention to the fact that information asymmetries are more likely to occur than in more tightly interconnected ones. Your ability to recognize and quickly adjust to changing conditions on the playing field can become a source of competitive advantage to you in your career game.

- *What can I do to develop and then deploy an increasing level of career agility?* As we described in the previous chapter, your career agility is determined by your ability to recognize and then leverage your potential sources of personal competitive advantage—it's about making the most of what you have. This requires you to do two things well. First, you must be able to conduct an honest inventory of your strengths and weaknesses, as well as of the opportunities and threats present in your career game. As was clear from our executive conversations, mentors can be of great value here. After all, a mentor who is not prepared to "tell it like it is" is not much of a mentor. Second, you must be able to see how you can play the game in a way that allows you to leverage your strengths to pursue opportunities while not exposing personal weaknesses or falling prey to career game threats.

Our contention is that you have prepared yourself to play when these questions are addressed and the answers are continually updated as circumstances change.

Although each career game of the executives who shared their experiences with us is—like yours—unique, there are some prevailing lessons that we think more broadly generalize across career games. One such lesson concerns how moves around first jobs are made. We talked with two individuals, Bryan Bell and Pasha Fedorenko, who were in the midst of seeking their first post-MBA jobs. As Bryan and Pasha described their searches, they were mostly focused on understanding what they need to do to convince employers that they are worthy hires. Even though both Bryan and Pasha made some savvy moves in their efforts to earn their first opportunities, as newly minted MBAs, neither was yet a particularly powerful career game player. What was interesting to us was how different elements of first jobs struck the executives we interviewed when they looked back on their early positions. Such was the case for Charlene Begley at GE and Dan Palumbo at Proctor & Gamble. With the benefit of hindsight, of course, they both emphasized the strategic value over the course of their careers of having first jobs with companies known for developing people. Some of the executives we talked to had opportunities to participate in programs designed for high-potential new hires. Others, like Brian Humphries, found that jobs that required interaction with high-level executives across a broad spectrum of the company—such as internal audit—were, in retrospect, valuable first moves. In each case, the positions were viewed as career accelerators.

A clear consensus prevails that self-awareness early in the career game is very important. Self-awareness helps you understand what you want out of the career game, it helps you identify gaps in your preparation, and it makes you open to career-refining moves to address those gaps. Virtually all of the executives we interviewed spoke about the things they learned about themselves early on and how they were able to respond in ways that advanced their career games.

Mentoring is important throughout the career game. Even the most senior executives we spoke with leveraged relationships with board members, other c-level executives, former professors, or others in order to experience occasional reality checks. Early in the career game, however, a particular sort of mentor is most useful. Some are fond of the image of Yoda, Luke Skywalker's mentor in the *Star Wars* movies, as the right model for the early career game.

Similar sorts of characters who have literally seen it all are invaluable at helping early-career game players develop their ability to understand context and to honestly take inventory of their weaknesses. As your game develops and you begin to make progress, you may find that you begin to outgrow this first mentor. Of course, if you have been playing the game well, you have been developing your professional network. As you do, you should be looking for the individual who will be your next mentor: the invisible hand. The invisible hand is that executive who is three or more levels above you on the organizational chart and who has become interested in helping you win at your career game. This mentor is high enough in the organizational chart to facilitate "disruptive" career-enhancing moves—the sorts of positions for which an individual might be "uniquely unqualified" and thus favorably positioned to learn the most.

Across your career, what makes an executive want to mentor you? The executives we interviewed were consistent in their descriptions of the sorts of players they want to help. They are quick to point out that their time is finite and that a number of subordinates may be vying for their attention as mentors. Earning a spot on a mentor's radar is assisted by understanding the career game—how can you help mentors recognize that they should invest in your success? Your ability to demonstrate passion and energy were frequently cited as important. Continually going above the minimum necessary for effective performance was also something that got players noticed. Finally, when executives concluded that players were in positions to help them improve at their own games (to help *them* learn), an edge in earning their mentorship was likely to be gained.

Regarding career moves, a number of points are useful. First, it is clear that our executives found international experience to be extremely valuable. For some, the value was in the way it changed their understanding of other people. For others, the value was in what it taught them about themselves—that they could find ways to survive and even thrive in unfamiliar surroundings. Second, the theme of "finding something to fix" early in one's career is, we think, something that will be useful to many. In some conversations, the "something to fix" was a broken part of the business; in Pasha Fedorenko's case, it was a hole in his résumé. In each case, the "fixing" created an opportunity to tell a great story. Great stories resonate throughout your career game. Third, the conversations offered some useful advice about moves. For example, the view that moves should reflect "running toward something, not away from something" makes great sense to us, as does the admonition to avoid jobs that may be career limiting; thinking about whether an opportunity has the potential to lead to other opportunities that interest you is very important. Finally, along this line of thinking, the advice that you should always have an exit plan in place—a way to get from where you are to a new opportunity that allows you to grow and contribute—is compelling.

The game starts early. Many of you are playing from positions that are the result of many, many moves. The good news is that the game is a long one and that you can still impact it. One overriding theme from our conversations seems to ring true for a broad scope of later game players. The title of Marshal Goldsmith's best-selling book, *What Got You Here Won't Get You There*, deftly sums it up. Players who are not able to adapt their games—to make second-half adjustments, if you will—are going to plateau, become frustrated, and find themselves suffering in middlescence. To us, this represents an agility deficit. If agility is not developed, then neither is the ability to make the changes from "what got you here" to what it is going to take to "get you there." Too many executives stall or actually derail because they have become wed to the moves and strategies that worked early in the game.

What moves can a later game player make? There are many. Some executives could focus on remediating any deficiencies in breadth of experience. This is the career state that might cause players to "move down to move up." Other moves could focus on further developing and refining agility. Leadership and influence are tools that are enacted differently from different positions on an organizational chart, and sometimes newly promoted executives evolve too slowly in their approaches to each. We noted that effective decision-making styles are elements of organization that operate differently according to the organizational level to which they are applied. Failure to recognize and then develop these new skills may contribute to a career stall or, worse, a blunder. We have offered suggestions about how to recover, should blunders occur.

We want to emphasize two important cautions regarding how you play your career game. One point that we cannot stress strongly enough is that you should not mistake our encouragement for players to be proactive and strategic with a suggestion that they play the game "below the board." Whereas a solid understanding of the game, its rules, and other player motives may sensitize you to potential unethical play by others, it is not our intent to in any way sanction playing outside of the rules. Second, it is possible that, in the short run, a career-agile player can rely on that savviness to create the impression of good performance. You should not mistake this focus on style over substance as being sufficient for success over the long run. Indeed, if style ends up being sufficient, some of the blame should be attributed to the employer for creating a game that is so easily manipulated. The behavior we are describing here is expressed in the career literature as *extreme careerism*. Extreme careerism has been defined as the pursuit of personal career advancement, power, and prestige through any positive or negative non-performance-based activity that an individual thinks will be effective. Typically, the moves made by an extreme careerist are intended to manipulate other players in the game.[1] Extreme careerism can also be thought of as taking the game below board. For example, efforts at impression management can be done fairly and above board—such as demonstrating modesty—or unfairly—such as casting blame for a failure on a coworker.

We suggest that the material we have shared with you can be collapsed into three critical success factors in the career game. First, as with any other game, a strong advantage goes to individuals who understand the game better than others. If readers will forgive one more sports analogy, one of the greatest hockey players of all time, Wayne Gretzky, has been famously quoted as explaining that his dad taught him to skate not where the puck was, but where it was going. That ability can come only from deep study of the game itself. Individuals who want to understand the career game better than others have to become expert at recognizing the condition of the playing field. They have to be able to recognize their career competitive advantages and be cognizant of how they can be leveraged in the marketplace. Understanding competitor motives is important, as is the ability to understand how to influence those in positions to impact the game toward your cause.

The second critical success factor is to develop the discipline around understanding the way that different career moves will impact your overall career game strategy. Doing this well requires developing a similarly deep understanding of how others will react to each move. Competitors for jobs, as well as coworkers and family members, are just a few of the other players whose reactions need to be anticipated, because those reactions can either enhance or detract from a move's effectiveness.

The final critical success factor involves efforts to improve career agility. Under our definition, career agility refers to the individual's ability to leverage a variety of competencies. As reviewed earlier, these competencies involve developing acumen in regard to diagnosing context—in other words, they aid in the continual evaluation and thorough understanding of the current condition of the game. As a result, agile players are prepared to make the right moves at the right times.

As you plan your next moves in your career game, we offer a few cautionary remarks intended to help you keep in perspective the effort that you spend planning. As Marius Kloppers told us, don't let the future distract you from your obligations today. Simply plotting for tomorrow is not sufficient. Others in your career game expect you to deliver results today. Your career game will evaporate if your energies are unevenly balanced toward future plans and away from contributing in your role today. As Dan Palumbo shared, you are wise to focus your efforts on building a reputation, not simply a résumé that records an impressive collection of titles. We are fond of the quote by Kaiser Aluminum founder Henry J. Kaiser, who said, "When your work speaks for itself, don't interrupt." The story that your work tells about you is what matters—and stories about impact matter much more than stories about your time as what some have referred to as "management tourists." Your odds of reaching whatever you consider to be a win in the career game are in your favor when you can balance performing today and strategizing for tomorrow.

NOTE

1. V. K. Bratton and K. M. Kacmar, "Extreme Careerism: The Dark Side of Impression Management," in *The Dark Side of Organizational Behavior*, ed. R. W. Griffin, A. O'Leary-Kelly, and R. D. Pritchard (San Francisco: Jossey-Bass, 2004).

INDEX

110–11, 112–13, 114–15, 116; and Chris-Craft Corp., 96, 110, 113–14, 116; at Erico International Corp., 110–11, 112–14; on financial services sector, 110–11, 115; on first job decisions, 77, 110–11; on Harvard Business School, 110–12, 115; and Indian Motorcycle, 96, 110, 116; at Price Waterhouse, 110–11, 112, 113, 114, 116; on risk, 110, 113, 115, 116, 117; on Wall Street employment, 77

Heidrick & Struggles, 201

Hewlett-Packard: Fiorina and Perez at, 194; Humphries at, 85, 131, 135, 136, 138, 142, 143–44; Hurd at, 85, 131, 142

Heyer, Steve, 120

Higgins, Monica: on constellation of mentors, 85

hockey, 48, 247

Home Depot: Blank at, 221, 223; Tomé at, 218, 219, 220–21, 223, 226

humility, 11, 217; Elop on, 55–56, 57, 58; Kent on, 149

Humphries, Brian, 136–45; on breadth of experience, 135–36, 137, 138–40, 142, 144–45; on cost structure, 143; at Digital Equipment, 136–41, 144; on early-career decisions, 136–37, 140, 244; at HP, 85, 131, 135, 136, 138, 142, 143–44; on internal audit work, 136–37, 141, 144, 244; on mentoring, 85, 140–43; 145; on path limiting career moves, 136; relationship with Jeff Clark, 141–42, 145; relationship with Mark Hurd, 85, 142

Hunter, Mark: "How Leaders Create and Use Networks," 80

Hurd, Mark, 85, 142

Hurricane Katrina, 5; and St. Bernard Project, 177–78, 186–91

Hymowitz, Carol: "As Managers Climb, They Have to Learn How to Act the Parts," 208, 218n2

Ibarra, Herminia: "How Leaders Create and Use Networks," 80

IBM: purchase of ISS by, 152, 156–57, 158

Ideo, 87

Immelt, Jeff: at GE, 14, 15, 124, 125, 165

Indian Motorcycle and Stephen Heese, 96, 110, 116

influencing other players, 86, 87, 89, 122, 211; influencing up, 213

information asymmetries: and asking questions, 50; assessment of, 51, 73–75, 95; defined, 38, 73, 242; between hiring managers and candidates, 50; and interconnectedness of markets, 77–78, 243; in job search situations, 49–50, 73–74, 76, 89; in labor markets, 76, 78; sharing of information, 89, 90; and signaling, 38–39, 50, 51n2

Intel: Barrett at, 123; Grove at, 123

international experience, 149, 151, 197, 199, 245

Internet, 152–54; blogs, 93, 121; social networking sites, 66, 79, 157. See also websites

Internet Security Systems (ISS): and Klaus, 5, 132, 152, 154, 155–57, 158

internships, 20–21, 26, 152–53, 158

Isdell, Neville, 146, 150

ISS. See Internet Security Systems

J. Crew, Drexler at, 123

Jim Walter Corp., 111

Jobs, Steven, 133, 176, 177

job-search situations: bluffs during, 93; campus career development staff, 92–93; candidate's current manager, 86, 88, 90; competitors in, 88–89; and family members, 89; hiring managers, 86, 91; information asymmetries in, 50, 73–74, 76, 89; negotiation phase, 49, 93, 94–95, 242; on-campus interviews, 88–89, 90, 92–93, 94; order of interviews, 38, 94; recommendations of candidates, 45, 93

Johnson, Fisk, 201

Johnson, Sam, 201

Jones, Reginald, 124

Jordan, Michael: on resilience, 213–14

JP Morgan Chase, 221; Dimon at, 122

Juniper Networks: Elop at, 52, 54, 55

Kacmar, K. M.: "Extreme Careerism," 247, 248

Kaiser, Henry J.: on work speaking for itself, 248

Kaneva and Klaus, 151–52, 157

Kasparov, Gary: on anticipating moves of opponents, 33, 36; How Life Imitates Chess, 10

Kent, Muhtar, 145–51; at Coca-Cola, 134, 135, 136, 145, 146–51; on continual learning, 150, 151; at Efes Beverage Group, 145–47, 150; on expansion into East Central Europe, 148, 151; on humility, 149; on international experience, 149, 151; on job performance and batting averages, 147, 150–51; on leadership, 148–49; on mentors, 150

Keough, Don, 150

Kim, W. Chan: Blue Ocean Strategy, 76

Klaus, Chris, 151–58; and computer games, 157, 158; on entrepreneurship, 153–54, 155–56, 157–58; at Georgia Tech, 152–55; on IBM,

CPSIA information can be obtained
at www.ICGtesting.com
Printed in the USA
BVHW03*1810190818
524997BV00001B/1/P